Imagining the Nation in Seventeenth-Century English Literature

This volume brings together new work on the image of the nation and the construction of national identity in English literature of the seventeenth century.

The chapters in the collection explore visions of British nationhood in literary works including Michael Drayton and John Selden's *Poly-Olbion* and Andrew Marvell's *Horatian Ode*, shedding new light on topics ranging from debates over territorial waters and the free seas, to the emergence of hyphenated identities, and the perennial problem of the Picts. Concluding with a survey of recent work in British studies and the history of early modern nationalism, this collection highlights issues of British national identity, cohesion, and disintegration that remain undeniably relevant and topical in the twenty-first century.

This book was originally published as a special issue of the journal *The Seventeenth Century*.

Daniel Cattell received his PhD from the University of Exeter, UK, and has been a Research Fellow on the AHRC-funded Poly-Olbion Project.

Philip Schwyzer is a Professor of Renaissance Literature at the University of Exeter, UK; his current projects include forthcoming editions of Michael Drayton's *Poly-Olbion* and the complete works of Humphrey Llwyd.

Imagining the Nation in Seventeenth-Century English Literature

Edited by
Daniel Cattell and Philip Schwyzer

LONDON AND NEW YORK

First published 2020
by Routledge
2 Park Square, Milton Park, Abingdon, Oxon, OX14 4RN

and by Routledge
52 Vanderbilt Avenue, New York, NY 10017

Routledge is an imprint of the Taylor & Francis Group, an informa business

© 2020 The Seventeenth Century

Chapter 3 © 2018 Philip Schwyzer. Originally published as Open Access.

With the exception of Chapter 3, no part of this book may be reprinted or reproduced or utilised in any form or by any electronic, mechanical, or other means, now known or hereafter invented, including photocopying and recording, or in any information storage or retrieval system, without permission in writing from the publishers. For details on the rights for Chapter 3, please see the chapter's Open Access footnote.

Trademark notice: Product or corporate names may be trademarks or registered trademarks, and are used only for identification and explanation without intent to infringe.

British Library Cataloguing-in-Publication Data
A catalogue record for this book is available from the British Library

ISBN13: 978-0-367-51088-6

Typeset in Minion Pro
by codeMantra

Publisher's Note
The publisher accepts responsibility for any inconsistencies that may have arisen during the conversion of this book from journal articles to book chapters, namely the inclusion of journal terminology.

Disclaimer
Every effort has been made to contact copyright holders for their permission to reprint material in this book. The publishers would be grateful to hear from any copyright holder who is not here acknowledged and will undertake to rectify any errors or omissions in future editions of this book.

Contents

Citation Information	vi
Notes on Contributors	viii
Introduction: visions of Britain *Daniel Cattell and Philip Schwyzer*	1
1 Imagining Britain: reconstructing history and writing national identity in *Englands Heroicall Epistles* *Sukanya Dasgupta*	16
2 Michael Drayton's *Poly-Olbion*: maritime England and the free seas debates *Sandra Logan*	33
3 The age of the Cambro-Britons: hyphenated British identities in the seventeenth century *Philip Schwyzer*	49
4 The religious geography of Marvell's "An Horatian Ode": popery, presbytery, and parti-coloured picts *Stewart Mottram*	62
5 "Neptune to the Common-wealth of England" (1652): the "Republican Britannia" and the continuity of interests *Willy Maley*	83
6 The archipelagic turn: nationhood, nationalism and early modern studies, 1997–2017 *Patrick J. Murray*	104
Index	115

Citation Information

The chapters in this book were originally published in *The Seventeenth Century*, volume 33, issue 4 (October 2018). When citing this material, please use the original page numbering for each article, as follows:

Introduction
Visions of Britain
Daniel Cattell and Philip Schwyzer
The Seventeenth Century, volume 33, issue 4 (October 2018) pp. 377–391

Chapter 1
Imagining Britain: reconstructing history and writing national identity in Englands Heroicall Epistles
Sukanya Dasgupta
The Seventeenth Century, volume 33, issue 4 (October 2018) pp. 393–409

Chapter 2
Michael Drayton's Poly-Olbion: *maritime England and the free seas debates*
Sandra Logan
The Seventeenth Century, volume 33, issue 4 (October 2018) pp. 411–426

Chapter 3
The age of the Cambro-Britons: hyphenated British identities in the seventeenth century
Philip Schwyzer
The Seventeenth Century, volume 33, issue 4 (October 2018) pp. 427–439

Chapter 4
The religious geography of Marvell's "An Horatian Ode": popery, presbytery, and parti-coloured picts
Stewart Mottram
The Seventeenth Century, volume 33, issue 4 (October 2018) pp. 441–461

Chapter 5
"Neptune to the Common-wealth of England" (1652): the "Republican Britannia" and the continuity of interests
Willy Maley
The Seventeenth Century, volume 33, issue 4 (October 2018) pp. 463–483

Chapter 6
The archipelagic turn: nationhood, nationalism and early modern studies, 1997–2017
Patrick J. Murray
The Seventeenth Century, volume 33, issue 4 (October 2018) pp. 485–495

For any permission-related enquiries please visit:
http://www.tandfonline.com/page/help/permissions

Contributors

Daniel Cattell University of Exeter, UK.

Sukanya Dasgupta Department of English, Loreto College (University of Calcutta), India.

Sandra Logan Department of English, Michigan State University, East Lansing, USA.

Willy Maley School of Critical Studies, University of Glasgow, UK.

Stewart Mottram School of Arts, University of Hull, UK.

Patrick J. Murray School of Critical Studies, University of Glasgow, UK.

Philip Schwyzer Department of English, University of Exeter, UK.

Introduction: visions of Britain

Daniel Cattell and Philip Schwyzer

ABSTRACT
This introductory essay situates *Poly-Olbion* (1612, 1622), Michael Drayton's vast chorographical and historical poem of England and Wales, in terms of its development as a poetic project, its structural choices, and its reception by early readers. It sets the tension in the text between the local and the national against the backdrop of a more fundamental seventeenth-century shift from national to regional description. By exploring the text's depiction of the ancient Picts, it also considers some of the difficulties that Drayton might have faced, had he managed to extend his poem north to Scotland.

This collection of essays on the image of the nation in seventeenth-century English literature finds its centre of gravity in *Poly-Olbion* (1612, 1622), a lavish, composite text that includes Michael Drayton's 15,000-line "Topo-chrono-graphicall" poem of England and Wales,[1] John Selden's learned prose "Illustrations", and the engraver William Hole's fantastical series of regional maps. *Poly-Olbion* was not a commercial success in its own day,[2] but its enduring power across time is testified by modern homages and imitations, including the twenty-first-century reimagining of Drayton's poem by Paul Farley.[3] The text remains a towering landmark in seventeenth-century literary imaginings of Britain, impressive not only for its scale and scope, but also its liminal position between two worlds. Conceived in the very different literary and political climate of the 1590s,[4] *Poly-Olbion* would not see the light of day until a change of dynasty and the crushing of Drayton's hopes for preferential royal treatment.[5] Drayton sensed that by then his moment for fortune and glory had passed, and he uses his preface "To the Generall Reader", not to endear himself to bookstall browsers, but to launch a scathing attack on "this lunatique Age", with its peverse fashions for coterie manuscript lyrics and "fantasies of forraine inventions", as well as its general flagrant disregard for the past.[6]

Drayton was entering his fiftieth year by the time Part 1 was published, and his rant could be read usympathetically as that of an embittered cultural stick-in-the-mud, hopelessly out of step with the pace of the changing world around him. Yet that view neglects that *Poly-Olbion* was simultaneously a culmination *and* a transformation, "genuine, and first in this kinde", as Drayton himself claimed.[7] It is the literary summation of what has traditionally been called (with obvious Anglocentric bias) the "discovery of England"[8] – the sixteenth-century advances in native cartographical and chorographical description that allowed the English to take, in Richard Helgerson's words, "effective visual and conceptual possession of the physical kingdom in which they lived".[9] While Drayton is sometimes presented as a one-dimensional Elizabethan nostalgic,[10] this view neglects the fact that his Janus-like poem also looks forward, anticipating the experiment in republicanism later in the century by presenting an image of the nation without the incumbent Stuart monarch at its head.[11]

The poem's fundamental structuring unit is the land. Drayton's drone-like muse flits from county to county, as the vocal, anthropomorphised landscape she encounters unlocks the memories of the particular histories and legends with which it is associated. But as the word "topo-chronographical" would suggest, the poem in fact wanders along the dual axes of chorography and chronography.[12] Though chorography is more conspicuous in its design and layout, chronology shapes many of the text's individual catalogues – of British and Saxon kings, Welsh princes, monarchs, military captains, voyagers – and also generates a degree of forward movement across songs, as Drayton begins with the arrival of the Trojan Brutus and then proceeds to work through the histories of the Britons, and, later, their Saxon displacers. Indeed, in Song 2 the tension between the ordering of space and the ordering of time generates friction, as the Hamble tries in vain to prevent the Itchen's retelling of the romance of *Bevis of Hampton*, which is set in later Norman times.[13]

Drayton's twofold topo-chronographical structure might have provided an ingenious means for sifting and sorting the vastness of his material. In practice, though, for some early readers, two for the price of one did not amount to the sale of the century. The Scottish laird William Drummond found in Drayton and his poem that "which is in most part of my Compatriots, too great an Admiration of their Country; on the History of which, whilst they muse, as wondering, they forget sometimes to be good Poets".[14] If for Drummond English (and Welsh) history in the poem was an unwelcome and poorly crafted diversion from less obviously historical matter – descriptions of landscapes and rivers, for instance – Ben Jonson believed that Drayton had not been zealous enough in describing England's famous historical figures: "Michael Drayton's *Poly-Olbion*, if he had performed what he promised, to write the deeds of all the worthies, had been excellent".[15] John Selden, invited by Drayton at a late stage to write a prose commentary on Part 1, and hence once of its earliest and most careful readers, suggests in his own preface that "*Gentlewomen* & their *Loves*" and "the more *Severe Reader*" would both find their tastes catered for in the text.[16] He perhaps sensed that Drayton's all-catering encyclopedic vision risked fragmenting under the strain of being pulled in different directions, as it also teetered precariously between two dynastic ages.

Nation and region

The accession of King James inaugurated a period of turmoil and disappointment in Drayton's life; his epistle to readers of the first edition refers to "the times since his Majesties happy comming in [... falling] heavily upon my distressed fortunes".[17] Yet while personal setbacks may have played a role, the significant delay in completing the first part of *Poly-Olbion* may also have been provoked by an expansion of the poem's plan to encompass the entirety of the island now ruled by the Stuart monarch. Where

Drayton's original intention may have been to describe the natural features of England alone, the poem as published in 1612 surveys Wales as well as the south of England, and the dedication promises Prince Henry that "May I breath to arrive at the Orcades (whither in this kind I intend my course, if the Muse faile me not) I shall leave your whole British Empire, as this first and southerne part, delineated".[18] Inevitably, for an early Jacobean work on a British theme, the poem contains various nods to the debate over closer union between England and Scotland, especially in Song 5, where the Severn resolves a feud between the rivers of Wales and England by declaring that the union of the kingdoms under a Stuart monarch dissolves all internal differences:

> By whom three sever'd Realmes in one shall firmlie stand
>
> As *Britain*-founding *Brute* first Monarchiz'd the land
>
> Why strive yee then for that, in little time that shall
>
> (As you are all made one) be one unto you all?[19]

Yet despite the topical nod to union, Drayton's idea of Britain (an ancient realm founded by the Trojan Brutus) is in many respects backward-looking, and his project of national description likewise chimes with sixteenth-century exemplars. He relied heavily on William Camden's *Britannia*, as well as Humphrey Llwyd's earlier *Breviary of Britain* (1573). In the background to Camden's and Llwyd's endeavours lay the illustrious if chastening example of John Leland (d. 1552), who had planned but never completed a pair of works on the geography and antiquities of Britain, the *Liber de topographia Britanniae primae* and *De antiquitate Britannica*.[20] As the titles of these works make clear, in the Tudor era the island of Britain presented itself as the natural subject of chorography, in spite of the absence of any form of political or regnal union between the kingdoms of England and Scotland. Although the devotion of these antiquaries to a mere "geographical expression" may seem quixotic, arguably Britain presented itself as a focus for nationalistic imagining in this period precisely because it represented an ideal that as yet lay out of reach.[21]

Drayton's dedication to the Prince of Wales refers to "your ... British Empire", but in its form and content the poem casts doubt over both the ownership and the unity of the nation. As Richard Helgerson noted in a seminal reading of *Poly-Olbion*, Drayton's real theme is regional particularity, and the poem was always bound to find its most sympathetic audience among representatives of the "country" (county land-owners) rather than the court.[22] Even where the poem's voluble rivers propound a putatively national vision – as when the Dart sings of the coming of Brutus, the Weaver praises the Anglo-Saxon heritage, or the Medway celebrates English conquests abroad – they do so in defence of local priorities and interests. The land is multiple, and internal difference is a matter for celebration, as in this catalogue of the various mottos of English counties in the twenty-third song:

> Quoth warlike *Warwickshire*, *Ile binde the sturdy Beare*.
>
> Quoth *Worstershire* againe, *And I will squirt the Peare*.
>
> Then *Staffordshire* bids *Stay, and I will Beet the Fire,*

And nothing will I aske, but good will for my hire.

Beane-belly Lestershire, her attribute doth beare.

And *Bells and Bag-pipes* next, belong to *Lincolneshire*.

Of *Malt-horse, Bedfordshire* long since the Blazon wan.

And little *Rutlandshire* is tearmed *Raddleman*.

To *Darby* is assign'd the name of *Wooll and Lead*.

As *Nottinghams*, of old (is common) *Ale and Bread*.[23]

Prior to the publication of the second part of *Poly-Olbion* in 1622, none of the counties mentioned in this extract (drawn from a much longer catalogue) had been the subject of printed surveys; indeed only Kent and Cornwall had received this distinction.[24] In 1622, however, William Burton's *Description of Leicestershire* provided an influential model for what would soon become a small flood of county surveys and chorographies, including William Dugdale's magisterial *Antiquities of Warwickshire* (1656), Robert Thoroton's *Antiquities of Nottinghamshire* (1677), Robert Plot's *Natural History of Staffordshire* (1686), James Wright's *History and Antiquities of the County of Rutland* (1684), and Thomas Habington's *Survey of Worcestershire* (which remained in manuscript). There were also more local surveys still, such as Richard Butcher's *The Survey and Antiquitie of the Towne of Stamforde, in the county of Lincolne* (1646). These treatises were motivated by the same pride in local history and particularity displayed by Drayton's hills and rivers, and their proliferation is in part the product of the same competitive impulse evinced by the landscape features in *Poly-Olbion*. The existence of a county survey became an indispensable token of shire-level patriotism. As Burton proclaimed, "rather then my native Countrie should any longer lye obscured with darkenesse; I have adventured (in some sort) to restore her to her worth and dignity".[25] The phrase bears echoes of Drayton's promise to his readers to reveal "the Rarities & Historie of their owne Country delivered by a true native Muse" – for Burton, however, the "country" means the county, and the name of the wider nation of which he might also consider himself a native is left unclear.[26]

Just as the publication of *Poly-Olbion* coincides with the rise of the seventeenth-century county survey, it marks the near-eclipse of the Elizabethan genres of national chorography and chronicle. The years immediately leading up to the first part of *Poly-Olbion* had seen the publication of Philemon Holland's English translation of Camden's *Britain* (1610) and John Speed's *History of Great Britain* (1611) and *Theatre of the Empire of Great Britain* (1611–12). After this high-water mark, there is remarkably little in the way of serious and innovative national description in the seventeenth century. Exceptions such as Richard Blome's *Britannia, or a Geographical Description of the Kingdom of England, Scotland and Ireland* (1673) tended to be both heavily derivative and emphatically shire-centric. In the field of British chorography, Camden's great work remained definitive and unsurpassed throughout the century, receiving a further lease of life from Edmund Gibson's revised and expanded edition of *Britannia* in 1695.

A shift from national to regional description characterises the chorographical poets who followed Drayton as well. The title of William Browne's *Britannia's Pastorals*

(1613–16) promises a survey of the island as a whole, but, as Gillian Wright notes, the poem "adumbrates a 'Britannia' with a clear bias towards the West Country and Wales, and, in particular, Browne's native Devon".[27] Later poems in the emerging topographical tradition are still more local in their professed scope, though they may, like Sir John Denham in "Cooper's Hill", detect indications of the state of the nation in the features of a provincial landscape. Denham's poem describes the particular sites and sights of Surrey, from the ruins of Chertsey Abbey to the iconic water-meadow of Runnymede, but also implies that any landscape in England would provide similar grounds for meditation on the whims of tyrants and the uneasy balance between law and power.

As the example of "Cooper's Hill" indicates, the regional focus of so much seventeenth-century chorography does not necessarily indicate a turn away from national themes. Indeed, it might be argued that only a deep confidence in the reality and endurance of the nation permitted antiquaries and poets to concentrate so exclusively on their own backyards. In Helgerson's reading of the county surveys, "the particularities ... constantly remind us of the whole of which they are part and from which they take meaning, even if only by difference. Nationalism is what ultimately justifies a project as particular as Dugdale's".[28] Alternatively, as Wright argues in regard to *Britannia's Pastorals*, the celebration of the region could expose the underlying weakness of the national idea: "rather than ... mutual reinforcement ... Browne's knowledge of Devon in fact works to undermine his depiction of Britannia".[29] The tensions between nation and region that ripple through the songs of *Poly-Olbion* would not be resolved either in politics or the literature of the later seventeenth century.

Problems with Picts

Scotland remained an enduring part of Drayton's vision for the completed *Poly-Olbion*. Having finished Wales and ventured as far north in England as Cheshire in Part 1, the poet vowed to Henry Stuart that he would reach "the Orcades" (Orkney).[30] Ten years later, and just making it with gritted teeth to the northernmost English counties of Northumberland and Cumberland, he obstinately announced to the deceased Henry's successor, Charles, that the project he had come to regard as a "strange *Herculean* toyle" was not quite done.[31]

> If meanes and time faile me not, being now arived at Scotland, I trust you shall see mee crowne her with no worse Flowers, then I have done her two Sisters, England, *and* Wales: *and without any partialitie, as I dare bee bold, to make the Poets of that Kingdom my Judges therin. If I arive at the* Orcades, *without sinking in my flight, your Highnesse cannot but say, that I had no ill Perspective that gave mee things so cleerely, when I stood so farre off.*[32]

As it turned out, means and time did fail Drayton, and any work begun on a Scottish continuation would never make it into print.[33] There are hints, though, even in this final unfulfilled promise, that the Scottish sister would never come in from the fringe and take her rightful place in this exclusive island sorority.[34] Drayton acknowledges the risks of partiality and perspective. Standing "*so farre off*" from his subject could well obscure the view, especially since the array of surrogates for actual travel that had served him well for England and Wales – richly detailed cartographical and chorographical works and an antiquarian circle that included luminaries such as William

Camden – would not provide anything like the same coverage north of the border.[35] Drayton's geographical location determined to a large extent the kinds and quality of materials, as well as the utility of support networks, available to him. It also conditioned the partiality of an Anglocentric outlook that he recognised would need to be overcome to do Scotland justice. Drayton had managed to offset, even overcompensate for, partiality as far as the Welsh sister was concerned, through the ardency of his own Cambrophilia, which helped propel the poem's passionate defence of the essential truths of Geoffrey of Monmouth's fabulous British history. Could Drayton turn Scotophile too?

One way of thinking about this question is to consider the extant poem's treatment of the Picts alongside that of other writers in the period. Long after the Picts had vanished as a distinct people following their amalgamation in the ninth century into the Kingdom of Scotland, these ancient inhabitants of northern Britain continued to provoke a variety of scholarly, literary and artistic responses that ensured their relevance and importance in forging early modern Scottish identities.[36] In the later seventeenth century, the English poet Samuel Butler could recoil in comic horror at how "The antient Picts made feasts / [Of] Sheperds Bums and womens brests".[37] But in the hands of the sixteenth-century Welsh antiquary Humphrey Llwyd, St Jerome's fourth-century account of cannibalism among the northwestern British tribe of the Attacotti was serious ammunition for the erudite.[38] "Pict" was a supple term. It might more generally denote an ancient and uncivilized inhabitant of Britain, a near synonym for "ancient Briton" like Rochester's "ancient Pict", the jilted onanist encouraging vegetative growth in St James's Park.[39] But, as Stewart Mottram's reading in this issue of the "parti-coloured" Pict in Marvell's "Ode" demonstrates, it could easily assume political resonance in its negative characterisation of a composite contemporary Scotsman.

A perceived threat to English identity from the prospect of Anglo-Scottish union may lie, as Andrew Hadfield has argued, behind the unflattering engravings of Picts which appeared, alongside images of their visibly more civilised southern neighbours, in the Frankfurt edition of Thomas Hariot's *Briefe and True Report of the New Found Land of Virginia* (1590).[40] But a desire to play to James's interests, so brilliantly managed by Shakespeare in *Macbeth*, surely also encouraged in some quarters an English re-evaluation of the Scottish identikit. In scholarly terms, that re-evaluation was already well underway by the time James acceded to the throne, thanks in large part to Camden's *Britannia*, which appeared in successively expanded editions from 1586, culminating in Philemon Holland's translation of 1610. With characteristic diplomacy, Camden conceded the difficulty of going against the near unimpeachable authority of Bede, who claimed that the Picts originated in the barbaric wilds of Scythia, and only later settled in northern Britain after the Irish had refused to accommodate them in Ireland.[41] However, reverence for Bede was not enough to mute Camden's careful survey of fragmentary linguistic evidence and extant Roman accounts which backed his strong inclination that the Picts were in fact an indigenous people:

> verie naturall Britans themselves, even the right progenie of the most ancient Britans: those Britans, I meane, and none other, who before the comming in of the Romans, were seated

in the North part of the Iland, and of those who afterwards, casting off the yoke of bondage (as they are a nation most impatient of servilitie) repaired unto these in the North.[42]

Camden recognised that "Briton" was a convenient umbrella term, one that concealed a wide range of distinct regional identities – the ancient British tribes, such as the Trinovantes and Iceni, who supplied *Britannia*'s larger chorographical section divisions and printed running heads, even where the correspondence between early modern county and ancient civitas was strained. As Philip Schwyzer argues in this issue, the Welsh adoption of the term "Cambro-Briton" by Llwyd and others in part offered the English and the Scottish a stake in a composite but communal identity. Camden may very well have taken his cue from Llwyd when he later minted the term "Pict-Britans", reflecting a contemporary vogue for hyphenated island identities back upon the diverse ethnic landscape of ancient Britain.[43]

Camden's reappraisal proved influential. The historian John Clapham thought the consanguinity of the Picts and the Britons "not improbable", and, applying the concept of nationhood somewhat incongruously to ancient Britain, suggested that the Picts' separation from "their civill Country-men" who remained within the boundaries of the civilising Roman province explained the later bitter enmity between these two peoples: "there being commonly no greater hatred, then that which is bred and nourished among the people of one Nation, when they are severed each from other by difference of maners and customes".[44] In like fashion, John Selden, glossing Severn's description of Pictish incursions against the Britons in Song 8 of *Poly-Olbion*, instructs the reader to "adhere to learned *Camden*, making the *Picts* very genuine *Britons*, distinguisht onely by accidentall name".[45]

Drayton, as we shall see, did not quite share Selden's unqualified support for Camden's thesis on the origins of the Picts. Drayton's subtle divergence on this question, set against a general reliance on *Britannia* throughout *Poly-Olbion*,[46] is due in no small part to the poem's heavy investment in Geoffrey of Monmouth's fabulous British history – a history whose truth status Camden with careful scholarship reluctantly dismantles.[47] Geoffrey's Picts are, as one writer puts it, "the savage villains of British history".[48] In *Poly-Olbion*, too, they seem at first sight little more than cartoonish Galfridian bogeymen, firstly on cue to illustrate Arthur's military prowess, as the legendary British king overruns "Scotland", pursuing his savage enemy "beyond Mount *Calidon*: There strongly shut them up whom stoutly he subdu'd".[49] Silencing through confinement in the island's northern extremities proves a temporary fantasy, however. The relentless incursions of "the remorselesse *Pict*, still wasting us with warre" push the floundering Britons to risky expediency:

The warlike *Saxon* then into the Land we drew;

A Nation nurst in spoyle, and fitt'st to undergoe

Our cause against the *Pict*, our most inveterate foe.[50]

The Galfridian Pict perhaps reaches his apex in Song 6, when the River Wye in her impassioned defence of the essential truths of the British history, figures the Picts, along with the Romans, the Saxons, and the Danes, as "a horrid raine / Deforming" the island. By placing the Picts in a company of historical invaders of unquestioned foreignness, the Wye effectively rejects out of hand Pictish claims to indigeneity. Regardless of the "rain" (or "reign") of their military and territorial successes, there is a refusal to entertain the possibility that the Picts might ever be taken for "verie naturall Britans". Instead, they hang over the island like a malevolent force, warping the "natural" shape of the land itself and making the survival of any testimonies to true indigenous cultural achievement all the more "miraculous".[51]

When Drayton does try to assimilate Camden's arguments within the poem, he finds a devious means to achieve consistency between the marauding Pictish outlander, on the one hand, and the "Pict-Britan" on the other. In the passage prompting Selden's endorsement of Camden's hypothesis, noted above, the Severn as Anglo-Welsh boundary celebrates the heroic resistance of the Britons, reflecting their ancient glory forward in time upon their early modern descendants, the Welsh:

> A hundred thirtie yeeres the Northerne *Britans* still,
>
> That would in no wise stoupe to *Romes* imperious will,
>
> Into the straitned Land with theirs retired farre,
>
> In lawes and manners since from us that different are;
>
> And with the *Irish Pict*, which to their ayde they drew
>
> (On them oft breaking in, who long did them pursue)
>
> A greater foe to us in our owne bowels bred,
>
> Then *Rome*, with much expense that us had conquered.[52]

As in Camden, the peoples of the north who successfully resist Roman efforts to occupy the entire island are said to be Britons. Critically, though, the expected designation has been changed from "Picts" to "Northerne *Britans*". Severn's "Northerne *Britans*" might still be thought of as Pict-Britons – a liminal, displaced people in the process of becoming "Picts" through a compelled disconnect that in time will produce divergent "lawes and manners" – were it not for the "*Irish Pict*" "breaking in" to underline that the former were never really Picts at all. The real Picts remain the Bedean interlopers arriving via Britain's large island neighbour. Severn's pronouns struggle to stand up to the complexities of this ethnographical navigation. From the outset, northern Britons ("theirs", "their", "them") are distinguished from the non-northern Britons ("us", "our"), who, in the context of a north-south divide in "lawes and manners", begin to sound suspiciously like an early modern amalgamation of English and Welsh. The fraught distinction finally bends under the strain of locating the emergence on the island of the Pict, now no longer a "horrid rain" falling from beyond, but an internally nurtured nemesis "in our owne bowels bred". The possessive pronoun here collapses the earlier insistence on "them" and "us", merging the "Northerne *Britans*" in whose "straitned Land" that "foe" is actually bred with their more southerly neighbours who come to feel its force.

Severn's politic confusion reminds us of the complexities that lay ahead for Drayton as his muse hovered over the Anglo-Scottish border. By way of contrast, Drayton's "old friend" William Warner illustrates in his *Continuance of Albion's England* (1606) how other English poets might have no qualms in awarding the Picts a proud place among Britain's indigenous ethnic identities[53]:

> Whether of Agathirsian Scythes, or Humbers Heere Remaigne,

> Or Brutaines, brave Recusants of the Romane servile Raigne,
>
> (The last the Likeliest) were the Picts exact dispute that will,
>
> Those curious Ambiguities we leave to others skill.[54]

Warner alludes to other supposed Pictish progenitors – the Scythian tribe of the Agathyrsi, Virgil's "pictique Agathyrsi" ("painted Agathyrsians")[55]; and Humber, legendary king of the Huns said by Geoffrey of Monmouth to have invaded "Scotland" before being defeated and drowning in the estuary that would take his name[56] – but his parenthesis assures the reader that an origin in the Britons themselves (styled as "Brutaines" to reflect their fabled descent from Brutus, mythical Trojan founder of Britain) is the most plausible. Warner warns that any account of the Picts would be necessarily "briefe, since Envie did provide / Their fame, if possible their Name, from Historie to hide",[57] echoing Drayton's River Dee, who condemns "*Caesars* envious pen" for producing an account of the Britons which deliberately exaggerated their barbarity for its own ends.[58] Like *Poly-Olbion*'s ancient Britons, Warner's Picts are "fame-wronged Men" with a legacy at risk of being wiped from the historical record. Warner's "hope" – that "neither Swords, nor fir'd Records, nor alterd names of all, / Nor Envies-selfe, this of their [the Picts'] worth extinguish" [59] – ultimately stands as a rousing cry for inclusive island identities. The problem facing Drayton, however, was that incorporating the Picts *"without any partialitie"* in a Scottish continuation of his chorography threatened unsettling the delicate balance arrived at between the English and the Welsh. Two sisters were company, but perhaps three would make an unruly crowd.

Drayton manages that delicate balance by allowing Albion's varied landscapes, peoples and cultures to cling to their individual identities even as they merge in a common geographical space and singular encyclopedic poem. As Sandra Logan observes in this issue, *Poly-Olbion*'s waterways retain their distinctiveness, even as they flow into more major rivers or even the sea. Similarly, the song contest between the Welsh/Britons and the English/Saxons over proprietal rights to the island of Lundy is both an opportunity to assert and celebrate cultural difference, and also an occasion to weave a greater unity that might contain these sub-identities without diluting them. As Severn proclaims, endorsing the myth that through the Tudor dynasty the descendants of Brutus had been restored to the throne: "Why strive yee then for that, in little time that shall / (As you are all made one) be one unto you all".[60] In Drayton's Albion, the fantasy of a unifying poetic perspective collapses time, transporting the reader to a summit "from whose height thou mai'st behold both the old and later times, as in thy prospect, lying farre under thee".[61] Each region inhabits its own groundhog day, bearing witness to the curious combination of fixity and motion perfectly captured in the gestures of the numerous nymphs and local deities populating the landscapes in William Hole's accompanying maps.

In this fantasy, which the tricky final sister never gets to spoil, the Welsh can remain "that unmixed race" offering a direct bloodline back to the ancient Britons.[62] The English, too, may inhabit a perpetual continuum with their Saxon forefathers, "boast[ing] themselves the Nation most unmixt".[63] Drayton's vision of restless stasis is a reminder that some literary constructions of the nation in the period are more rooted in time than others. Warner, anticipating Defoe's satire on English xenophobia and pretensions to racial purity,[64] recognises more prosaically: "We Modernes are compounded of them both [i.e. Welsh and Scots], *Picts, Romaines*, and / *Armoricanes, Danes, Normaines*, all once breeding in this land".[65] Here, unlike in *Poly-Olbion*, the island's past racial and ethnic diversity appears definitively severed from its hybrid present, as singular "Modernes" defined only by their relative position in time replace the multiple former peoples of shared geographies.

The essays in this issue all address, in different ways, the construction of the nation and national identity across a range of seventeenth-century literary texts. Two share a focus on works by Michael Drayton. Sukanya Dasgupta's textual springboard is *Englands Heroicall Epistles* (first edition 1597), a collection of imaginary paired verse epistles by famous historical figures which ran through several editions and revisions during Drayton's lifetime. Pushing against more simplistic constructions of Drayton as a patriotic author, she argues that his appropriation of the past had a subversive underbelly particularly apparent in the "generic manipulations" of the *Epistles*. Sandra Logan returns to the magnum opus itself, widening *Poly-Olbion*'s sphere of concern beyond the limits of the island landmass to explore how the representation of waterways encodes attitudes towards overseas imperialist expansion. Philip Schwyzer takes a broader view of the period, examining the reasons behind the emergence and decline of the "Cambro-Briton", a hyphenated identity adopted by Welsh writers, but not fully appreciated by their English neighbours.

The two essays which follow take us forward in time to the English Republic. Stewart Mottram unravels the complex religious geography of Marvell's "Ode" (1650), tracing a more exclusively anti-Catholic focus that eschews the anti-Presbyterianism of contemporaries John Milton and Marchamont Nedham, and also anticipates the religious politics of Marvell's later work. Willy Maley locates in "Neptune to the Commonwealth of England", a minor poem prefixed to Marchamont Nedham's 1652 English translation of John Selden's *Mare Clausum* (1635), a vision of British overseas expansion that bridges republicanism and royalism and remains painfully relevant today. Lastly, Patrick Murray offers a detailed review of scholarship on nationalism and nationhood in the early modern period over the last twenty years.

Notes

1. "Topo-chrono-graphicall" is the term coined by Drayton's friend George Wither in the title of his dedicatory verse to Part 1 to describe the poem's dual axes of chorography and chronology (Drayton, *Poly-Olbion*, Part 2, "*To his Noble Friend*, Michael Drayton, Esquire, upon his Topo-chrono-graphicall Poeme").
2. There were enough unsold sheets from Part 1 (1612) for the new printers of Part 2 (1622) to be able to create complete copies from the two printings without resetting the first text. Part 2 was also sold as a standalone text with its own letterpress title-page, presumably for readers who already owned the first part. Drayton complained in the Preface to Part 2 that certain booksellers had resorted to selling incomplete copies of Part 1, "because it went not so fast away in the Sale, as some of their beastly and abominable Trash" (Drayton, *Poly-Olbion*, Part 2, "*To any that will read it*").
3. Paul Farley's contemporary reimagining of Drayton's poem, known under working titles that include *The Electric Poly-Olbion* and *The People's Poly-Olbion*, is forthcoming. For an already published excerpt, see Farley, "*from* The Electric-Poly-Olbion".

4. The first mention of the poetic project in progress is by Francis Meres in 1598 (Meres, *Palladis Tamia: Wits Treasury*, 281^r). In his sonnet sequence *Idea* (1594), Drayton had already transformed from being a passive consumer of of classical chorography ("Reading sometyme, my sorrowes to beguile, / I find old Poets hylls and floods admire" ["Amour 20"]) to a native chorographical poet himself, and the catalogue of English rivers presented there ("Amour 24") has been called "a miniature *Poly-Olbion*" (Aubin, *Topographical Poetry*, 19).
5. The reasons behind Drayton's failure to secure the favour of James I (VI) are unclear. His *To the Majestie of King James. A Gratulatorie Poem* (1603) was among the first published poetic works to celebrate the succession of the Scottish king, and Henry Chettle suggested that year that Drayton had been indecorous in the timing of his bid for royal patronage: "Thinke twas a fault to have thy Verses seene / Praising the King, ere they had mourn'd the Queene" (Chettle, *Englands Mourning Garment*, D2^r).
6. Christine Barrett observes that, "It is a wonder that anyone who read Drayton's note 'To the Generall Reader' ... actually bought the book" (*Poetics of Cartographic Anxiety*, 90). The preface does have a certain shock value, however, and we might give Drayton some credit for recognising the text's commerical limitations and willing a select group of potential readers to see themselves mirrored in his image of the text's ideal consumer, a skilled, intelligent reader with a strong interest in his native land.
7. Drayton, *Poly-Olbion*, Part 1, "To The High And Mightie, *Henrie, Prince Of Wales*". "Genuine" here means natural or native ("genuine, *adj.*^{1} [1a], in *OED Online*. Oxford: Oxford University Press, 2018. <http://www.oed.com>, accessed 5 May 2018).
8. See Chapter 2, "The Elizabethan Discovery of England", in Rowse, *The England of Elizabeth*, 49-86.
9. Helgerson, "The Land Speaks", 51.
10. See e.g. d'Haussy, *Poly-Olbion ou l'Angleterre*, and Hardin, *Michael Drayton*.
11. It is remarkable to consider that Drayton never mentions the incumbent monarch James anywhere in his poem. The Thames's "Catalogue of those, the Scepter heer that swayd" in Song 17 abruptly ends after Elizabeth (Drayton, *Poly-Olbion*, 17.109).
12. In the seventeenth century, chronology and geography were sometimes referred to as "the two eyes of history". The motto on the frontispiece of Abraham Ortelius's *Parergon* (1595 edition), an historical atlas of ancient lands, declared: "Historiae oculus geographia" ("Geography [is] the eye of history"). See the discussion in Goffart, *Historical Atlases*, 104, 129 n. 141.
13. "Besides, the Muse hath, next, the *British* cause in hand, / About things later done that now shee cannot stand" (Drayton, *Poly-Olbion*, 2.251-2).
14. Drummond, *Works*, 227. As John Kerrigan notes perceptively of this passage in Drummond, "'my compatriots' is at odds with 'their country'. Was Drayton a fellow-Briton or an alien Englishman?" (Kerrigan, *Archipelagic English*, 148).
15. Jonson, "Informations to William Drummond", ll. 17-18.
16. Drayton, *Poly-Olbion*, Part 1, "From the Author of the *Illustrations*".
17. Ibid., "To the Generall *Reader*".
18. Ibid., "To the High and Mightie, *Henrie, Prince of Wales*". In 1598, Meres had described a more limited (though still daunting) project, confined to the description of "all the forests, woods, mountaines, fountaines, rivers, lakes, flouds, bathes and springs that be in England" (Meres, *Palladis Tamia: Wits Treasury*, 281^r).
19. Drayton, *Poly-Olbion*, 5.67-8, 5.77-8.
20. Leland and Bale, *Laboryouse Journey*, D7^v, D8^v.
21. On British nationalism in the sixteenth century, see Schwyzer, *Literature, Nationalism and Memory*.
22. Helgerson, "The Land Speaks".
23. Drayton, *Poly-Olbion*, 23.261-70.
24. Lambarde, *Perambulation of Kent*; Carew, *Survey of Cornwall*. In addition, John Norden published brief descriptions of Middlesex and Hertfordshire in the 1590s. These were not

full-scale county surveys, however, but contributions to a larger, unrealized national chorography, the *Speculum Britanniae*.

25. Burton, *Description of Leicester Shire*, ¶2ᵛ.
26. Drayton, *Poly-Olbion*, Part 1, "To the Generall *Reader*". Burton approaches national nomenclature with a shrug, referring within a few lines in the preface to Speed's *History of Great Britaine* as "Historie of England" (¶2ᵛ) and "History of Brittaine" (¶2ʳ).
27. Wright, "Whose Pastorals?"; see also Mottram, "William Browne".
28. Helgerson, "The Land Speaks", 75.
29. Wright, "Whose Pastorals?".
30. Drayton, *Poly-Olbion*, Part 1, "To the High and Mightie, *Henrie, Prince of Wales*".
31. Ibid., 30.342.
32. Ibid., Part 2, "To the High and Mightie, *Charles* Prince of Wales".
33. Drayton's Scottish literary acquaintances evidently believed that Drayton had made progress on a Scottish continuation. In a letter written shortly after Drayton's death in 1631, William Drummond of Hawthornden instructed the poet and courtier William Alexander, first earl of Stirling, to seek out and collect these surviving fragments for publication in Scotland (Newdigate, *Michael Drayton*, 188-9).
34. Drayton's sororal metaphor may be rooted in the biblical figuring of the neighbouring kingdoms of Israel and Judah as sisters (see e.g. Jeremiah 3:6-10). The same comparison is made in early religiously inflected references to England and Scotland, and their respective churches, as sisters (see e.g. Clapham, *Sinners Sleepe*, 58, and Willet, *Ecclesia triumphans*, ¶7ᵛ). In Geoffrey of Monmouth's *History of the Kings of Britain*, the island is of course initially divided among three brothers, the sons of the Trojan émigré Brutus (2.1).
35. As an illustration of the problem, Camden's *Britannia* in the 1610 Philemon Holland translation devotes some 578 pages to describing the counties of England, 59 to those of Wales, but only 45 to the regions of Scotland. Drayton's special interest in Wales spurred him to go far beyond these sample proportions in gathering material in Part 1 for seven "Welsh" songs (almost a quarter of the total of 30 published songs). Whether he would have found the enthusiasm and resources for a similarly thorough treatment of Scotland remains doubtful.
36. For an accessible overview of this topic, see Hudson, *The Picts*.
37. Butler, "History", 172. Butler ultimately takes his cue from St Jerome's fourth-century report of the cannibalism of the Attacotti, a tribe of north-west Britain: "Why should I speak of other nations when I myself, a youth on a visit to Gaul, heard that the Atticoti, a British tribe, eat human flesh, and that although they find herds of swine, and droves of large or small cattle in the woods, it is their custom to cut off the buttocks of the shepherds and the breasts of their women, and to regard them as the greatest delicacies?" (St Jerome, *Letters and Selected Works*, 393-4).
38. Llwyd's target was Hector Boece, whose *Scotorum historia* (1527) he viewed as a fabricated history of ancient "Scotland" that often glorified the Scots by falsely attributing to them the achievements of the Britons, ancestors of the early modern Welsh. Llwyd deploys St Jerome's account to make a mockery of the "holsome lawes, & institutes" Boece claimed were in Scotland at this time (*The Breviary of Britayne*, 43ᵛ). It appeared that in the scholarly recovery of the history of the island's peoples there was only a finite amount of fame, and giving to one of those peoples, as Boece had done, meant taking away from another.
39. Rochester, "A Ramble in St. James's Park", l. 14.
40. Hadfield, *Matter of Britain*, 73. Based on the paintings of John White, who had accompanied Hariot on the 1585 voyage to north America, these images were redrawn for publication by the Frankfurt printer and engraver Theodor de Bry. In the series of engravings, the Picts' less backward neighbours are not named, but, as Hadfield presumes, these are surely Romanised Britons.

41. Bede, *Ecclesiastical History*, 1.1. Bede's account of Pictish origins remained highly influential, and was drawn on by later seventeenth-century writers including Milton, who rehearsed the story of the Picts' supposed Scythian origins (Milton, *History of Britain*, e.g. 79).
42. Camden, *Britain*, 115. I quote from Holland's translation, but Camden already presents the argument in the original 1586 edition of *Britannia* (30-4).
43. Camden, *Remaines*, 8.
44. Clapham, *Great Britannie*, 142.
45. Drayton, *Poly-Olbion*, §. 8.315.
46. Critics have often somewhat harshly suggested that the poem is fundamentally a versification of Britannia (see e.g. Parry, *Trophies of Time*, 108; Herendeen, *William Camden*, 214; Levy, Tudor Historical Thought, 222; Boon, "Camden and the *Britannia*", 17)
47. See Gourvitch, "Drayton's Debt". Camden's *Britannia* is not quite the uncomplicated demolition of the Brutus story and other Galfridian myths it is sometimes taken to be. Camden admits to having personally defended the Brutus story in the past, and is careful not to be seen to have "impeached that narration", instead framing objections to it as the opinions of others. He eventually reaches the kind of intellectual compromise which might have satisfied (and also influenced) Drayton: "Let Antiquitie heerein be pardoned, if by entermingling falsities and truthes, humane matters and divine together, it make the first beginnings of nations and cities more noble, sacred, and of greater majestie" (Camden, *Britain*, 8-9).
48. Hudson, *The Picts*, 216.
49. Drayton, *Poly-Olbion*, 4.274-5.
50. Ibid., 8.349, 8.354-6. The notion that the Britons first brought in the Saxons as hired warriors to fight against the Picts may be traced back to Gildas.
51. Ibid., 6.336-7, 6.333.
52. Ibid., 8.309-16.
53. The phrase "my old friend" is Drayton's in his elegy "To Henry Reynolds" (1627). Drayton writes here of Warner's poetry: "though his lines were not so trim'd, / Nor yet his Poem so exactly lim'd / And neatly joynted ... / ... some passages there be / In him, which I protest have taken me, With almost wonder, so fine, cleere, and new / As yet they have bin equalled by few".
54. Warner, *Albion's England*, 345.
55. Virgil, *Aeneid*, 4.146.
56. Geoffrey of Monmouth, *History of the Kings of Britain*, 2.1.
57. Warner, *Albion's England*, 345.
58. The Dee asks whether the Britons could be "So ignorant ... and yet so knowing warre", as attested by Caesar's descriptions of their skilled use of chariots, and their deployment of sharpened wooden stakes to impede the Roman advance across the Thames (Drayton, *Poly-Olbion*, 10.307; Caesar, *Gallic War*, 4.33, 5.18). For a discussion of the problems Drayton faced in having simultaneously to rely on, but also discredit, the earliest authentic written source on the Britons, see Curran, Jr., "History Never Written".
59. Warner, *Albion's England*, 345, 373.
60. Drayton, *Poly-Olbion*, 5.77-8.
61. Ibid., Part 1, "To the Generall *Reader*".
62. Ibid., 9.183.
63. Ibid., 4.381.
64. Defoe, "The True-Born Englishman". Defoe suggests that the English are "the most scoundrel race that ever lived; / A horrid crowd of rambling thieves and drones" (191), and sketches a composite English identity in which each ethnic facet lends a unique characteristic:

    Fierce, as the Briton; as the Roman, brave;

    ...

    The Pict has made 'em sour, the Dane morose;
    False from the Scot, and from the Norman worse.
    What honesty they have, the Saxons gave them (197).
65. Warner, *Albion's England*, 374.

Acknowledgments

Research for this article was supported by an AHRC Research Grant for *The Poly-Olbion Project* (2013-16; PI Andrew McRae). We are grateful to Andrew McRae for his advice and support in compiling this collection of essays.

Disclosure statement

No potential conflict of interest was reported by the authors.

Bibliography

Aubin, R. A. *Topographical Poetry in XVIII-Century England*. New York: Modern Language Association, 1936.
Barrett, C. *Early Modern English Literature and the Poetics of Cartographic Anxiety*. Oxford: Oxford University Press, 2018.
Bede. *The Ecclesiastical History of the English People*, edited by Judith McClure and Roger Collins. Oxford: Oxford University Press, 2008.
Boon, G. C. "Camden and the *Britannia*". *Archaeologia Cambrensis*, 136 (1987), 1–19.
Butler, S. "History". In *Samuel Butler, Satires, and Miscellaneous Poetry and Prose*, edited by René Lamar. 172–175. Cambridge: Cambridge University Press, 1928.
Burton, W. *The Description of Leicester Shire*. London, 1622.
Caesar, J. *The Gallic War*, translated by H. J. Edwards. Cambridge, MA: Loeb Classical Library, 1917.
Camden, W. *Britain*, translated by Philemon Holland. London, 1610.
Camden, W. *Britannia Siue Florentissimorum Regnorum, Angliae, Scotiae, Hiberniae, Et Insularum Adiacentium Ex Intima Antiquitate Chorographica Descriptio*. London, 1586.
Camden, W. *Remaines of a Greater Worke, Concerning Britaine*. London, 1605.
Carew, R. *The Survey of Cornwall*. London, 1602.
Chettle, H. *Englands Mourning Garment*. London, 1603.
Clapham, H. *The Sinners Sleepe Wherein Christ Willing Her to Arise Receiveth but an Untoward Answer*. Edinburgh, 1596.
Clapham, J. *The Historie of Great Britannie*. London, 1606.
Curran, J. E. Jr."The History Never Written: Bards, Druids, and the Problem of Antiquarianism in *Poly Olbion*". *Renaissance Quarterly*, 51 (1998), 498–525.
Defoe, D. "The True-Born Englishman". In *The Earlier Life and the Chief Earlier Works of Daniel Defoe*, edited by Henry Morley, 175–218. London: George Routledge and Sons, 1889.
Drayton, M. *Ideas Mirrour*. In *The Works of Michael Drayton*, 5 Vols, edited by J. William Hebel et al., corrected edition, 1:95–124. Oxford: Basil Blackwell for the Shakespeare Head Press, 1961.
Drayton, M. *Poly-Olbion*. Vol. 4 of *The Works of Michael Drayton*, 5 Vols, edited by J. William Hebel et al., corrected edition. Oxford: Basil Blackwell for the Shakespeare Head Press, 1961.
Drayton, M. "To Henry Reynolds". In *The Works of Michael Drayton*, 5 Vols, edited by William J. Hebel et al., 3:226. Oxford: Basil Blackwell for the Shakespeare Head Press, 1961.
Drummond, W. *The Works of William Drummond, of Hawthornden*, edited by John Sage and Thomas Ruddiman. James Watson: Edinburgh, 1711.
Farley, P. "*From* the Electric-Poly-Olbion". In *The Map and the Clock: A Laureate's Choice of the Poetry of Britain and Ireland*, edited by Carol Ann Duffy and Gillian Clarke. London: Faber & Faber, 2016.
Geoffrey of Monmouth. *The History of the Kings of Britain*, edited by Michael D. Reeve, translated by Neil Wright. Woodbridge: Boydell, 2007.

Goffart, W. *Historical Atlases: The First Three Hundred Years, 1570-1870*. Chicago: University of Chicago Press, 2003.
Gourvitch, I. "Drayton's Debt to Geoffrey of Monmouth". *Review of English Studies*, 4 (1928), 394–403.
Hadfield, A. *Shakespeare, Spenser, and the Matter of Britain*. Basingstoke: Palgrave Macmillan, 2004.
Hardin, R. *Michael Drayton and the Passing of Elizabethan England*. Lawrence, KS: University of Kansas Press, 1973.
Haussy, A. d'. *Poly-Olbion Ou l'Angleterre Vue Par Un Élisabéthain*. Paris: Klincksieck, 1972.
Helgerson, R. "The Land Speaks: Cartography, Chorography, and Subversion in Renaissance England". *Representations*, 16 (Autumn, 1986), 50–85.
Herendeen, W. H. *William Camden: A Life in Context*. Woodbridge: Boydell & Brewer, 2007.
Hudson, B. T. *The Picts*. Chichester: John Wiley, 2014.
Jerome, St. *St. Jerome: Letters and Select Works*, edited by Philip Schaff and Henry Wace. Oxford: James Parker, 1893.
Jonson, B. "Informations to William Drummond of Hawthornden". In *The Cambridge Edition of the Works of Ben Jonson*, 7 vols, edited by David Bevington, Martin Butler, and Ian Donaldson. Cambridge: Cambridge University Press, 2012.
Kerrigan, J. *Archipelagic English: Literature, History, and Politics 1603–1707*. Oxford: Oxford University Press, 2008.
Levy, F. J. *Tudor Historical Thought*. San Marino, CA: Huntingdon Library, 1967.
Lambarde, W. *A Perambulation of Kent Conteining the Description, Hystorie, and Customes of that Shyre*. London, 1576.
Leland, J., and John B. *The Laboryouse Journey & Serche of Johan Leylande, for Englandes Antiquitees*. London, 1549.
Llwyd, H. *The Breviary of Britayne*, translated by Thomas Twyne. London, 1573.
Meres, F. *Palladis Tamia: Wits Treasury*. London, 1598
Milton, J. *The History of Britain, that Part Especially Now Call'd England*. London, 1670.
Mottram, S. "William Browne and the Writing of Early Stuart Wales". In *Writing Wales, from the Renaissance to Romanticism*, edited by Stewart Mottram and Sarah Prescott, 91–107. Farnham: Ashgate, 2012.
Newdigate, B. H. *Michael Drayton and His Circle*. Corrected Edition. Oxford: Basil Blackwell for Shakespeare Head Press, 1961.
Parry, G. *The Trophies of Time: English Antiquarians of the Seventeenth Century*. Oxford: Oxford University Press, 1995.
Rochester, J. W. "Earl Of. A Ramble in St. James's Park". In *Rochester, Selected Poems*, edited by Paul Davis, 41–45. Oxford: Oxford University Press, 2013.
Rowse, A. L. *The England of Elizabeth: The Structure of Society*. 2nd edition. Basingstoke: Palgrave Macmillan, 2003.
Schwyzer, P. *Literature, Nationalism, and Memory in Early Modern England and Wales*. Cambridge: Cambridge University Press, 2004.
Virgil. *Aeneid*. A. In *Eclogues. Georgics. Aeneid: Books 1-6*, translated by H. Rushton Fairclough, revised by G. P. Goold. Cambridge, MA: Loeb Classical Library, 1916.
Warner, W. *A Continuance of Albion's England*. London, 1606.
Willet, A. *Ecclesia Triumphans: That Is, the Joy of the English Church*. Cambridge, 1603.
Wright, G. "Whose Pastorals? William Browne of Tavistock and the Singing of Britannia". In *Archipelagic Identities: Literature and Identity in the Atlantic Archipelago, 1550-1800*, edited by Philip Schwyzer and Simon Mealor, 43–52. Aldershot, Ashgate, 2004.

Imagining Britain: reconstructing history and writing national identity in *Englands Heroicall Epistles*

Sukanya Dasgupta

ABSTRACT
The idea that in the Tudor era the English people became proudly conscious of their national language and history, has been challenged by critical interventions that suggest how England as a nation had to be "written": the act of writing can construct imagined boundaries, both to appropriate and exclude. In *Englands Heroicall Epistles*, Drayton replaces Ovid's mythological figures in the *Heroides* with specific well-known English historical personas who provide, through their letters, different perspectives on English history. I will contend that Drayton's assertion of national identity and patriotism is done verbally and semantically, while his allegiance to oppositionist politics is rendered generically and subversively by a remarkable manipulation of the genre of historical poetry in the *Heroicall Epistles*: this in turn reflects his deep engagement with ideas of history and the construction of national consciousness in early modern England.

I

In his study of Michael Drayton over a century ago, Oliver Elton intriguingly observed: "Into Drayton, English as he was, had sunk the Renaissance feeling of the wreck and destruction accomplished by Time upon beauty, and power, and noble, visible monuments, and the glory of the great".[1] I would like to use Elton's epithet for Drayton – "English as he was", as the starting point of my analysis on Drayton's ideas of national identity in *Englands Heroicall Epistles*. Indeed, how *English* was Michael Drayton? How successful was he in his attempts to forge a sense of national consciousness, given his engagement with oppositionist politics?[2] What kind of politics did he engage in exactly? Richard Helgerson identifies Drayton as a member of a generation of professional poets who developed genres that made the beginning of the English nation-state conceivable.[3] I will contend that Drayton's assertion of national identity and patriotism is done verbally and semantically while his allegiance to oppositionist politics is rendered generically and subversively by a remarkable manipulation of the genre of historical poetry in *Englands Heroicall Epistles*.

The Tudor period has long been associated with the process of the "discovery of England" when the English people became acutely aware of their culture, their geographical location and their exclusivity, fueled not merely by expansive texts like Camden's

Britannia, but also by evolving material practices like cartography, historiography, biblical rhetoric, standardization of language and the work of the Society of Antiquaries. Adrian Hastings asserts that England "presents the prototype of both a nation and a nation-state" in the pre-Enlightenment era.[4] In 1565, planning the subjugation of Ireland, Sir Thomas Smith identified what he believed were the three true bands of a commonwealth: "our tongue, our laws and our religion".[5] This spirit seems to be reflected in what is now a well anthologized speech by John of Gaunt in Shakespeare's *Richard II*:

> This precious stone set in a silver sea
>
> Which serves it in the office of a wall
>
> Or as a moat defensive to a house,
>
> Against the envy of less happier lands,
>
> This blessed plot, this earth, this realm, this England...[6]

It is interesting to note how Gaunt specifically celebrates "England", that "precious stone set in a silver sea", as a geographically consolidated entity that does not take cognizance of other cultural and geographical spaces that include Wales, Scotland and Ireland. On the contrary, this "scepter'd isle" is a "fortress built by Nature for herself/ Against infection and the hand of war...".[7] Yet, as the critical interventions of Richard Helgerson, Claire McEachern, David Baker, Andrew Hadfield and Bernhard Klein have proved, the new emerging "English" nation and notions about nationhood were bound to be rendered problematic and complex by the growth of empire and the question of "Britishness", even if that was to serve English material interests.[8] "Britain" or "England" was a multivalent trope and as Helgerson has persuasively argued, while the kingdom took on a number of names like Albion or Britannia or Poly-Olbion, the national territory denoted by these names was in a state of flux.[9] England, like other nations, had to be constructed, created as "imagined communities" (to use Benedict Anderson's telling phrase), even "written" by Sidney, Spenser, Drayton, Hakluyt and others, and Philip Schwyzer makes the cogent assertion that "Englishness" was (and indeed still is) a "relational identity".[10] At the same time, even in an age of emerging nationhood, English men and women often drew their primary identity from the town, the local community, the county or the parish. Local consciousness often emerged as a dynamic site of negotiation where broader changes were interrogated, modified and adapted to the needs of smaller communities. J. G. A. Pocock's seminal article "British History: A Plea for a New Subject" (1975) grapples with the problematic intellectual dynamics of reconciling a pluralistic approach in British history to the history of an increasing English dominion.[11] My intention will be to trace how Michael Drayton negotiated these simultaneously existing and complex ideas of nationhood through his historical poem *Englands Heroicall Epistles*, to write and construct a picture of a nation that offers the reader an alternative way to view the "Rarities and Histories of their own country".[12] I wish to analyze two sets of epistles, those between Mortimer and Isabel and between Surrey and Geraldine, as case studies to corroborate my argument that Drayton engages in oppositionist politics generically in a way none of his contemporaries do, articulating and presenting ideas of nationhood that were both complex and innovative.

The importance of history as a key component of national identity has been recognized by many historians and theorists of nationhood. Florian Kläger, for instance, points out that imagined communities "are endowed, through the narrative configuration and interpretation of the past, with a common history. It is with reference to this constructed history that the collective is meant to understand, justify and orientate itself in the present".[13] However, in order to serve national purposes, history must be reconstructed and indeed "written" by the nation's authors. The publication of this shared past and the construction of English consciousness were achieved largely through the works of the chroniclers of the era, but also through literature as portrayed by the playwrights, poets and polemicists of the day. For subjects and sovereigns, the emergent nation state made the study of English history a matter of pride, interest and a source of self-definition. Viewed in the context of this process of national consolidation and national self-definition, the vogue for history in the late sixteenth century appears as an important component of the cultural project of imagining an English nation. Paul Ricouer points out how history is more a matter of representation than documentation.[14] Historiography therefore plays a key role in the formation of national identity, not because it carefully records the past, but because it distorts historical facts in ways that allow societies to construct national myths out of them. The history play, chorographical poems, hagiography, fictitious letters based on the amorous liaisons of English historical characters as in *Englands Heroicall Epistles* or any other kind of historiography moulds past material into a subjective narrative: ultimately what seems like a lack of veracity metamorphoses into a constructed national history. Living at a time of rapid social, economic and political change, early modern English readers looked to the past for the roots that would stabilize and legitimate their new identities. Drayton was quick to realize that recognizing a common past was fundamental for the unification of local or particularistic attitudes into wider, national concerns. Even if we grant, as modern theorists of the nation like Ernest Gellner have, that nations are constructed and invented, and as an ideology and as a language "nationalism" is relatively modern, it is hard to neglect the fact that the past is, in many ways, essential for the emergence of national identity.[15] The past as it is imagined by the emergent nation plays a crucial role in its self-conception. A *belief* in a shared past is a precondition for the creation of a nation.[16]

When Drayton chose to write *Englands Heroicall Epistles* in 1597 (revised with the incorporation of new epistles in 1598 and 1599 and republished several times thereafter till 1619) he must have been well aware of the fact that writing about English history in the late 1590s could carry with it immense potential as well as risks, depending on his choice of subject matter. Here he conspicuously appropriates the Ovidian verse epistle and ingeniously constructs it into a specifically English textual product. Based on close but inventive readings of a range of chronicle sources and juxtaposed with an extended generic, stylistic and structural meditation on the *Heroides*, it was destined to be amongst the most popular of Drayton's works in his own lifetime. This collection of epistolary exchanges also represents the culmination of what Lindsay Ann Reid has referred to as "Elizabethan Anglo-Ovidianism".[17] Although Drayton acknowledges that the literary antecedent of the Epistles is Ovid's *Heroides*, he parenthetically observes, "…whose Imitator I partly professe to be".[18] This work engages in a highly productive and transformative relationship with Ovid's *Heroides*. Of Drayton's many telling departures from Ovid's work, the one that is especially innovative is his replacement of mythological characters with personalities drawn from different ages of English history, placing them in the heroic genre. Drayton takes an ostensibly neutral and politically conservative stand by declaring at the outset that he has "interwoven matters Historicall" merely so that his poems are not considered "Braynish" or unduly passionate. Sequenced chronologically, the epistles are putatively written by royal or noble, specifically English couples, whose stories were mined from the annals of English history. The very title of Drayton's poem hints at the generic manipulations that become evident as the work progresses. The term "heroicall" has epic implications; the linking up of English historical material (all the characters are taken from English history) with heroic poetry confirms the implicit admixture of epic purpose in all of Drayton's poems dealing with English history:

> *The Title (I hope) carrieth Reason in it selfe; for that the most and greatest persons herein, were English; or else, that their Loves were obtained in England. And though (Heroicall) be properly understood of Demi-gods ... yet it is also transferred to them, who for the greatnesse of Mind come neere to Gods.*[19]

By drawing exclusively on English historical personages and by making English history a context for his epistles, Drayton ensured that his work would be popular among the general public and that national sentiment would be aroused by recounting the chivalric deeds, military achievements and noble lineage of his characters. At the same time, however, Drayton subtly undercuts the patriotic, nationalistic attitude of his military English heroes in a number of innovative ways (for instance by using paired, gendered epistles), problematizing the reader's response to the notion of a masculine national identity. Ovidianism provided a means of extracting the feminine complaint, the voice of alterity, from chronicle history and drawing it into a discussion about English nationhood. Georgina Brown argues for a new form of historical complaint that uses the Ovidian feminine voice.[20] It is to this nuanced, subversive undercurrent in the text that I now wish to turn. My contention here is to explore the ways in which Michael Drayton uses history and the strategy of paired epistles in *Englands Heroicall Epistles* to project not only a deeply entrenched and challenging sense of national consciousness, but what I will argue, was a unique poetic and political agenda as well.

Needless to say, the creation of a new national identity would involve selecting stories that would highlight some players and erase others. Drayton's subjective version of historical facts may lack veracity, but it gives us valuable insights into the fabrication of a national history. Drayton was intensely aware of this: his decision to frame each letter with a contextualizing *argumentum* and a scholarly gloss on weighty "matters historicall" attempts to imbue the new vernacular work with an aura of established authority. The history of England is unravelled through the reigns of monarchs in moments of crisis but the effect is not to celebrate kingship. Drayton's epistles start with the Plantagenet kings (Henry II, John, the Black Prince) and their paramours and extends through the crisis of Richard II's fall and its turbulent aftermath, culminating in the valedictory epistles exchanged by Lady Jane Gray and her husband, Gilford Dudley. I would argue that Richard Hardin's optimistic assertion that Drayton's epistles are marked by "a spirit of confident patriotism" needs to be qualified.[21] Indeed there are many passages in the epistles that seem to support Hardin's contention at a superficial level. Written at a time when the "emergent nation-state made the study of English history a matter of pride and interest as well as an essential source of self definition", and when the Tudors sponsored official histories that constructed a myth of ancient descent to authenticate their questionable claim to the throne, many of the writers of *Englands Heroicall Epistles* do view themselves consciously as English public figures endowed with nationalistic and patriotic virtues.[22] Queen Katherine's legitimacy as a French and English queen for instance, authorizes her pursuit of the Welsh Owen Tudor. In context of the succession debates of the entire Elizabethan period, Wales came to serve as the touchstone and repository of true Britishness in the imagination of sixteenth-century writers. The anxious reinscriptions of cultural and political heritage in the pursuit of national legitimation are evident in Katherine's association with Owen Tudor as she attempts to resuscitate the ancient British line. Yet the proliferation of royal narratives and heterogeneous social dialogue found in the epistles counters and indeed challenges the idea of singular sovereignty and monarchical authority, bringing to the forefront pluralist images of the nation that embodies the concept that sovereignty is shared between the king and the people.

Before one turns to the epistles themselves however, something may be said about Drayton's political inclinations or the apparent lack of them. Drayton's poetic programme is so radically different from that of his contemporaries that it is impossible to classify him as belonging to any faction, party or group; in this context I would argue that there was no "Michael Drayton and his Circle" in the way Bernard Newdigate suggests, simply because Drayton did not ally himself with any literary or political "circle".[23] At a time of escalating conflict between the Crown and Parliament, Court and Country, Drayton seemed to resist categorization or placement on either "side" by maintaining links with Royalists and the Country faction simultaneously. Yet his affiliation to oppositionist politics is affirmed through his network of associates and friends, many of whom later had links with the "Country" party and who were in most cases anti-court. Drayton's engagement with oppositionist politics is rendered problematic by the fact that his political attitude is rarely explicit and couched within the purview of his poetic practice.

Like many of his contemporaries, Drayton wrote a considerable amount of historical verse, but what is interesting is the range of genres he chose and experimented with when dealing with historical material. Edward II's reign was often alluded to during both Elizabeth's and James's time and would have relevance for an Elizabethan audience, given the Queen's favours towards the Cecils over the older nobility. As Lily Campbell points out, a document popularly entitled *Leicester's Commonwealth* (1584), written in all probability by Robert Parsons, compared Queen Elizabeth's partiality towards her favourites with Edward II's "excessive favour towards Peter Gaveston and two of the Spencers". In a later work, Parsons even suggested that "Princes may for good cause be deposed", arguing that deposed monarchs were often succeeded by much better ones, as in the case of Edward II, who was followed by Edward III. Marlowe's play *Edward II* was published in 1591, while in 1598 Peter Wentworth's *A Pithie Exhortation to her Maiestie for Establishing her successor to the Crowne* was published posthumously. Echoing Parsons's view, Wentworth contends that although Edward II was ruled by the "lewde counsell" of the Spencers and Gaveston, he was not deposed by his son but by "his Nobilitie and commons".[24] It is also worth noting that from 1595,

Lord Burghley left notes in manuscript form on the reign of Edward II.[25] Thus Elizabeth could no longer view historical precedent, particularly the ruling of monarchs by royal favourites and their consequent deposition, as remote and distant. The dangers of civil war was a common theme in Elizabethan literature, and as David Norbrook argues, Lucan's poem *Pharsalia* or *Civil War* "did become identified with a particular kind of political grouping that, while not specifically antimonarchical, had distinct hankerings after a severely limited monarchy".[26] Towards the end of Elizabeth's reign, republican ideas became fashionable in the intellectual circles of the Earl of Essex and among those who had been connected with Philip Sidney. However, a republican culture that erased the signs of kingship was never forged. The development of the Privy Council and the frequent meetings of Parliament made England what Kevin Sharpe calls "a mixed polity", where, however, the monarch remained the hub of a network of clientage and patronage.[27] The emergent "Country" faction comprised many people like John Selden and Edward Coke, who firmly believed in the supremacy of the common law. Like Camden, Selden and Jonson, Drayton shared the political anxieties of the last years of Elizabeth's reign. Parallels between the past and present, particularly between ancient Rome and contemporary England, were frequently made, and could often be disturbing. Jonson's *Sejanus his Fall*, with its account of the suppression of Roman liberty under Tiberius and his favourite Sejanus, is a case in point. Instead of setting his poem in imperial Rome, Drayton chooses the reign of Edward II from the chronicles of Holinshed as the background to the epistles between Mortimer and Isabel in *Englands Heroicall Epistles*. In her last years Queen Elizabeth faced widespread accusations that she had surrendered control of her realm to favourites, particularly to Robert Cecil, who was said to have risen at the expense of the old nobility. By highlighting the repercussions arising out of the rule of favourites, Drayton issues a warning against repeating past mistakes.

II

The reign of Edward II provided Drayton with the subject matter for the complaint poem *Piers Gaveston* (later revised as the *Legend of Pierce Gaveston), Mortimeriados*, and *The Barons Warres*, as well as the epistles between Isabel and Mortimer in *Englands Heroicall Epistles*. It is to these epistles that I now wish to turn. By presenting history through the medium of letters, Drayton is not only able to furnish different points of view regarding the same incidents or situations, but the gender dialectics that this device of "pairing" generates, become in turn a reflection of the historical dialectics that form the basis of the epistles. The women, through their interpretations of "history", offer a different perspective and often a critique of the kind of "history" presented by the men. While discussing the "single line of dialogue", Mikhail Bakhtin writes:

> In such a line, every utterance, while focussed on its referential object, at the same time displays an intensive reaction to another utterance, either replying to it or anticipating it. This feature of reply and anticipation penetrates deeply into the intensively dialogic utterance.[28]

He further adds that such an utterance appears to be taking in the intentions of the speaker and "reworking" them. Although here Bakhtin is not referring to the epistolary method, his definition may be profitably applied to the relational character of the letter form. The unit in *Englands Heroicall Epistles* is not the dramatic monologue incorporated in a single letter, but the letter together with its reply. Each unit provides two versions of history, one from a male and the other from a female point of view. This dialogism implies a "third–person" analysis by the writer which combines with individual psychological introspection on the parts of the characters.

It is precisely this merging of historical and personal elements that marks Drayton's most innovative departure from Ovid's *Heroides*. The sense of national consciousness expressed by the women writers is instructively contrasted to the idea of nationhood offered by the men, and the epistles between Queen Isabel and Mortimer are a case in point. Isabel's epistle to Mortimer begins after Mortimer has escaped to France. Outraged by Edward's preference for male favourites, Isabel's letter begins on a note of personal lament for the absent Mortimer, soon to be replaced by indignation at being refused the marriage bed by the "*English* Edward":

Did Bulloyne once a Festivall prepare,

For England, Almaine, Cicill and Navarre?

When France envi'd those Buildings (onely blest)

Grac'd with the Orgies of my Bridall Feast,

That English Edward should refuse my Bed,

For that lascivious shameless Ganimed?[29]

Interestingly, by referring here to Edward Carnarvon, the first Prince of Wales of English blood, who married her in a ceremony attended by the kings of England, Cicill and Navarre, Queen Isabel establishes her position in the English royal family, referring to herself as "Englands Queene" and thus paving the way for her apparent patriotism for England later in the epistle. Scorning her husband's economic mismanagement and his inability to pursue an aggressive foreign policy she laments that the "Princely Jewels" of England are given away to "Beggers-Brats, wrapt in our rich Perfumes" like Gaveston. Isabel also makes a pointed reference to the lands that had been conquered by Longshanks and are now being given away:

Did LONGSHANKS purchase with his conqu'ring Hand,

Albania, Gascoyne, Cambria, Ireland?

That young CARNARVAN (his unhappie Sonne)

Should give away all that his Father wonne,

To backe a Stranger, proudly bearing downe

The brave Allies and Branches of the Crowne?[30]

She reminds Mortimer of Edward I's dying wish that Gaveston, the "proud Gascoyne" should be banished, never to step on English soil again. Though personal and intimate in tone, the political resonances of such an utterance are clear: Isabel, herself of French origin, adopts an indignant and specifically English nationalistic tone in her criticism and disparagement of this foreigner. Despite her lament and despair at Mortimer's being absent, Isabel deliberately catalogues all those who have defended England in the past: the brave Normans, bold Britans, big-bon'd Almans, stout Brabanders and the Pickards.[31]

Mortimer's public declarations in his reply to her not only show him to be endowed with tremendous heroic and patriotic virtues, but his English lineage is emphasized upon in contrast to Gaveston's French ancestry: his Grandsire Roger Mortimer reinstated the Round Table at Kenilworth after the Order of King Arthur's Table and thus "Princely Order honour'd England more / Than all the Conquests she atchiev'd before". Assuming a public, rhetorical stance, Mortimer asserts that while the ancestral seat of the Mortimers at Wigmore flourished, the Scots did not dare "set foot on English ground", which is then contrasted to the English blood being "stayned" at Banocksbourne where the Scots "Made lavish Havocke of the English Blood" who were led by Edward II.[32] The greater involvement of Mortimer in the realm of public affairs, his constant reference to heroic deeds, his military achievements and his noble lineage, clearly make him view himself as a public figure even when expressing private emotions. Furthermore, Mortimer envisions the establishment of an English empire and longs to subjugate Scotland and France for the glory of England:

A thousand Kingdomes will we seeke from farre,

As many Nations waste with Civill Warre,

Where the dishevel'd ghastly Sea-Nymph sings,

Or well-rig'd Ships shall stretch their swelling Wings,

And drag their Anchors through the sandie Fome,

About the World in ev'ry Clime to rome

And those unchrist'ned Countries call our owne,

Where scarce the Name of *England* hath been knowne.[33]

The importance given to Mortimer in Drayton's historical poem *Mortimeriados* (1596) is not from a psychological perspective but a heroic and even mythic one, in keeping with the epic tenor of the work. In the very next year, however, Drayton presents Mortimer from a radically different perspective in *Englands Heroicall Epistles*. In the epistles between Mortimer and Queen Isabel, Mortimer counters Isabel's despair with dreams of his future military ascendance. Asserting that he has not been banished from England, but rather England has been banished from him, Mortimer "fashions" a self that is comparable to "the Skie-attempting DEDALUS".[34] Here he is not presented in mythic terms, but rather as a personality whose imagination shapes experience and whose individual mind shapes the version of national history he presents. Although in exile, Mortimer sees himself as an integral part of this patriotic and military venture. It is a hypothesis that he constructs in order to come to terms with his banishment.

It is perhaps instructive to note at this juncture that Drayton is stressing many aspects of Mortimer's character that might have encouraged identification with the increasingly rebellious Earl of Essex, whose popularity was based on his belief that England should pursue a militant foreign policy in order to, among other things, vanquish the forces of Catholic Spain. In the late 1590s, the supporters of Essex were trying to create a faction opposed to the court consisting of Catholics and left-wing Puritans. Many of Drayton's patrons and dedicatees belonged to, or at least had political affiliations with, this group. A large portion of Drayton's early work was, for instance, dedicated to the Harington family. Related to the Sidneys and to Francis Bacon, these already important family connections of the Haringtons were further cemented by Lucy Harington's marriage to Edward Russell, the third Earl of Bedford in 1594, the year Drayton began dedicating some of his works to her. The Earl of Bedford, a prominent member of the Essex faction, participated in the Essex rebellion in 1601, for which he was fined and his estate entailed upon the next heir. But Drayton's awareness of the close ties between Bedford and Essex did not make him remove the dedication to the Earl in the subsequent editions of 1598, 1599, 1600 and 1602. The supporters of the Earl of Essex were also becoming increasingly critical of Elizabeth's apparent partiality towards the Cecils. The deposition of Richard II was frequently seen as an analogy to the overthrow of the Queen. That Shakespeare's play dealing with the deposition and murder of Richard II was arranged to be performed by Essex's supporters the night before his return to London from Ireland, and the probable use of the deposition scene (never printed during Elizabeth's reign) in Essex's rebellion, have been noted by several critics.[35] The political implication of this cannot be ignored: without making any direct statement about his own political affinities, the idea of connecting epistles about a deposed king with a dedicatee who was an Essex sympathiser had clear political connotations. Drayton was clearly aligning himself with individuals who were associated with Essex, or felt a special allegiance to him.

The second pair of epistles that I wish to focus on to illustrate Drayton's unique sense of nationalism is the one between Henry Howard, Earl of Surrey and Lady Geraldine. It has been pointed out that the inclusion of this pair of epistles violates Drayton's overall design of writing about English monarchs, and it may have been incorporated to make the work "less susceptible to political interpretation".[36] While this is entirely possible, there seems to have been a more serious motive behind Drayton's insertion of these epistles in a work that was primarily historical and political in nature: I contend that it was to offer a new definition of nationalism. Surrey's single epistle was incorporated in 1598 while its corresponding epistle was included in the 1599 edition. Surrey's epistle was the only one written by a man that was initially introduced without a corresponding epistle by a woman. It did not deal strictly with "historical" or political matters but with the theme of poetry, in accordance with Surrey's vocation. In 1599, political events may have encouraged Drayton to incorporate the reply from Geraldine. It was in this year that the Earl of Essex returned to England after his abortive Irish campaign. In the annotation to the Geraldine epistle, Drayton states that she was related to the Earl of Essex, since the family of the Fitz-Geralds was originally English.[37] By connecting the patriotic Geraldine with Essex around whom a political storm was already brewing from 1598, Drayton was clearly inviting a political interpretation. The case of the Surrey-Geraldine epistles also hints at Drayton's use of gender dialectics to comment on contemporary politics. Drayton often thwarts one's expectations of achieving a sense of national consciousness and pride by these recollections of military prowess by interestingly offering a contrastive study here between the male and female letter writers. While Surrey's epistle was introduced and indeed could exist independently in 1598 without inviting any political interpretation, it acquired a political dimension on being paired with Geraldine's in 1599.

In his letter written to Geraldine from Italy, Surrey proffers a different kind of national consciousness to that of Mortimer. Writing to Geraldine from Tuscany, and calling for a quintessentially English culture that will be superior to the Italians he begins his epistle by acknowledging the "smoothnesse" of Italian verse, but insists that his "Native Tongue" is no less excellent:

> Though to the Tuscans I the smoothnesse grant,
>
> Our Dialect no Majestie doth want,
>
> To set thy praises in as high a Key,
>
> As *France*, or *Spaine*, or *Germanie*, or they.[38]

This patriotic note echoes throughout Drayton's works: the Muse in *Poly-Olbion* is a "true native Muse", while his Odes are in the "old English Garbe".[39] Similarly Surrey asserts that there is no reason why

> My Countrey should give place to *Lumbardy*;
>
> As goodly flow'rs on *Thamesis* doe grow,
>
> As beautifie the Bankes of wanton *Po*;
>
> As many Nymphs as haunt rich *Arnus* strand,
>
> By silver *Severne* tripping hand in hand:
>
> Our shade's as sweet, though not to us so deere,
>
> Because the Sunne hath greater power there.[40]

After tracing his impressive lineage, Surrey points out that he has yet another, and indeed more important, identity. If his earldom proves "insufficient" for Geraldine, he has something far more valuable to offer her: he is "one of great APOLLO's Heires": Drayton's exalted notion of a poet finds expression in Surrey's declaration:

> When Heav'n would strive to doe the best it can,
>
> And put an Angels Spirit into a Man,
>
> The utmost pow'r it hath, it then doth spend,
>
> When to the World a Poet it doth intend.
>
> That little diff'rence 'twixt the Gods and us,
>
> (By them confirm'd) distinguish'd onely thus:
>
> Whom they, in Birth, ordaine to happy dayes,
>
> The Gods commit their glory to our prayse;
>
> T'eternall Life when they dissolve their breath,

We likewise share a second Pow'r by Death.[41]

Surrey's heroism and martial prowess in the political sphere is paralleled to his success in the linguistic sphere: the glorification of England and the English language is achieved through his verse. Surrey is putting forward a new idea of patriotism and national pride: through the writing of English poetry. He refers to "beauteous Stanhope", "famous Wyat" and "sweet-tongued Bryan" only to reiterate that if he is truly inspired he can supersede them all.[42] The poet not only defines and protects English identity here but Surrey becomes an expression of Drayton's patriotism, of England's destiny. Although he is unlike the militant Mortimer, we have here an equally strong sense of national consciousness and pride in being "English" though this is to be expressed through his verse. Surrey tells Geraldine his poetic skills can be used to recreate a *permanent* Florence (my italics) protected by Apollo, should the city in time lose her fame:

My Lines for thee a *Florence* shall erect,

Which great APOLLO ever shall protect,

And with the Numbers from my Penne that falls,

Bring Marble Mines, to re-erect those Walls.[43]

The constant emphasis on the eternising power of Surrey's "Verse" and the "sacred Pow'r" of his "Inke"[44] offers us new and innovative ways of looking at national consciousness.

In her response, incorporated in 1599, Geraldine replies fittingly by making a disparaging reference to unpatriotic Englishmen who:

In their Attyre, their Gesture, and their Gate,

Found in each one, in all Italionate;

So well in all deformitie in fashion,

Borrowing a Limbe of ev'ry sev'rall Nation;

And nothing more then England hold in scorne,

So live as Strangers whereas they were borne.[45]

Yet interestingly Geraldine, while recognizing Surrey's public and national status as a poet, does not profess to love him because of his national stature, asserting that "If in your Verse there be a pow'r to move, / It's you alone, who are the cause I love".[46] Generically, the device of paired epistles allows Drayton to compare the public, elaborately rhetorical, patriotic stance taken by the men to the more private, subversive and deconstructive stance taken by the women. This is an interesting device by which Drayton is able to contrast male and female states of mind. Although the women, chosen from two hundred years of English history, constitute a diverse group, Drayton unites them in their common desire to concentrate on concrete experience and historical facts. The women writers of the epistles deliberately resist flattery, realizing it opens the way to semantic manipulation, and through their interpretations of history often offer a critique of the kind of history presented by the men. For instance, although Edward the Black Prince describes himself as "*England's* Heire", Alice, Countess of Salisbury sceptically rejects his public, hyperbolic stance by asserting: "Let John and Henry, Edwards instance be, / Matilda and faire Rosamond for me".[47] For Lady Jane Grey, monarchy and fame have no attraction for "where the Arme is stretch'd to reach a Crowne, / Friendship is broke, the dearest things throwne downe".[48] Rosamond's epistle to Henry II perhaps best demonstrates how she refuses to be a passive spectator, equipping herself with a pen as a heroic counter instrument to Henry's sword in order to write a letter that becomes a legalistic critique of sovereign power. Splitting the body natural from the body politic and demanding an explanation as to why a king's body natural should not be subject to law, the dialogical fabric of the letters allows women like Rosamond to put their discourse on a par with, the king's, to have the right to speak and converse about sovereignty to a point when Henry's singular control as monarch is questioned: he asks her, his subject, to "raze" his name, obliterate his sovereign identity if it offends her and he offers her the power he has earlier wielded over her.[49] The women thus deliberately reject their public selves, their patriotic achievements, each one opting for a private stance, thereby offering a critique of the male point of view and their notions of English history. These monarchs and noble Englishmen, meant to inspire a sense of patriotic zeal and national pride in the minds of the audience, are suddenly seen as men to whom their mistresses are mere victims of desire: Matilda flees to a nunnery only to be pursued by King John, while Edward IV views Jane Shore as a material commodity by comparing her beauty to rubies, pearls and diamonds. Drayton does not merely move from the historical to the personal, but rather gives history a human angle by viewing the historical *through* the personal, with the paired epistles reflecting gender encounters and giving the women letter writers an agency that their Ovidian and English prototypes lacked. It becomes clear, then, that for Drayton there are competing, even contradictory and gendered ways, of being "English".

After the Queen's death and with James on the throne, Drayton compulsively revised all the works written during Elizabeth's reign. By doing so, Drayton indicates his keen interest in contemporary political affairs. *Englands Heroicall Epistles* ran into several editions up to the Folio edition of 1619. By the end of the sixteenth century, a varied and somewhat ambiguous range of attitudes had developed towards the court. Malcolm Smuts points out how works of Roman historians like Tacitus were often used to comment on court politics, one of the most provocative historical analogies being Sir John Eliot's reference to the Duke of Buckingham as "Sejanus" in the Parliament of 1626.[50] Writers did not draw only on classical precedent to analyze political behaviour. Often historically distant English monarchs were referred to, and these analogies acquired a pointed contemporary significance, especially during periods of crisis. When John Hayward, for instance, wrote the prose history *The First Part of the Reign of Henry IIII* in 1599, John Chamberlain wrote to Dudley Carlton: "Here hath been much descanting about it why such a storie shold come out at this time, and many exceptions taken, especially to the epistle which was a short thinge in Latin dedicated to the erle of Essex".[51] The subversive use of history was the first step towards challenging royal authority, which later helped to fuel parliamentary and public critiques of the Stuart court. Drayton's unsuccessful bids for royal patronage and his political inclinations resulted in a progressive alienation and isolation from court during the reign of James

I. Prince Henry died unexpectedly in 1612, and this led to Drayton further distancing himself from the court, now that Henry's patronage was no longer available. Unlike his younger contemporaries Browne, Wither and Christopher Brooke, Drayton seems to indicate that his basic commitment is not to politics, but to the poetic craft itself. This is borne out by the diligent and almost compulsive revision of all his works. This fundamental catholicity of temperament allows him to have a range of patrons that can include, among others, Catholic sympathisers and Royalists. At the same time, though by no means a Puritan, his alignment with the more radical and assertive Protestant politics of his time points to a root affinity with oppositionist politics that begins during Elizabeth's reign and crystallizes in James's time into anti-court and "Country" politics. It is this dichotomy that makes him incorporate political designs and statements in apparently apolitical poetry. One way of reading Drayton is to recognize the fact that this "apolitical" poetry becomes an implicit vehicle for a political purpose, particularly the politics of the "Country" faction. When Drayton dedicates a work to an influential patron with courtly connections, there is almost always a simultaneous address to the "Reader" or the "gentlemen of Britain". From early in his career, Drayton seems to be assuming a stance beyond the network of the aristocratic patronage system and looking beyond it to the general reading public. Thus when we analyse Drayton's patronage pattern from Elizabethan to Jacobean times, it may be concluded that it reflects the sharpest possible modification of the monarch-centred patronage system to a point where it virtually *excludes* the monarch. As David Norbrook has suggested, in his growing aversion for James, Drayton shared the feelings of a large number of his peers who were alienated from the Court and formed a kind of "poetic opposition".[52] Although Norbrook cautions that in this period it is misleading to speak of any formal "opposition based on a coherent ideology", it is a well-established fact that there were Puritan and "Country" leanings among the court and related circles. There was a strong Protestant element in Warwickshire, primarily because of the Dudley brothers Ambrose and Robert, who had a wide following among the country gentry. King James had given Warwick Castle to Fulke Greville in 1604. Although there was "no sign of a broad, open opposition movement in Warwickshire before 1640", behind the scenes, "contacts were being made between disgruntled local men and national 'opposition' figures".[53] As his range of patrons and associates indicate, it is almost certain that Drayton was in contact with these members of the local gentry in his native county.

While it is true that in Drayton's epistles the historical material is carefully selected and arranged, it is practically impossible to agree with Richard Hardin that the primary purpose of the work was to "look forward to the culmination of history in the greatness of his own age".[54] Drayton's political motive and his "increasingly oppositional politics", noted by Curtis Perry among others, are indicated in the first 1597 edition of the epistles itself.[55] Here four sets of epistles refer to the reigns of Edward II, Richard II and Henry VI, all of whom were ultimately deposed. In the late 1590s the supporters of Essex were becoming increasingly critical of Elizabeth's apparent partiality towards the Cecils and the deposition of Richard II was frequently seen as an analogy to the overthrow of the queen. In the 1597 edition, Richard makes the dangerous admission that his deposition was justified and the politically volatile lines referring to him as a "barraine trunk" were deleted in the 1599 edition.[56] Raphael Lyne argues that in *Englands Heroicall Epistles*, poetic, prosaic and pedagogical print conventions "are recruited to a patriotic cause", but this is not an overt mode of political engagement.[57] Diana Barnes asserts that the work articulates in a more general fashion "pluralist ideas of community and sovereignty".[58]

Analysing the phenomenon of Elizabethan nostalgia, Leah Marcus contends that the conscious reconstruction of the past in early Jacobean literature often became a political device for commenting on the present and carried with it an oppositional charge: "After her death ... the image of the queen signified political difference from James: she stood for nationalism and local identity".[59] The emergent nostalgia involved reviving not only memories and idealised images of the late queen, but also revaluating Elizabethan courtiers and writers, many of whom had, in fact, oppositionist affinities during her reign. Sidney, Spenser, Essex and Walter Ralegh, among others, became reference points for nostalgia for Elizabethan culture. Drayton's innovations in treating history, both in terms of content and form, create an apparent sense of patriotic pride and it is clear that he had a large national audience in mind, to whose popular sentiment he had to cater. On the other hand, this text strongly reflects Drayton's political concerns, sometimes at the level of local communities, with political spaces occupied by those who aligned themselves with the "Country" party during the reign of James I. Yet Drayton's political attitude is couched so much within the purview of his poetic practice that it is often easy to miss the subversive element in his work, the anti-establishment attitudes and the political statements in his apparently apolitical poetry. What seems like Drayton's orthodox and conservative stand are really carefully crafted political arguments; the subversive elements and generic manipulations in *Englands Heroicall Epistles* demonstrate the use of fiction to point to political and patriotic ends in a completely new way. The history of England is told through the reigns of kings but the plurality of narratives results in unravelling monarchical authority rather than celebrating it. The public longing for the narratives of strong male heroes who embody national prowess through their military achievements and their mastery of women are presented, only to be juxtaposed by counter narratives written by women, which in turn reflect Drayton's deeply ironical reconstruction of history and writing of national identity, fraught with tensions and anxieties about his notions of nationhood.

Notes

1. Elton, *Michael Drayton*, 110.
2. I am inclined to concur with Curtis Perry and Jane Tylus that Drayton was indeed engaged in oppositionist politics though I argue that it was in a way different from that suggested by Perry and Tylus. See Perry, *Making of Jacobean Culture*, 168, and Tylus, "Jacobean Poetry and Lyric Disappointment", 189.
3. Helgerson, *Forms of Nationhood*, 129.
4. Hastings, *The Construction of Nationhood*, 4.
5. Dewar, *Sir Thomas Smith*, 157.
6. Shakespeare, *Richard II*, 2.1.46-50.
7. Ibid., 2.1.43-44.
8. See McEachern, *Poetics of English Nationhood*; Baker, *Between Nations*; Hadfield, *Shakespeare, Spenser and the Matter of Britain*; Gordon and Klein, eds., *Literature, Mapping*.
9. Richard Helgerson, *Forms of Nationhood*, 8.
10. Anderson, *Imagined Communities*; Schwyzer, *Literature, Nationalism and Memory*, 3.
11. Pocock, "British History".

12. Drayton, "To the General Reader", *Poly-Olbion*, in Drayton, *Works*, vol. 4, v*. All references to Drayton's works are from this edition, henceforth referred to by volume and page number.
13. Kläger, *Forgone Nations*, 1.
14. Ricouer, *Reality of the Historical Past*, 2.
15. Gellner, *Nations and Nationalism*.
16. See Hertel, *Staging England*, 78.
17. Reid, *Ovidian Bibliofictions*, 165.
18. Drayton, *Works*, vol. 2, 130.
19. Ibid.
20. Brown, *Redefining Elizabethan Literature*, 185.
21. Hardin, "Convention and Design", 35.
22. Rackin, *Stages of History*, 4.
23. Newdigate, *Michael Drayton and his Circle*.
24. Campbell, "Use of Historical Patterns", 145, 152, 155.
25. *Calendar of State Papers, Domestic Series, 1595–1597*, 158.
26. Norbrook, *Writing the English Republic*, 24, 40.
27. Sharpe, *Remapping Early Modern England*, 201.
28. Bakhtin, "Discourse Typology in Prose", 189.
29. Drayton, *Works*, vol. 2, 161–162.
30. Ibid.
31. Ibid., 163.
32. Ibid., 169.
33. Ibid., 170.
34. Ibid., 168.
35. Campbell, "The Use of Historical Patterns", 165.
36. Brink, *Michael Drayton Revisited*, 60.
37. Drayton, *Works*, vol. 2, 293.
38. Ibid., 277.
39. Ibid., vol. 4, v*; vol. 2, 346.
40. Ibid., vol. 2, 283.
41. Ibid., 280.
42. Ibid., 281.
43. Ibid.
44. Ibid., 280.
45. Ibid., 291.
46. Ibid., 289.
47. Ibid., 180, 183.
48. Ibid., 298.
49. Ibid., 143.
50. Smuts, "Court-Centred Politics", 22.
51. *Letters of John Chamberlain*, vol. 1, 70.
52. Norbrook, *Poetry and Politics*, 198.
53. Hughes, *Politics, Society and Civil War*, 112.
54. Hardin, "Convention and Design", 39.
55. Perry, *Making of Jacobean Culture*, 168.
56. Drayton, *Works*, vol. 5, 114.
57. Lyne, *Ovid's Changing Worlds*, 147.
58. Barnes, *Epistolary Community*, 58.
59. Marcus, *Puzzling Shakespeare*, 184.

Disclosure statement

No potential conflict of interest was reported by the author.

Bibliography

Anderson, B. *Imagined Communities*. London: Verso, 1983.
Baker, D. J. *Between Nations: Shakespeare, Spenser, Marvell and the Question of Britain*. Stanford: Stanford University Press, 1997.
Bakhtin, M. "Discourse Typology in Prose". In *Problems of Dostoevsky's Poetics. Readings in Russian Poetics: Formalist and Structuralist Views*, edited by L. Matejka and K. Pomorska. Cambridge, MA: MIT Press, 1971.
Barnes, D. G. *Epistolary Community in Print, 1580–1664*. Surrey: Ashgate, 2013.
Brink, J. *Michael Drayton Revisited*. Boston: Twayne, 1990.
Brown, G. *Redefining Elizabethan Literature*. Cambridge: Cambridge University Press, 2004.
Campbell, L. B. "The Use of Historical Patterns in the Reign of Elizabeth". *Huntington Library Quarterly* 1, no. 2 (1938): 135–167. doi:10.2307/3815999.
Dewar, M. *Sir Thomas Smith: A Tudor Intellectual in Office*. London: Athlone Press, 1964.
Drayton, M. *The Works of Michael Drayton*. Edited by J. William Hebel, et al. 5 vols. Oxford: Basil Blackwell for The Shakespeare Head Press, 1931–1941.
Elton, O. *Michael Drayton: A Critical Study*. London: Archibald Constable and Company Ltd, 1905.
Gellner, E. *Nations and Nationalism*. 2nd ed. Ithaca, NY: Cornell University Press, 2008.
Green, M. A. E., ed. *Calendar of State Papers, Domestic Series, 1595–1597*. London: Longmans, Green., 1869.
Gordon, A., and B. Klein, eds. *Literature, Mapping and the Politics of Space in Early Modern Britain*. Cambridge: Cambridge University Press, 2001.
Hadfield, A. *Shakespeare, Spenser and the Matter of Britain*. Basingstoke: Palgrave Macmillan, 2004.
Hardin, R. F. "Convention and Design in Drayton's *Heroicall Epistles*". *Publication of the Modern Language Association* 83, no. 1 (1968): 35–41. doi:10.2307/1261231.
Hastings, A. *The Construction of Nationhood: Ethnicity, Religion and Nationalism*. Cambridge: Cambridge University Press, 1997.
Helgerson, R. *Forms of Nationhood: The Elizabethan Writing of England*. Chicago: University of Chicago Press, 1994.
Hertel, R. *Staging England in the Elizabethan History Play: Performing National Identity*. London: Routledge, 2016.
Hughes, A. *Politics, Society and Civil War in Warwickshire 1620–1660*. Cambridge: Cambridge University Press, 1987.
Kläger, F. *Forgone Nations: Constructions of National Identity in Elizabethan Historiography and Literature: Stanihurst, Spenser, Shakespeare*. Trier: Wissenschaftlicher Verlag, 2006.
Lyne, R. *Ovid's Changing Worlds: England's Metamorphoses, 1567–1632*. Oxford: Oxford University Press, 2001.
Marcus, L. *Puzzling Shakespeare: Local Reading and Its Discontents*. Berkeley: University of California Press, 1988.
McClure, N., ed. *The Letters of John Chamberlain*. Philadelphia: American Philosophical Society, 1939.
McEachern, C. *The Poetics of English Nationhood, 1590–1612*. Cambridge: Cambridge University Press, 1996.
Newdigate, B. *Michael Drayton and His Circle*. Oxford: Basil Blackwell, 1941. reprinted 1961.
Norbrook, D. *Writing the English Republic: Poetry, Rhetoric and Politics 1627–1660*. Cambridge: Cambridge University Press, 1999.

Perry, C. *The Making of Jacobean Culture: James I and the Renegotiation of Elizabethan Literary Practice.* Cambridge: Cambridge University Press, 1997.

Pocock, J. G. A. "British History: A Plea for A New Subject". *The Journal of Modern History* 47, no. 4 (1975): 601–621. doi:10.1086/241367.

Rackin, P. *Stages of History: Shakespeare's English Chronicles.* Ithaca, NY: Cornell University Press, 1990.

Reid, L. A. *Ovidian Bibliofictions and the Tudor Book.* Surrey: Ashgate, 2014.

Ricouer, P. *The Reality of the Historical Past.* Milwaukee: Marquette University Press, 1984.

Schwyzer, P. *Literature, Nationalism and Memory in Early Modern England and Wales.* Cambridge: Cambridge University Press, 2004.

Shakespeare, W. "Richard II". In *William Shakespeare: The Complete Works*, edited by P. Alexander. London: English Language Book Society, 1964.

Sharpe, K. *Remapping Early Modern England: The Culture of Seventeenth-Century Politics.* Cambridge: Cambridge University Press, 2000.

Smuts, M. "Court-Centred Politics and the Uses of Roman Historians, C.1590–1630". In *Culture and Politics in Early Stuart England*, edited by K. Sharpe and P. Lake, 21–45. London: Macmillan, 1994.

Tylus, J. "Jacobean Poetry and Lyric Disappointment". In *Soliciting Interpretation: Literary Theory and Seventeenth-Century English Poetry*, edited by E. D. Harvey and K. E. Maus, 174–198. Chicago: University of Chicago Press, 1990.

Michael Drayton's *Poly-Olbion*: maritime England and the free seas debates

Sandra Logan

ABSTRACT
Attending to *Poly-Olbion*'s river dynamics, I argue that, implicitly opposing natural, inevitable unionization, Drayton demonstrates through visual and poetic means that any viable empire is forged by deliberate local choices about conjunction and affiliation. Further, I show that by reconfiguring Saxton's maps, rejecting politically defined boundaries and perceptions, and situating three major rivers as the organizing features of the landscape and the empire, Drayton ultimately defines Britain as inherently and universally maritime. Moreover, linking *Poly-Olbion* to *mare clausum* and *mare liberum* debates, I reveal that Drayton situates the flow of self-aware rivers into the sea as an extension of Britain beyond its land boundaries. He thereby suggests that the eventual mixing of British waters with the larger oceans establishes the basis of Britain's local and global maritime rights, linking regional autonomy and conjunction by choice with claims to both local offshore dominion and global freedom of navigation and trade.

Michael Drayton's *Poly-Olbion* has long been recognized as a poetic project with powerful political implications, especially concerning the relationship between historical myths and geopolitical realities, unionization or separatism, centralized or decentralized sovereign authority. Considering the implications of river dynamics within the politicized, personified landscape of Britain has been a fundamental aspect of such scholarship, and these debates make visible the multifarious and sometimes irreconcilable perspectives embodied by Drayton's British landscape, and the many rich interpretive possibilities offered by his chorographic and cartographic epic. Certainly, Drayton is anything but univocal in this long, complex poem, and it is safe to assume that his own views, values, and perspectives shifted to some extent in the course of his two decades or more of composition. The songs register modes of exchange and interaction within the landscape that vary from the fully cooperative to the contentious, and if the sea lies beyond Britain's territorial purview, it nevertheless surrounds the land mass and plays a significant role, as both the maps and the Songs make clear.[1] John Speed's map of "The Invasions of England and Ireland" (1627) reveals the vulnerability of the "island nation" because of its extensive seacoast. Like all "contact zones", it is a site of almost inevitable confrontation, the terms of which must constantly be negotiated. The coastal aspect of the nation provided benefits and opportunities as well, enabling England's participation in exploration and trade, and Drayton, in both his Songs and the accompanying maps, situates his Britain in relation to the sea, addressing both the positive and negative potential of Britain's land/sea interface.

Here, I consider how the poem, particularly Part 1, resists notions of natural affinities and shared identities associated with pro-union positions, but nevertheless suggests that a united Britain might be built by pact or choice, for strategic economic purposes, while retaining inherent and indelible difference.[2] Further, in conjunction with the unionization debates, a less-recognized set of debates was raging in the period of the poem's composition. These debates focused on whether the oceans of the world, both the high seas and coastal waters, could be claimed and controlled by nations in the same way that land-territory was.[3] These debates offer an additional and intriguing layer to our understanding of Drayton's project, when we recognize his frequent representation, not only of river interactions within the landscape of Britain, but also of *river/sea dynamics*. For as much as he locates rivers as emerging from and bearing the qualities of particular landscapes, he also offers frequent depictions of rivers confronting and surviving their interactions with the sea. The poem thus seems to engage with questions both of whether and how union could effectively be achieved, and of Britain's capacity to control its local waters, and claim a place on the broader global seas. Drayton was, I suggest, thinking and writing not only about domestic imperialism or unionization, but also about a more ambitious global imperialist project for Britain, and here I will consider how these local and global objectives may be understood as closely linked through the representational strategies of the poem.

In tracing this conjunction of debates, I follow two intertwined lines of investigation. I trace how the debates about control of local and global waters are centrally important to Drayton's depiction of England as a maritime nation in Part 1 of the poem, and how his allusions to the terms of those debates meld apparently conflicting perspectives, align English and Scottish positions, and encourage cooperation. River identities, as Drayton depicts them, are distinct, and remain so even as they join with larger river bodies; similarly, larger rivers retain their identities as they enter or encounter the sea. This suggests that the qualities of the land, borne by the rivers, extend beyond the boundary of the land itself. Moreover, if the conjunctions of rivers serve as a metaphor for the joining of regions and nations, it is important to recognize that his river conjunctions are most often enacted by choice – at times as a willfully political choice that sometimes flouts geographic reality. Drayton may have recognized force as a failed policy, given the frequency with which he articulates its temporary success and eventual failure, and seen pragmatic alliance or unity as a more viable option. The key would be to promote the benefits of unification, rather than the losses, and this, I think, brings the two questions together: how did the free seas debates serve as an encouragement toward unification or alliance by choice, supportive of regional distinction and difference, and how did this willing union align with a British bid for global maritime viability?[4]

Drayton was consistently attentive to England's aqueous nature, as scholarship on the river dynamics of the poem recognizes. The maps created by William Hole for *Poly-Olbion* eliminate most signs of human occupation as well as the political boundaries emphasized in his source maps, allowing the land to assume its natural configuration.[5] Hole's maps are predominantly oriented to show the heads of rivers as they emerge from the land, to trace their gathering of tributaries and their passage through the landscape, and to depict the mouths where their waters confront and flow into larger aquatic bodies. Rivers thereby become the organizing feature of the regions presented.[6] The Songs similarly trace these emergences and relationships, and detail the resources that enrich the rivers in their origins and courses. The regional scope of rivers would seem to establish natural associations and divisions, since rivers do have limited draw and flow. However, Drayton offers a more complicated sense of the shape of the landscape than mere regionalism would itself suggest. He presents his virtual empire of Britain as oriented around two main waterways – the Severn River and the Thames River – that flow into the North (British) and Irish (Hybernian) seas to the east and west. Even rivers not connected to these main seaward-flowing rivers, such as those of Songs 1 and 2, which flow southward, and those of Songs 9–11 which flow westward, all eventually meet the sea – either the English Channel or the Irish Sea.

In each case, the relationship between inland and maritime regions can be inferred from the references to these major waterways, and often the point is made explicitly. For example, when Drayton reaches the midlands in Song 13, he depicts the Forest of Arden as touching the Trent (through the tributary Tame) with one "hand" and the Severn (through the tributary Avon) with the other. Thus, even the landlocked heart of the midlands, which Selden calls "Middle-Engle ... for equality of distance from the inarming Ocean", is connected, through these ocean-bound rivers, to the North Sea and Irish Sea respectively. Drayton's songs and maps thereby offer a view of Britain as, in effect, entirely maritime in its orientation, with even these inland regions connected to the ocean-lapped coasts. In his depiction, there is no part of England that does not join with the sea.

Drayton and the free seas debates

In the debates about control of the world's oceans, two conflicting positions shaped national policy: the seas could not be possessed or controlled by any nation – the *mare liberum* position – or they could be apportioned and controlled – the *mare clausum* position. Two terms are especially important in these debates: jurisdiction and *dominium*. Jurisdiction, a form of national legal authority, treated the coastal waters as a buffer around the nation, defensible during war, but not truly the property of the nation, and thus not subject to taxation or licensing, and open to any and all in terms of access and resource use, such as fishing and other peaceable purposes. Jurisdiction applied to local waters, and was compatible with the policy of *mare liberum* – the freedom of the high seas, since it avoided making a territorial claim. *Dominium*, by contrast, defined the coastal waters as a form of property that the claiming nation could occupy or use for its own sole benefit, controlling and limiting access through taxes, licenses, and fines. *Dominium* was compatible with the policy of *mare clausum* – the closed seas policy – which supported territorial claims on the high seas. The question was whether this kind of proprietary claim could be made over either coastal waters or the high seas. Both local and global concerns and claims were fundamentally economic, involving off-shore fishing rights and broader navigational and trade rights, but the security of a nation's ships on the high seas, and the security of the nation itself along its coasts, were also important considerations.

At the global level, papal bulls had already defined the rights of Spain and Portugal to claim the lands and oceans of the world, granting them *dominium* over the seas and exclusive trade rights, dividing the world more or less evenly between these two growing global empires.[7] At the local level, the question was mainly whether a nation could assert *dominium* over territorial or coastal waters, and whether they could therefore control the fishing rights and other rights of access. And fishing was incredibly lucrative – the wealth of the Dutch through fishing was compared in the period to Spain's gains through the plunder of new-world silver and gold.[8] Nations tended to adhere to one policy for both local and global waters. Those who wished to claim *dominium* over their coastal waters adhered to *mare clausum* policy, and accepted Spanish and Portuguese control of the high seas. Those who wished to assert their rights to navigate and trade on the high seas and in foreign territories accessed through such navigation, or to fish off the coasts of other nations, rejected the idea of *dominium* on the high seas or locally, adhered to *mare liberum* policy, and accepted mere jurisdiction over coastal waters.

For several centuries up through and including the Elizabethan era, England had generally held to a policy of *mare liberum*, accepting mere jurisdiction over coastal waters in order to defend their freedom to navigate on the high seas. Scotland, much less interested in global trade and heavily reliant on a local fishing economy, held to a *mare clausum* position.[9] England's idea that there must be coherence between local and global policies was brought implicitly to an end in 1609, when James I/VI issued a statute asserting England's *dominium* over its territorial waters, aligning English and Scottish policies. This statute required that all foreign fishing vessels obtain yearly license to fish English and Scottish waters, a new policy which was to be enforced by undesignated punishments. While the statute was general, the Dutch appear to have been the main target, given the pressure their fishing put on English coastal waters, their ongoing expansion into new and unclaimed fishing grounds, and their domination of the sea fishing industry.[10] Juridical debates and challenges erupted in response to this statute, adding to the already circulating treatises and documents supporting the various positions.[11] Drayton is thought to have composed the majority of Part 1 of *Poly-Olbion* in 1609–12, a period marked by the issuance of this statute, the heightening of these debates, and the publication of the first major treatise in support of free seas policy, the Dutch jurist Hugo Grotius' 1609 *Mare Liberum*, to which James's statute was apparently a response.[12] As David Armitage argues in his introduction to the treatise, Grotius' support for the freedom of trade and navigation "sparked a wider, more enduring controversy regarding the foundations of international relations, the limits of national sovereignty, and the relationship between sovereignty (*imperium*) and possession (*dominium*)".[13] Drayton would almost certainly have been aware of Grotius' text and the controversies it intensified as he worked on Part 1 of his poem.

In *Mare Liberum*, Grotius shows no direct interest in asserting the Dutch right to fish English coastal waters. He mainly focuses on negating the Portuguese claim to *dominium* over their granted portion of the seas, and their claim to exclusive trade rights in the East Indies, refuting *mare clausum* arguments to do so. His general arguments establish the impossibility of claiming either possession or exclusive use of the seas, arguments based on distinctions between land and sea, and thus between those things that "could be appropriated and those that remained common in nature".[14] He argues that the sea is as unbounded as the air (and similarly infinite), and that like the air, it was created for common use.[15] It cannot be occupied in the way that land or other finite territory can be occupied; because it is unfixed, its surface boundaries and therefore the boundaries of possession cannot be accurately or effectively determined, and thus the sea cannot be divided and apportioned in any reliable and definable way.

His distinction between *rivers* and *seas* in making this argument is central to an understanding of Drayton's poem in relation to the free seas debates. Grotius, drawing on classical legal arguments, asserts that "The sea ... is in the number of things which are not in merchandise and trading, that is to say, which cannot be made proper [property]", and that therefore, "The people of a country might possess a river as included within their bounds, but so they could not possess the sea".[16] Where ancient legal precedent allows for the rights of the nation in regard to coastal seas, such rights extend only to protection and jurisdiction, argues Grotius, not to *dominium* or proprietary right.[17] James's statute rejected this view, asserting English *dominium* and a *mare clausum* policy over coastal waters, while implicitly continuing to hold to a *mare liberum* policy on the open seas, supportive of England's broader trade and exploration interests.

Two main points here are pertinent to my reading of *Poly-Olbion*: I want to suggest that Drayton mobilizes Grotius' recognition that rivers are included as part of sovereign territory, and are therefore under the *dominium* of nations, but challenges Grotius' notion that rivers are possessed only to the boundary of the land.[18] Drayton demonstrates in his elaboration of river dynamics and river-sea confrontations that the edge of the land is not, in fact, the boundary of rivers – they retain their unique identities as they flow into the foreshore, carrying with them the qualities they have gathered in their waters. Further, this retention of identity figures in the poem's challenge to the idea of unification-through-conquest, instead emphasizing division and independence, with tributary rivers joining major rivers – or refusing to do so – through deliberate rather than natural conjunction, retaining their distinctiveness and difference even in the face of confluence. Drayton's representation of willing cooperation and shared resources among distinct, autonomous rivers and regions suggests that the divided regions of England – and implicitly Scotland – might be moved toward a more stable unity by such means than would be achieved through forced unification based on sovereign claims, martial force, or a rhetoric of natural similarities. The second point related to the free seas debates concerns how the depictions of river/sea dynamics in the poem align closely with the arguments made by Grotius concerning the nature of the broader seas. Drayton emphasizes that the ocean eventually absorbs the waters of all nations via their rivers' outflows into the larger salt body. His depiction of the multiplicity of the ocean's waters seems to suggest that, once this mixing has been accomplished – which only happens beyond the foreshore – no *one* nation can lay claim to those oceanic waters, which are literally made up of waters from *all* nations. Through these various depictions, he reconciles the notion of a *mare clausum* policy in local waters – the foreshore – with a *mare liberum* policy on the high seas.

Distinction, identity, and choice

The distinction and choice involved in river and thus regional conjunctions is exemplified in the story of the River Dart. The Dart, a river in Devonshire depicted in the map for Song 1, claims sovereignty over a number of other rivers in the region, not through volume or size, but through historical contribution. Although not as large as nearby rivers such as the Tamar, the Exe, or even the Torridge, emerging low on the Dartmoor plains and fed by only one tributary, the Dart's retelling of the story of Brute brings under her sway a series of small rivers that remain separate from the larger dominant ones. For instance, moved by the Dart's role in history, the Teign abandons her intent "To sing the Danish spoyles committed on her shore", in order to pay to the Dart "those high respects belonging unto her" (1.512; 522), although the Teign follows a course completely separate from the Dart's. Similarly, the Axe and the Otter commit their allegiance to the Dart, despite the fact that their waters do not actually flow into that river (1.541–543). These allegiances transcend mere geographic reality, allowing Drayton to privilege one aspect of history over another – the earliest British identity over later Danish influence. Such allegiances are clearly not natural or inevitable, since the rivers themselves do not physically conjoin. Rather, the rivers choose to join together through emotionally charged but rational determinations. Moreover, the historical conditions that inspire their choices – the conquests of Britain by the Danes and the Saxons – have clearly failed as the means of gaining permanent dominion over the territory. Human political history, itself marked by violent conquest and reconquest, is overwritten by regional river dynamics, sovereignty is asserted only over willing subjects who choose to submit, and Dart's authority remains limited to the region through which she flows.

Drayton offers a more problematic representation of river and river/sea dynamics in his description of the River Exe. This river, which gathers tributaries much like other rivers in this region, is "invited" by the Teign to join in tribute to the Dart. However, rather than paying homage to the Dart, the River Exe gathers tributaries as it flows southward at an accelerating pace, almost as though the "sovereign" river lacks necessary control. As these rivers "assist the *Ex*, so *Ex* consumeth these; / Like some unthriftie youth ... / that keeps a needless port" (532–534). Compared to a landlord who impoverishes his tenants, the Exe consumes their resources and his own, which "with most vaine expense upon the Prince is throwne: / So these, the lesser Brooks unto the greater pay; / The greater, they againe spend all upon the Sea" (538–540). While the sea does not conquer or overcome the river in this case, any more than it does in most other instances, there is a suggestion that some rivers (or patrons) attract followers without actual desert, abuse the tribute paid to them, and waste it in paying homage to the greater power of the sea. Drayton depicts the sea as the more powerful body in this relationship, not because it is an active conquering force, but because the Exe foolishly squanders his resources in a bid for personal favor, rather than casting his forces in with the Teign and the Dart.[19] Drayton does not pursue this metaphor, but he does create a brief moral lesson in the uses and abuses of micro-sovereignty, as well as a cautionary anecdote, briefly sketched, of the futility of pandering to the more powerful sovereign – in this case, Neptune or the sea. A similar moral lesson emerges in the tale of the River Chore (Cober), which meets the sea on the southeast coast of Cornwall earlier in Song 1. The Chore is, "transform'd into a Lake, / Through that impatient love shee had to entertaine / The lustfull *Neptune* oft (1.142–144). Chore's sexual incontinence has an effect similar to that of the Exe's self-interested squandering of resources, allowing Neptune to dominate where more resilient rivers withstand his fierce aggression. The moral lesson of the spendthrift Exe returns in Song 16 in a more explicitly human form, where "The 'idle

Gentry' (342) of the day are wasteful and irresponsible, drawing the 'publique wealth ... drie' (344) with their 'insatiate pride' (346) and spending the kingdom's gold on 'foolish foraine things' (345) such as Persian silk and Indian tobacco".[20] Here, the positive effects of trade afforded by Britain's maritime interface is undermined by human weakness, parallel to the metaphorical weakness of the spendthrift river Exe, who rejects regional coalition in order to seek personal favour. The overarching moral implication is that succumbing to the temptations of the sea, whether material or social, can undermine a more cooperative commitment to the greater good.[21]

The tension between coalition and independence arises elsewhere as well. The Tamar, a much larger river than the Dart, gathers a vast train of tributary rivers in her sweep down toward "The French Sea" as it is called in the poem. The Lynher, one of these tributaries, initially remains aloof from the Tamar, but when she sees "her Sovereigne ... approach the surgefull deepe, / To beautify her fall her plenteous tribute brings" (1.212–214), a choice that "honours Tamer much" (1.215) and that influences other rivers to lend their support to the Tamar as well. Thus, rather than allowing the Tamar to enter the sea unsupported, keeping to their own independent course, these other rivers join her and lend her their strength. The Plym is the last river to join the Tamar just before the "sovereign" river plunges into Plymouth Bay, which takes its name from this small, local tributary. The bay's name suggests the Plym's retention of identity and its presence in the coastal waters despite joining with the Tamar. The willful, deliberate, and cooperative nature of this interaction is much more typical than the runaway flow and self-serving outflow of the River Exe. Conversely, in a quite different and much more explicit resistance, the Torridge appears about to join the Tamar, but, warned that she can't compete with the sovereignty of the greater river in the southern regions of Dartmoor, turns north, gathers her own retinue, and flows into the Severn Sea, where Torridge "maist live admir'd, the mistress of the Lake" (1.279–280). This choice to maintain sovereignty emphasizes the independence and divisions even in micro-regions, as well as the deliberate choices of conjunction and direction that negate the idea of inevitable union.

Like the Torridge, flowing northward through Cornwall, the River Hayle has a powerful identity that she maintains even in her "quick recourse to the Severne Sea", where she can be found "With *Neptunes* Pages oft disporting in the Deepe". (1.111–13). The playful nymph of the Hayle engages in sexual congress with Neptune, successfully maintains her autonomy, and apparently controls their interactions, unlike the River Chore. On the map for this section Hayle is pictured arising, not from the land-framed river as do most of her sister-nymphs, but from the sea into which it empties, facing her own river mouth, a dolphin-mounted oceanic figure trumpeting at her back. Thus, on the map as in the song, the Hayle's nymph disports lustily while retaining her voice and individual character. She uses that voice to counter the lament of St. Michael's Mount over his lost land and power,[22] and to enumerate the many attractions of the region through which her river flows – diamonds, sea-holm, the Main-Amber, and the Burien Trophy. She thereby refutes St. Michael's claim that the wealth of the land has been lost through the nymph's interactions with Neptune, and emphasizes that the rivers are linked to and bear in their waters the qualities of the land, which then make their way to the sea (1.116–30).

Similarly, in Song 5, as the River Cowen (Cywyn) flows from the north (Welsh) bank toward the Severn near that river's mouth, lesser rivers join his stream and Cowen, "as their generall head / Their largess doth receive, to bear out his expence: / Who to vast *Neptune* leads this Courtly confluence"(5.216–18). Here, his joining is directly with the ocean rather than with the Severn, and he flows outward like one monarch entering the court of another, retaining his identity, his retinue, and his royalty in the process.[23] Milford Haven, at the mouth of the Clethy (Cleddau) River, is touted as a matchless harbor, decked with islands "That from the *British* shores by *Neptune* are embrac't; / Which stem his furious Tides when wildiest they do rave, / And breake the big-swolne bulke of manie a boystrous wave" (5.318–20). Again, then, the river does not lose its identity in entering the sea, and the qualities it bears are retained. Throughout these Songs, rivers carry the character of the land toward and into the sea, withstanding the ocean's aggressions, dropping easily into its calmer bays, or gleefully cavorting in its waters, coherent bodies that change constantly yet remain ever themselves, even as they pass the boundary of the land and mingle with the ocean's waters in the foreshore.

The association of resources with rivers is a constant aspect of the poem. Rivers that feed the Severn (the primary westward flowing river) in its major outflow connect with the larger flood in various ways. The Bristol Avon draws on in a quiet course toward Bath, willingly supported by the rivers that join her – "the lustie *Froome*, the first of floods that met / Faire *Avon* . . . "; the "cleere *Chute*" which "kindly came" to be carried down to Bristol; and the Mendip, "Which is the only store, and Coffer of her Mines . . . " (3.227–31; 249–50). The micro-regions associated with the various rivers supply the Bristol Avon, serving as storehouses for specific resources, just as "in some rich mans house his severall charges lie", with "provisions there, of Fish, of Fowl, and Neat; / His cellars for his wines, his Larders for his meate . . . here againe / Cribs. Graners, Stables, Barnes . . . " (3.253–58). This section situates the Bristol Avon as a country lord whose lands and rivers fill his larders, with the tributary rivers enriching the larger river by contributing their waters and their resources to its bounty (3.251–60).[24] Here Drayton makes explicit the relationship between the specific qualities and resources of individual rivers, and the collective wealth of the larger river which relies upon and carries these qualities and resources forward. The conjunctions are deliberate and willing, not forced, inevitable, or "natural" in the sense of being propelled by an irresistible condition of nature – rather, they are joinings by choice. The reliance of the "Lord" on these tributes reveals the importance of specific tributaries for particular resources and characteristics, emphasizing the aggregational nature of each region, and the importance of their differences and unique inherent qualities.

A more contentious relationship emerges in Song 14, when the Warwickshire Avon meets the Severn, here still fully a river, but approaching the point where it will open into the Severn Sea or Severn Estuary. The Warwickshire Avon is far less cooperative than the Bristol Avon, apparently resentful of the Severn's sovereign manner. Initially, the Severn is identified as the Avon's "soveraigne Queene", as though there is no question concerning the lesser river's submission. However, the various rivers that sweep down to watch their conjunction and "partake the joy that there is seene" come, not to watch the Avon submit, but rather, "*their* greatnesse to attend" (emphasis added), suggesting that allegiances are divided and that the two rivers are seen as nearly equal (14.63–65). The power of the Severn is obvious: she moves past Gloucester and gathers tributary rivers as "upon her course she wantonly doth straine, / Supposing then her selfe a Sea-god by her traine" (14.190–91; 193–194). The description continues in this vein: "She *Neptune*-like doth float upon the bracky Marsh", shaded by the "woody

Bowers" of "Faire *Micklewood*" (14.195; 202; 197), her power nearly divine. Yet, Severn's hubris alienates those who might have willingly served her: "*Severne* (on her way) so large and head-strong grew, / That shee the Wood-Nymph scornes, and *Avon* doth pursue" (14.203–204). The capacity of both the wood-nymph and the Avon to challenge a river as powerful as the Severn suggests that these relationships have not been naturally and inevitably settled by the water's flow – the Wood-nymph turns away from the Severn to support the Avon in her challenge.

In this interaction, the Severn marshals tidal force near the widening of her channel, asserts her authority over the lesser river, and establishes her superior power: "Like *Thetis* goodlie selfe" she "majestically glides"; while "Upon her spacious breast tossing the surgefull Tydes, / To have the River see the state to which she growes,/And how much to her Queene the beautious Avon owes" (14.213–16). Nevertheless, Avon remains capable of deciding and must be persuaded to commit to this union, while the Severn's force in confronting the sea emphasizes the autonomy of rivers in such interactions. This image of Severn as working to gain the support of lesser rivers, and the triumphant image of the Severn challenging the power of the seas, epitomizes the general thrust of Drayton's river/sea dynamics throughout Part 1.

Even while the political realities of the tension between Wales and England emerge in various ways throughout *Poly-Olbion*, the Severn maintains her identity as a powerful sovereign force, attracting allegiance from both sides and retaining her impartiality. We see this in Songs 4 and 5, where the amassed rivers of Cornwall and Wales, all of which feed the Severn, gather to contest which region may lay claim to the Isle of Lundy. Despite this contention, the Severn transcends these differences, fed by tributaries from both sides that are repeatedly portrayed as willingly joining with the larger river and accepting her sovereignty.[25] As the rivers Tamar and Hayle enter from the south, so the River Teme does from the north. The Teme, like the Avon, initially resists the Severn, approaching "with water ... so ranke, / As though she would contend with *Sabryne*, and doth crave / Of place (by her desert) precedencie to have" (7.238–240). However, "chancing to behold the others godlike grace" (7.241), Teme "So strongly is surpris'd with beauties in her face / By no meanes she could hold, but needsly she must showe / Her liking; and her selfe doth into *Sabrine* throwe" (7.242–244). Following Severn's inspiring account of the strength and resilience of the *Cambrians* (Welsh) in the face of various conquests in Song 8, Teme gathers all her tributary rivers, "Her native *Shropshire* leaves, and bids those Townes adiew, / Her only soveraigne Queene, proud *Severne* to pursue" (8.415–416). Other rivers enter the Severn directly: "*Camlet* commeth in, a Mountgomerian mayde, / Her source in *Severns* bankes that safely having layd" (8.443–444), followed by the River Mele (Meole or Rea Brook), who "her great Mistris next at *Shrewsbury* doth meet, / To see with what a grace she that faire towne doth greet" (8.445–446). The Severn River, whose head lies in the Cambrian Mountains in Wales, is thus depicted as a unifying agent through the willing, self-directed cooperation of her tributaries, carrying with her the identities, values, and virtues of all the rivers and regions from both Wales and England that feed her course. Further, this willing cooperation stands in contrast to the human history recounted in these Songs, which emphasizes the temporary success of conquests, and the resilience of the native "Cambrians" in the face of foreign invasion. Drayton, it appears, supports only a form of unionization that would encourage and allow for natural difference and distinction.

In *Poly-Olbion*, the Severn River becomes the "Severne Sea" at the point where modern geography identifies the Severn Estuary (approximately at the city of Gloucester), and this sea extends, in Drayton's depiction, all the way out to Land's End, where the River Hayle dallies with "*Neptunes* Pages" (1.112–13). Drayton presents domestic waterways as contributing to superior rivers as a form of tribute and patronage while retaining autonomy, and similarly, the multifarious Severn remains whole despite such contributions, gradually transformed into a sea body, distinct and identifiable despite the meeting with the larger ocean and the salination of its waters. Indeed, the map to Song 1 features a female figure that must be Sabrina, Goddess of the Severn, seated on Neptune's tail and held in a comfortable embrace by the sea god. In Song 5, the river relinquishes her sovereignty but nevertheless retains her identity as, joining Neptune, "She with extended armes unbounds her ancient seat: / And turning lastlie Sea, resignes unto the Maine / What sovereigntie her selfe but latlie did retain" (5.104–106). Like the sportive River Hayle, the Severn willingly accepts Neptune's embrace, and just as her own tributaries delivered their resources into her waters, so she delivers all into the waters of the sea. If the fate of the Severn River suggests the capacity of the regions of Britain to retain their diverse identities as their rivers meet the sea, it also indicates that eventually, even a river as great as this will dissipate into the ocean. When Drayton depicts Severn's sovereignty and autonomy melding, finally, with the sea, it is not through a loss of chastity or virtue, nor a loss of self. Rather, having "growne too great" – that is, expanded too far beyond her banks – she cannot any longer sustain her sovereignty, or authority over the sea that pushes against her, but must at last acknowledge the ocean's greater power (5.103). The expansion of the river into the sea leads to a gradual dissipation of sovereignty, until the Severn becomes salty, implicitly remaining herself, but submitting at last to the ocean's dominion, as so many have submitted to hers. In both visual and poetic terms, Drayton asserts the complex identity of regional rivers, and troubles the idea of a stable ocean, depicting instead the insistent presence of multiple local fluvial identities melding with the sea in the coastal waters surrounding the land.

There is undoubtedly a give and take as Neptune makes his aggressive advances, sometimes sweeping in where land once stood, as St. Michael's Mount laments, sometimes overcoming the force of a river as powerful as the kingly Thames, whose song of England's kings is interrupted by the "Tide" which, "retiring soon, did strongly thrust him out" (17.356). Nevertheless, the majority of rivers enter the foreshore intact and autonomous, but eventually, beyond these territorial waters, the distinctiveness can no longer be detected and Neptune comes to dominate. In depicting these distinctive, autonomous but conjoined river outflows, Drayton makes a strong case for the extension of the characteristics of the land beyond the boundaries of the land – not an unlimited extension, but one that makes it possible to include the foreshore in the proprietary claims on land and rivers. Drayton can be understood, in that sense, to support arguments for *mare clausum* policy in the foreshore – these waters are *British*, and indelibly marked as such by the fresh territorial waters flowing outward from land to sea.

An international coalition

The other question in the debates about the freedom of the seas focuses on whether the high seas can be claimed as, in effect, national territory. We can readily recognize from the final outcome of the Severn in Song 5 that Drayton makes no suggestion that rivers retain their integrity beyond a reasonable (though unspecified) distance from the land.[26] He does not seem to be suggesting that Britain has a natural, legal, or divinely asserted claim to the high seas – Britain is limited by the multiplicity of the ocean's waters, just as other nations are. However, although Britain cannot claim *dominium* of the seas, the rivers of other nations acknowledge the inherent greatness of British rivers at several moments in the poem, much as we see in the interactions between tributary rivers and the greater rivers that they join within the nation. For example, the power of the Thames (the major eastward flowing river) is strongly conveyed in Song 15, where it is predicted that this important river will gain the support of all the regions through which he passes, and will likewise draw international deference as he mingles with rivers from other nations in the sea:

The *Skeld*, the Goodly *Mose*, the rich and viny *Rheine*,

Shall come to meet the Thames in *Neptunes* watery Plaine.

And all the *Belgian* Streames and neighboring Floods of *Gaul*,

Of him shall stand in awe, his tributaries all. (15.109-112)

This prediction of future domination asserts a powerful role for rivers in connecting not only local, but global regions, offering a view of willing submission that strongly echoes the willing conjunctions of rivers as they make their commitments to their local sovereign floods.[27] In acknowledging this mingling of rivers in the North Sea, Drayton suggests that the oceans are multiple in their sources and character, like the rivers he has depicted throughout the poem. As the marginal note to the above cited passage from Song 15 indicates, the rivers *Skeld, Mose*, and *Rheine*, "al three ... of greatest note in the *Lower Germany*, cast themselves into the Ocean, in the Coast opposite to the mouth of the *Thames*". Similarly, the rivers of Belgium and Gaul flow outward into the oceans, choosing to submit to Britain but free to choose otherwise.[28] Moreover, this vision of the Thames parallels the depiction of Prince Henry as future ruler of the "three seas" and of the three realms of Britain in the dedicatory poem.[29] Drayton is thus fairly explicit in suggesting that England might rise as the sovereign nation which leads a global alliance; there is a strong indication that he sees this as a real possibility, an objective potentially more successful than repeating the struggle for *dominium* over each other's territory, which has consistently offered temporary, rather than permanent, gains.

This idea resonates in Song 18, the last song in Part 1, which depicts the marriage of the Thames and the Medway, a courtly celebration that marks their conjunction as they flow, from their separate courses, into the Thames Estuary. Interestingly, these rivers never actually unite – they mingle only in the bay of their outflows.[30] While the authority of the Thames is reasserted in this final song, and the Thames and Medway hold court together in their shared bay, it is the Medway rather than the Thames that sings of British conquests in the regions surrounding the seas of Britain, and as far away as the Levant. Highlighting the melding of identity under the Normans, Medway begins by recounting how the "renowned spirits ... of English *Norman* blood ... bore her [England's] fame so farre", and who joined in "Holy warre ... The Sepulcher to free" (18.118–128, emphasis in original). The Medway thus seems to answer the Andredsweald's just-expressed lamentations about the Danish conquest of England by emphasizing the success of England in its own conquests.[31] The role of the Medway in this tale of conquests is made explicit:

> This *Medway* still had nurst those navies in her Road,
>
> Our Armies that had oft to conquest borne abroad;
>
> And not a man of ours, for Armes hath famous been,
>
> Whom she not going out, or coming in hath seen:
>
> Or by some passing Ship, hath newes to her been brought,
>
> What brave exploits they did, as where, and how, they fought. (18.109-114)

As we can see, the Medway does not join with, but oversees and supports these expeditions and returns, praising past imperialist efforts, but not herself participating in them. There is thus no claim that the oceans are controlled by England's river presence within them, no hint that a local claim to *mare clausum* policy would naturally extend into the oceans of the world. Rather, this celebration emphasizes the broad scope of English martial history, and situates it as reliant upon access to the seas.[32] That this song of conquest begins with the Normans suggests not only the martial capability of the English, but their potential vulnerability should they fail to embrace their own expansionist potential.[33] We can surmise that, through his relation of the deep history of English imperialism, Drayton was sufficiently interested in establishing a long-standing historical precedent of free passage on the high seas, that he elides the Norman conquest of England in order to invoke England's conquests of others under Norman rule. Through this imperialist narrative, he justifies a *mare liberum* policy in the expanses of the ocean, as a counter to the *mare clausum* claims by Spain and Portugal, and distinct from the *mare clausum* claims over coastal waters, which he seems to support throughout the poem.

However, this idealized history of martial glory is a story of temporary gains which omits the history of reconquests and losses that defined England's boundaries in Drayton's day. The idea that conquest and forced subjection are failed strategies in the long term is conveyed throughout the poem in more local contexts, just as the history of English expansionist gains and losses is an important context to this part of the poem.[34] Given his depiction of cooperative river dynamics as the primary mode of interaction, as well as this idea that in international contexts, England's superiority will be recognized, this final song seems to suggest that Drayton is proposing a model of both submission and alliance on the international level as well – to the putative benefit of all concerned. Unity between Scotland and England would help both nations to secure their coastal waters against Dutch, French, Spanish, and other fishing venturers, as well as against other kinds of foreign threats – a strong argument for *mare clausum* in the foreshore, which James's statute instituted. In terms of global interests, standing united against Spain and Portugal would benefit all nations interested in free access to navigation and trade. Drayton seems to situate England as the natural leader in both contexts, linking local and global debates.

In recognizing that all sovereign territories with rivers are situated similarly to England, Drayton affirms the vision of individually defined territorial waters as local and distinct, but as also eventually contributing their qualities and natures to the greater global seas. He thereby reconciles *mare clausum* and *mare liberum* views, refuting the notion that a consistent policy for coastal waters and the wider oceans was necessary. *Mare clausum* is a local claim, while *mare liberum* is a negation of global territorial, jurisdictional or dominion-based claims. Coastal waters can be protected as though they were extensions of the land, whose qualities they carry, but the high seas contain the waters of all nations, fluidly mixing and moving, and therefore are not subject to national control. Drayton's poetic depiction of both local and global presence melds and reconciles the apparently oppositional views, situating dominion over territorial waters and freedom of the high seas as compatible notions.[35] If the ocean that batters English shores comprises the very waters that have washed the shores of India or the Americas, it is also comprised of local river waters with their individual characters. Thus, Drayton suggests, not only may England – or his imagined Britain – lay irrefutable claim to its own territorial waters, but through the mixing of British rivers with the surrounding ocean, it has also always been present in, and rightfully may navigate upon, the global seas. His quaint chorographic epic offers a metaphorical but highly strategic vision of persistent distinction and difference which carries forward from the most inland reaches of England into the seas, as well as of mutually beneficial domestic alliance and transnational partnership, which he mobilizes in support of England's maritime global opportunism.

Notes

1. Klein, "Maritime Olbion; or, "*th'Oceans Island*" (forthcoming), affirms the importance of the sea in the representational strategies of the poem, and offers an insightful reading of key aspects of the poem in relation to the sea.
2. McEachern, *Poetics of English Nationhood*, 138-191, argues that Drayton supported the idea of union. Herendeen, *From Landscape to Literature*, 302-303, addresses cooperative union in the poem. For other perspectives on the unionization question, see Kilgour, "Writing on Water", who sees the poem aiming toward forced union (287-94); Ewell, "Drayton's 'Poly-Olbion'", who sees an idealized, unified Albion; and Revard, "Design of Nature", who considers Drayton's a straightforward hierarchy.
3. Armitage, *Ideological Origins*, 61-124.
4. See Armitage, *Ideological Origins*, Ch. 4, for arguments concerning Britain as a maritime nation. Fulton, *Sovereignty of the Sea*, details the maritime concerns of England across history. Cormack, *Power to do Justice*, 227-290, addresses the expansion of sovereignty to maritime contexts. On river/sea dynamics, see also Herendeen, *From Landscape to Literature*, 258-62.
5. I have used Hebel's edition of *Poly-Olbion*, in *Works of Michael Drayton*, vol. 4. Herendeen, *From Landscape to Literature*, 292-3, notes that "Drayton formulates a historic nationalism based in geographical nature". McRae, *God Speed the Plough*, notes that Drayton fixes "attention on the land itself" (255). Mendyk, "Early British Chorography", establishes the more historical tradition of sixteenth-century chorography. Although Helgerson suggests that Drayton endeavors to "find and assert continuity", but (seemingly unintentionally) creates "a picture of discontinuity and mutual hostility", he nevertheless emphasizes aspects of *Poly-Olbion* that are central to my own analysis, including the

multiplicity of sovereigns, and "antipathy to royal centralism" (*Forms of Nationhood*, 140-141).

6. On rivers as vectors of spatial interaction and connection, see McRae, "Fluvial Nation".
7. The 1493 declarations favored Spain, but the following Treaties of Tordesillas (1494) and Zaragoza (1529) between Spain and Portugal made a more equal division and resolved the disputes of these two nations. The terms that apply to these claims are "sovereignty" (*imperium*) and "possession" or "ownership" (*dominium*).
8. Fulton, *Sovereignty*, 87. Klein, "Maritime Olbion", offers an overview of the significance of trade and exploration as a context for the poem.
9. Armitage, *Ideological Origins*, 108.
10. See Fulton, *Sovereignty*, 123-125; 150.
11. Fulton, *Sovereignty*, 86-88; 147-150.
12. Hebel, *Works*, vol. 4, Introduction, viii. For Grotius' *Mare Liberum*, I have used *The Free Sea*, ed. Armitage. Grotius mainly refutes the Portuguese claims to "exclusive access to the East Indies" (xv).
13. Grotius, *The Free Sea*, Introduction, xv.
14. Grotius, *The Free Sea*, Introduction, xvi.
15. Grotius, *The Free Sea*, 25.
16. Grotius, *The Free Sea*, 30. Possession or "physical seizure (*possessio*) leading to use (*usus*)" is the precursor to *dominium* (ownership), as Armitage explains (xiii; xvi-xvii). Use can loosely be equated to improvement.
17. Grotius, *The Free Sea*, 31.
18. McRae, "Fluvial Nation", 113, addresses the internal contestation of river "ownership" which included distinctions between "'navigable' and 'non-navigable' rivers", and claims for either proprietorship or use by the Crown, landowners, and the commons.
19. Helgerson, *Forms of Nationhood*, 141, takes up this river's unthriftiness as well, situating the squandering of resources as an expression of Drayton's antipathy to sovereign centralism.
20. See Klein, "Maritime Olbion; or, "th'Oceans Island".
21. In addressing the poem's representation of such a multiplicity of identities, Hadfield notes "*Poly-Olbion* ... articulates the fear" that "national, regional, and racial differences stubbornly refuse to break down", which might negatively affect the "hopes of unionization" ("Spenser, Drayton", 597). He nevertheless affirms the relative indelibility of such identities.
22. He explains to the Muse that the sea had been admitted by the "*Genius*" of the forest, who now has nearly overcome the land entirely, drawing out her "intrailes" and thrusting "his gripple hand into her golden mawe" (1.99-106).
23. The gender shifts are a bit tricky here, although the river is clearly designated female when introduced in 5.205-214; the metaphor defining the Cowen as like a "general" at 5.216 signals a shift in the gender referent for these two lines, with the masculine pronoun suddenly inserted despite the identification of the river as female.
24. The parallels with the country-house poem are obvious, but here, there appears none of the irony of that genre's tendency to celebrate laborless production and generous donation of resources to a human overlord.
25. However, see Schwyzer, "Map of Greater Cambria", where he notes the complexities of identifying a clear natural border between England and Wales, which was defined most anciently by the Severn, but which political realities of the succeeding centuries had redrawn.
26. The Glamorgan Promontory, mentioned as the last protector of the Severn against the "Ocean's power" (5.101-102), stands at approximately 150 kilometers from where the Severn becomes salinized. Parts of both Wales and Cornwall lie a significant distance west of this promontory, so the claims of coastal dominion, though not specified, must be understood as relatively modest, especially compared to the arguments made by Welwod in *An Abridgement of All Sea Laws* a few years later, for a 100-mile limit.

27. The dynamics differ significantly from Spenser's depiction of international rivers at the wedding celebration of the Thames and the Medway in *FQ* 4.11. There, the great rivers of the world merely join the procession, with no indication that they pay homage to or subject themselves to the Thames. The acknowledgement of superiority here echoes the willing submission of smaller rivers to greater ones elsewhere in Drayton's poem.
28. See Drayton, *Poly-Olbion*, 15.109-110.
29. Drayton, *Poly-Olbion*, prefatory materials, iv. On unification as central to the larger imperialist project of England, see Armitage, *Ideological Origins*, 100-103; for refinements of this line of argument, particularly concerning the Protestant position, see Boruchoff, "Piety, Patriotism, and Empire". Hadfield recognizes the tensions, in both Drayton's *Poly-Olbion* and Edmund Spenser's *The Faerie Queene*, between territorial expansion and the integrity of "pristine identity and moral authority" ("Spenser, Drayton", 582).
30. Given geographic realities, this is anything but an obvious union. See Joan Fitzpatrick, "Marrying Waterways", 84.
31. The Andredsweald, or ancient Forest of Andred, invokes the Danish conquest of England, describing "The heavy Danish yoke, the servile English bare" (18.72). Medway's song of English conquest covers lines 117-652. Certainly the Norman conquest is not without its negative aspects, although Drayton does not seem to address them here.
32. It should be noted, however, that many of the expeditions she mentions, such as the early crusades, were land-based rather than sea-based, although Mediterranean routes were used in the later crusades.
33. Hadfield, "Spenser, Drayton", articulates the tensions between the necessity of expansion and the dissipation of identity.
34. On the conflicted national history of conquest and reconquest, see Hadfield, "Spenser, Drayton", 591.
35. Welwod, *Critique*, in Grotius, *The Free Sea*, 74, ends by acknowledging that he is concerned only with asserting the right to territorial claims in local waters (to a 100-mile distance), while he accepts freedom of navigation on the high seas. Drayton prefigures this final position of Welwod's 1613 treatise, although he is undoubtedly more conservative in the reach of national claims.

Disclosure statement

No potential conflict of interest was reported by the author.

Bibliography

Armitage, D. *The Ideological Origins of the British Empire*. Cambridge: Cambridge University Press, 2000.

Boruchoff, D. A. "Piety, Patriotism, and Empire: Lessons for England, Spain, and the New World in Richard Hakluyt". *Renaissance Quarterly* 62, no. 3 (2009): 809–858. doi:10.1086/647349.

Cormack, B. *The Power to Do Justice: Jurisdiction, English Literature, and the Rise of Common Law, 1509-1625*. Chicago: University of Chicago Press, 2008.

Drayton, M. *Poly-Olbion*. In *The Works of Michael Drayton,* 5 Vols, edited by J. William Hebel. Vol. IV. Oxford: B. Blackwell, 1933.

Ewell, B. C. "Drayton's '*Poly-Olbion*': England's Body Immortalized". *Studies in Philology* 75, no. 3 (1978): 297–315.

Fitzpatrick, J. "Marrying Waterways: Politicizing and Gendering the Landscape in Spenser's *Faerie Queene* River-Marriage Canto". In *Archipelagic Identities: Literature and Identity in the Atlantic Archipelago, 1550-1800,* edited by P. Schwyzer and S. Mealor, 81–91. Abingdon, UK: Routledge, 2004.

Fulton, T. W. *The Sovereignty of the Sea: An Historical Account of the Claims of England to the Dominion of the British Seas, and of the Evolution of the Territorial Waters*. Edinburgh: William Blackwood and Sons, 1911.
Grotius, H. *Hugo Grotius, The Free Sea, Translated by Richard Hakluyt, with William Welwod's Critique and Grotius's Reply,* edited by David Armitage. Indianapolis: Liberty Fund, 2004.
Hadfield, A. "Spenser, Drayton, and the Question of Britain". *The Review of English Studies* 51, no. 204 (2000): 582–599. doi:10.1093/res/51.204.582.
Helgerson, R. *Forms of Nationhood: The Elizabethan Writing of England*. Chicago: University of Chicago Press, 1992.
Herendeen, W. H. *From Landscape to Literature: The River and the Myth of Geography*. Pittsburgh, PA: Duquesne University Press, 1986.
Kilgour, M. "Writing on Water". *English Literary Renaissance* 29, no. 2 (1999): 282–305. doi:10.1111/j.1475-6757.1999.tb01151.x.
Klein, B. "Maritime Olbion; or, 'th'Oceans Island'". Forthcoming.
McEachern, C. *The Poetics of English Nationhood, 1590-1612*. Cambridge: Cambridge University Press, 1996.
McRae, A. "Fluvial Nation: Rivers, Mobility and Poetry in Early Modern England". *English Literary Renaissance* 38, no. 3 (2008): 506–634. doi:10.1111/j.1475-6757.2008.00136.x.
McRae, A. *God Speed the Plough: The Representation of Agrarian England, 1500-1660*. New York: Cambridge University Press, 1996.
Mendyk, S. "Early British Chorography". *Sixteenth Century Journal* 17, no. 4 (1986): 459–481. doi:10.2307/2541384.
Revard, S. P. "The Design of Nature in Drayton's *Poly-Olbion*". *Studies in English Literature, 1500-1900* 17, no. 1 (1977): 105–117. doi:10.2307/450424.
Schwyzer, P. "A Map of Greater Cambria". *Early Modern Literary Studies* 4, no. 2 (1998): 1–13.
Spenser, E. *The Faerie Queene*. Edited by A. C. Hamilton. London: Longman, 1995.

🔓 OPEN ACCESS

The age of the Cambro-Britons: hyphenated British identities in the seventeenth century

Philip Schwyzer

ABSTRACT
In the late sixteenth and early seventeenth centuries, Welsh writers including the antiquary Humphrey Llwyd, the bard Gruffudd Hiraethog, and the epigrammatist John Owen began referring to themselves as Cambro-Britons. The term was quickly adopted and popularised by English writers, often in ways that show an imperfect grasp of the intentions behind the hyphenated phrase. Whereas the Welsh had hoped that the English and Scots would adopt similar hyphenated identities, English writers tended to interpret "Cambro-Briton" as an intensified and potentially comical expression of Welshness. Though Welsh writers largely ceased to employ the term after the 1620s, the use and misuse of "Cambro-Briton" in English texts continued unabated throughout the century.

One effect of the 2016 Brexit referendum was to throw into the limelight some stark contradictions in the structure of national identity in the UK – and to precipitate more. According to post-referendum polling, voters in England who identified themselves as more English than British were overwhelmingly likely to vote Leave.[1] Voters who felt more British than English, or simply British rather than English, voted in the majority to Remain. In Wales and Scotland, however, the position was reversed. Voters in those countries who identified primarily as Welsh or Scottish opted in the majority to Remain, whilst those who identified primarily or exclusively as British were more likely to vote Leave.[2] As these figures suggest, the general crisis of national identity in twenty-first century Britain is both characterised and exacerbated by persistent asymmetries. Welshness, Scottishness, and Englishness are generally assumed to be cognate identities, whether defined by descent or country of residence; yet these national identities are not configured in the same way in relation to Britishness, nor to one another, nor to the various ethnic and religious identities with which they may coincide.

For the English, since the eighteenth century, the distinction between Englishness and Britishness has tended to present itself as that between a cultural or ethnic identity on the one hand and a civic or political identity on the other. There is thus comparatively little difficulty in regarding oneself as equally English and British (as a plurality of England's inhabitants do and have long done).[3] Scottishness and Welshness, however, present a more complex mixture of ethnic and civic elements, and Britishness, from the

---

This is an Open Access article distributed under the terms of the Creative Commons Attribution License (http://creativecommons.org/licenses/by/4.0/), which permits unrestricted use, distribution, and reproduction in any medium, provided the original work is properly cited.

perspective of these nations, can be associated with English cultural hegemony as much as with the political union. To be equally Scottish and British is thus a rather more challenging stance to adopt than the equivalent position in England, and it is no surprise that fewer people in Scotland confess to this compound identity. One way of cutting through this web of asymmetries would be to argue that, from the differing perspective of each British nation, "Britishness is just Englishness writ large".[4] Yet these asymmetries in the structure of national identity significantly predate the eighteenth century, when the conventional coupling of Englishness and Britishness first took hold. The structural crisis of national identity within Britain is not at all new, though recent referenda have made it once again news. This article will focus on a period when the meanings and relationships between terms like Welsh, English, and British were in flux, as they are today – and will explore an attempt to resolve that earlier crisis (ultimately, I shall argue, a failed attempt), by an innovative piece of hyphenation: the term "Cambro-Briton".[5]

In 1572, the Cologne press of Johann Birkmann printed the first early modern treatise on the topography and antiquities of Britain, Humphrey Llwyd's *Commentarioli Britannicae descriptionis fragmentum*. The title page attributes the work to "Auctore Humfredo Lhuyd, Denbyghiense, Cambro-Britanno". This earliest printed instance of the hyphenated Latin term *Cambro-Britannus* was swiftly followed by the first example of the English equivalent. Published in London a year later, Thomas Twyne's translation, *The Breviary of Britain*, names the author as "Humphrey Llwyd of Denbigh, a Cambre Britayne". On both the Latin and the English title pages, the name of Britain appears twice, first with reference to the entire island, and then with reference to a particular national community within it. "Cambro-Britanno" thus describes a relation of part to whole. Although Llwyd had died in 1568 (the posthumous publication of his research being overseen by his friend, Abraham Ortelius), it appears likely that Cambro-Briton was his preferred term, at least in the context of this work, both for himself and for the Welsh people generally. The Latin text includes further reference to "meis Cambrobritannis".[6] Twyne, not overly familiar with the term, translates this phrase as "my countrymen the Britons in Wales".[7]

Llwyd's earlier history of Wales, *Cronica Walliae* (1559), features no reference to Cambro-Britons. In that text Llwyd, like other Welsh and English writers of the Middle Ages and sixteenth century, tends either to use the terms "British" and "Welsh" interchangeably (as in "the Britons or Welshmen"), or uses "Britons" to refer to an ancient people whose modern descendants include the Cornish and Bretons as well as the Welsh.[8] There is no hint in *Cronica Walliae* that the modern inhabitants of Scotland and England are also in some sense Britons. Yet Llwyd's turn from Welsh history to British chorography in *The Breviary of Britain* seems to have necessitated a more nuanced approach to national nomenclature. In a work surveying Britain as a whole, Llwyd may well have reasoned that to reserve the name of Britons for only one (or two) of the island's peoples would be both divisive and confusing. Likewise, to skirt the question of British identity entirely, and refer only to the Welsh, English, and Scots, would defeat the treatise's purpose in celebrating the island's glorious Brythonic heritage.[9] The innovative hyphenation of Cambrian and Briton suggests the existence of a range of different kinds of Britons. Although Llwyd does not employ the terms Anglo-Britannus and Scoto-Britannus in his work, the existence of these national communities is implied and in a sense conjured into being by the coinage "Cambro-Briton".

Although Llwyd was the first Welsh writer to identify himself in print as a Cambro-Briton, he did not coin the phrase single-handed. The potential for compounding the names of Wales and Britain seems to have attracted the collective interest of a community of scholars and poets based in early Elizabethan Denbighshire, including Llwyd, the bard Gruffudd Hiraethog, and the prominent humanist William Salesbury.[10] In 1561, Gruffudd presented the gentleman Richard Mostyn, a sometime absentee in England, with a poetic anthology entitled *Lloegr drigiant ddifyrrwch Brytanaidd Gymro*.[11] The title may be translated literally as "Entertainment for a British Welshman dwelling in England". The phrase "British Welshman" might be taken to suggest that Welshness is the broader of the two identities, and that only certain Welshmen (perhaps those living in England?) are British. Probably, however, Gruffudd is simply reversing the expected order of noun and adjective, a common technique in Welsh poetry ("*hydref ddail*"). Whatever the grammatical relation, Gruffudd's *Brytanaidd Gymro*, like Llwyd's *Cambro-Britannus*, forms a compound phrase from two terms which had heretofore been regarded as largely synonymous. Gruffudd and Llwyd were well known to one another, and discussions between them, perhaps extending to Salesbury and others, are likely to lie behind Llwyd's eventual public adoption of a Cambro-British identity.

The new phrase "Cambre Britayne" or Cambro-Briton first came to the notice of English readers through Llwyd's *Breviary of Britain*, and a number of early uses involve direct or indirect reference to Llwyd's works. In a letter of 1574 to the French Protestant scholar Hubert Languet, Sir Philip Sidney refers to Llwyd as "our poor Cambro-Briton" (*miserum nostrum cambrobritannum*) and seeks to defend Llwyd against Languet's strictures, whilst getting in some jokes of his own at the Welsh antiquary's expense.[12] Although there is no evidence in the letter that Sidney was directly acquainted with Llwyd's scholarship beyond what Languet had reported to him, his use of the term *Cambrobritannus* (which Languet does not employ in his letter to Sidney) suggests that he knew this to be Llwyd's term of preference; it is not clear whether Sidney understands the term to refer to the Welsh generally, or more specifically to one recently deceased Welsh author. Echoing Llwyd's own "meis Cambrobritannis", Sidney's use of the possessive pronoun involves an expression of affinity or kinship shading – as in a good many English examples that follow in the seventeenth century – into condescension.

Among Llwyd's staunchest admirers in the early seventeenth century was the poet Michael Drayton, an avowed Cambrophile. In the front-matter of his *Poly-Olbion* (1612) – a poem which, like Llwyd's *Breviary* and William Camden's *Britannia*, sets out to survey the whole of Britain – Drayton includes a special address to "My Friends, the Cambro-Britons". Understanding that Welsh readers may be particularly interested in the poetic representation of their own nation, the preface is intended to help them "without difficulty understand, how in this my intended progresse, through these united kingdomes of great Britaine, I have placed your (and I must confesse) my loved Wales..." Although Drayton applies the term "Cambro-Britons" to the Welsh generally, he also includes special reference to "my much loved (the learned) Humfrey Floyd" whose influence has inspired him "to uphold [the] auncient bounds" of Wales.[13] The epistle carries echoes of Llwyd's title pages, with the close positioning of "great Britaine" in relation to the more geographically localised "Cambro-Britons". The idea of the

Cambro-Briton is also closely tied to the theme of antiquity "which Wales may highly boast of". Like both Llwyd and Sidney and before him, Drayton couples the term with a possessive pronoun, the first of several in the brief preface ("my friends the Cambro-Britons", "my ... Wales", "my ... Floyd"). This locution serves to heighten the sense of affinity between the English writer and his Welsh audience, a connection already implicit in the term Cambro-Briton. At the same time it conveys – intentionally or otherwise – a whiff of condescension, further heightened by the poet's professed concern that his Welsh readers may find the poem difficult to understand.

In the 1612 edition of *Poly-Olbion*, Drayton's largely positive address to the Cambro-Britons is countered on the facing page by the more severe opinion of the legal scholar John Selden, who supplied the learned annotations to Drayton's songs. Drayton and Selden were drastically mismatched in their approaches to the British past. In his own epistle to the readers of the book, Selden begins by disclaiming any faith in the British History, with its "intollerable Antichronismes, incredible reports, and Bardish impostures":

> Being not very Prodigall of my Historicall Faith, after Explanation, I oft adventure on Examination, and Censure. The Author, in Passages of first Inhabitants, Name, State, and Monarchique succession in this Isle, followes Geffrey ap Arthur, Polychronicon, Matthew of Westminster, and such more. Of their Traditions, for that one so much controverted, and by Cambro-Britons still maintayned, touching the Trojan Brute, I have (but as an Advocat for the Muse) argued; disclaiming in it, if alledg'd for my own Opinion.[14]

Like Drayton, Selden associates the Cambro-Briton with a love for the ancient past, but in this case that love is unmasked as a devotion to false traditions. His annotations contain several further references to the Cambro-Britons, sometimes disparaging their credulity – "These things are the more enforst by Cambro-Britons, through that universall desire, bewitching our Europe, to derive their bloud from Trojans" – at other times more neutrally, as when he applies the term to the great (Cambro-Norman) medieval authority, Gerald of Wales.[15]

Poly-Olbion thus provides a range of interconnected meanings and connotations of the term Cambro-Briton, including:

(a) A term associated specifically with the scholarship and national vision of Humphrey Llwyd;
(b) A term deemed to demonstrate politeness and respect;
(c) A term highlighting the Welsh love of the past;
(d) A term applicable to Welsh people in the past;
(e) A term appropriate when highlighting the stubbornness and foibles of the Welsh, especially as regards antiquity;
(f) A condescending term, in which mock-respect provides matter for more or less affectionate amusement.

To deal for the moment with sense "a", the term Cambro-Briton or Cambro-Britannus would continue to be associated specifically with Llwyd throughout the seventeenth century. Robert Burton in *The Anatomy of Melancholy* (1621) cites "Humfry Lluyd ... [a] Cambro-Brittaine himselfe" on the Welsh fondness for dairy products, and the antiquary William Burton defers to "the learned Cambro-Britan, Humphrey Lhuyd".[16] Writing after the Restoration in celebration of the Stuarts' Welsh descent, Percy Enderbie describes "Mr. Floyd, or Lloyd, a Cambro-Brittaine", as "one who for his knowledge may justly challenge an eminent place amongst our Antiquaries", but differs with him on the etymology of Britain.[17] With or without specific reference to the author, the term "Cambro-Briton" often connotes a Llwydian vision in which the Welsh language and cultural community embody an otherwise unavailable link to the antique and early medieval past. John Speed in his *History of Great Britain* (1611) discusses the predilection of the ancient Britons for painting themselves blue, "which colour the Cambro-Britannes doe yet call glace".[18] The close association of the Cambro-Briton with Welsh antiquity misled some English writers into believing the term was itself antique; thus Richard Johnson could write of "Saint David, the Champion for Wales, at that time entituled Camber-Britannia".[19]

Although Llwyd may have coined the phrase, he claimed no monopoly on it, and a number of other Welsh writers in the late sixteenth and early seventeenth century would define themselves or their language as *Cambro-Britannus* or *Cambro-Britannicae*, especially when addressing an international or European audience. The compound term is applied to the language formerly known as Welsh in Siôn Dafydd Rhys's ground-breaking grammar, *Cambrobrytannicae Cymraecaeve Linguae Institutiones et Rudimenta* (1592), and subsequently in Thomas Wiliems' manuscript *Thesaurus Linguae Latinae et Cambrobrytannicae* (c. 1620) and John Davies of Mallwyd's *Antiquae linguae Britannicae, nunc communiter dictae Cambro-Britannicae, à suis Cymraecae vel Cambricae, ab aliis Wallicae rudimenta* (1621). The term was applied posthumously to the Welsh Catholic Owen Lewis (d. 1594), Bishop of Cassano and founder of the English College or (as he had planned to call it) *Seminarium Britannicum* at Rome. The inscription on the marble plaque over his grave at the English College begins "*D. O. M. Audoeno Ludovico Cambro-Britanno...*" and proceeds to a long list of his ecclesiastical and academic positions.[20] It is tempting to suppose that the notorious controversy between English and "British" students at the College, gleefully recorded by Anthony Munday in *The English Roman Life*, may have prompted Lewis to define his national identity with particular care.[21] The phrase occurs again at the English College in the epitaph of the Catholic exile and suspected Gunpowder conspirator Hugh Owen (d. 1618), memorialised as *Hugoni Odoeno Nobili Cambro Britanno Carnaviensi*.[22]

In his will, the Hugh Owen who was buried in Rome disinherited his nephew and presumptive heir John Owen, who had written vehemently against the Catholic Church. Yet their differences did not extend to national nomenclature, for in all of the many editions of Owen's epigrams (the first in 1606), the author is identified on the title page as Cambro-Britannus. In later seventeenth-century literature the compound epithet is applied to Owen as frequently as it is to Llwyd, and he exerted a powerful influence over other Welsh epigrammatists and poets. Sir John Stradling acknowledged Owen as his inspiration, and in his own *Epigrammatum Libri Quatuor* (1607) addressed his Welsh relatives and connections (including his cousin Sir Edward Stradling, from whom he would inherit the estate of St Donat's in 1609) as *Cambrobritanni*.[23] In the second decade of the seventeenth century, the poets John Davies of Hereford and Hugh Holland of Denbighshire identified themselves as Cambro-Britons in verses contributed to English publications.[24] The Welsh clergyman and future Bishop of Gloucester,

Godfrey Goodman, did not apply the title to himself, but instructed the English readers of his *Fall of Man* (1616) that it was proper to refer to "the Cambro-Britaines (whom we improperlie call Welsh)".[25]

Although the list of Welsh writers who employed the term is fairly extensive, it is not necessarily indicative of a wider embrace of the hyphenated identity in Elizabethan and Jacobean Wales. Tellingly, most of the authors mentioned above participated in one or several of a small number of overlapping communities, connected by geography as well as by various scholarly, religious, or familial ties. The term seems to have originated in Denbighshire, home not only to Gruffudd Hiraethog and Llwyd in the mid-sixteenth century but to Holland and Goodman in a later generation. Most of the others who employed the term also hailed from North Wales (Thomas Wiliems and Hugh and John Owen from Caernarfonshire, Siôn Dafydd Rhys and Owen Lewis from Anglesey.) Catholicism provides a further link between not only the priests Owen Lewis and Hugh Owen, but also Hugh Holland and Siôn Dafydd Rhys (both of whom travelled in Italy), and probably Thomas Wiliems; Llwyd's religious sympathies remain somewhat murky, but he served with Hugh Owen in the household of the Catholic Earl of Arundel, and the two apparently travelled together to the continent in 1566.[26] Even an apparent outlier like John Stradling, who was born in Bristol, is connected to these networks by more than one link, dedicating epigrams to both John Owen and Siôn Dafydd Rhys, who had earlier dedicated his Welsh grammar to Sir Edward Stradling. In light of the web of relationships that binds the majority of Welsh writers who favoured the hyphenated phrase, there is little reason to suppose that the term "Cambro-Briton" was ever in very widespread use in seventeenth-century Wales.

However, the term was never really intended for domestic consumption. Humphrey Llwyd had adopted it in a treatise written for an international scholarly audience. Most later writers who used the phrase (including John Owen, Stradling, Holland, John Davies of Hereford, Goodman, and the authors of the Roman epitaphs) were likewise writing primarily for non-Welsh eyes, be they those of English readers or continental Europeans. These were the audiences to whom the epithet's implicit argument – that Britishness was the common identity of the island's inhabitants, rather than something specific to the Welsh – was directed. The union of the crowns under James VI and I added urgency and pith to the argument, as seen in Owen's 1606 epigram "Cambro-Britannus":

Tecum participant in nomine Scotus et Anglus
Iam tu non solus, Walle, Britannus eris.

[Scot and Englishman join in a name with you,

Now, Welshman, you will not be the only Briton.][27]

Sir John Stradling a year later makes the same point in an imitative epigram:

Anglo-Britannus, Scoto-Britannus, Cambro-Britannus
Una acclememus voce, Britannus ego.

[Anglo-Briton, Scoto-Briton, Cambro-Briton,

Let us proclaim with one voice, *I am a Briton*.][28]

Owen's and Stradling's optimistic epigrams highlight a striking and rather poignant absence in national nomenclature. Where were the Anglo-Britons and the Scoto-Britons? By comparison to Cambro-Briton, these parallel compounds remain surprisingly rare throughout the seventeenth century. It is true that John Price, the Catholic classical scholar and editor of Apuleius, referred to himself as "Anglo-Britannus" or "Anglo-Britannicus", and the literary celebrity James Howell described himself as "Brit-Anglo" in at least one printed work.[29] Yet both Price and Howell were of Welsh extraction (the former born to Welsh parents in London, the latter hailing from Carmarthenshire), and it seems likely that in each case they were using "Britannus" as a synonym for "Welsh". For these writers, "Anglo-Britannus" or "Brit-Anglo" did not connote an English Briton, but something closer to Anglo-Welsh (a notoriously problematic hyphenation in itself). The question of Howell's mixed identity was subsequently resolved, with or without his consent, on his monument in Temple Church, describing him as Cambro-Britannus.[30]

There are a handful of further examples, hardly indicative of a widespread cultural movement. The printer Henry Holland called himself "Anglo-Britannus" on the title page of his *Heroologia Anglica* (1620); but he may have done so in part to distinguish himself from his avowedly Cambro-British contemporary Hugh Holland, as well as to provide a counterpoint to John Davies of Hereford, who in a poem included in the work ascribes himself Cambro-Britannus. The antiquary Sir Henry Spelman, who had written in tempered support of Anglo-Scottish union, also described himself as Anglo-Britannus.[31] John Selden's *Jani Anglorum*, published before his contribution to *Poly-Olbion*, refers to the laws of "Anglo-Britannia" in the extended title; yet the term apparently struck readers as so obscure that an English translation later in the century includes a substantial endnote explaining the phrase (with reference, inevitably, to "Cambro-Britannia"). Slightly more willingness to identify as Anglo-British was seen in writers based on the continent; a short lived Dutch journal *Mercurius Anglo-Britannus* was published in The Hague in 1648, and throughout the century a number of English students at continental universities registered as Anglo-Britanni.[32] By and large, however, even English writers who fully grasped the implications of the term Cambro-Briton were reluctant to adopt the parallel compound term for their own nation. Thus, the clergyman William Sclater quotes Humphrey Llwyd on the "temper of his countrimen, the Cambro-Britannus" and proceeds to draw a contrast with "wee, Britans of t'other race" – a striking but by no means unusual degree of reticence regarding the relationship between Englishness and Britishness.[33]

Yet whilst English writers showed very little interest in identifying themselves as Anglo-Britons, their enthusiasm for the phrase Cambro-Briton continued unabated throughout the century. In some cases, the phrase was taken (as Llwyd had intended it) as a hallmark of British unity. Arguing in 1642 for full political union between England, Scotland and Ireland, Henry Parker observed that "if the name of Hiberno-Britaines may not be applyed to the Irish, as Cambro-Britaines is to the Welsh; yet now Scottish, English, Welsh, and the mixt Irish being so indifferently blended in Ireland ... it must be wilfull neglect in us, if we do not close yet more amiably together".[34] Even as he upholds the Cambro-Briton as an embodiment of the principle that all should follow, Parker stops short of arguing that other British nations should adopt comparably hyphenated identities. In his catalogue of united British peoples, the Cambro-Britons stand apart, paradoxically distinct from their British peers by their greater commitment to union. The same point may be made regarding the joyful chorus of the royalist song *The Cock-crowing at the Approach of a Free Parliament* (1659):

> Then of with your pots English, Irish, and Scots,
> And loyall Cambro-brittaines,
> From Lobster-like Jump
> And the head-playing Rump
> You'l soon have an acquittance.[35]

English poets also found the phrase useful in laying claim to historical Welsh achievements from the period before the Acts of Union. Charles Fitz-Geffry's 1596 elegy for Sir Francis Drake, which features a catalogue of great English travellers by land and sea, includes among their number "Renowned Madocke, Princes sonne of Wales,/Brave Cambro-britton uncontrol'd by might".[36] The legend of Madoc, son of Owain Gwynedd, and his twelfth-century voyage to America is recorded in Richard Hakluyt's *Principal Navigations* (1589), where Humphrey Llwyd (the first reporter of the tradition, in *Cronica Walliae*) is among the sources cited. The mention of Llwyd may have prompted Fitz-Geffry to write "Cambro-Briton", but chiefly the phrase serves as a way of including the Welsh Madoc within a list of English adventurers. A similar end is in view in Christopher Brooke's *The Ghost of Richard III* (1614), where the tyrant laments that "Richmond comes on... / Seeing the Back of his great enterprize, / With Cambro-Brittaines, men of taintlesse Name".[37] Here the use of the hyphenated term both casts the contest for the English throne as a British matter, and recognises the Welsh stake in the question. Whereas Shakespeare's Richard III castigates Richmond's followers as "a scum of Britons", lumping together the Welsh and Bretons as unwelcome foreigners, Brooke's Richard is forced to acknowledge that the Welsh at least are fellow-countrymen.[38] The passage may even hint at a parallel between Henry Tudor and James I as bringers of British unity.

Rather more common, however, are texts in which the Cambro-Briton is exposed to mockery, the hackneyed terms of humiliation made the more acute by the supposed dignity of the long-winded title. The game here is to point out that, despite the politically correct phrase considered "proper" nowadays, the Welsh are still the Welsh; the old rules still apply. In 1609 we find William Rowley reviving a timeworn national stereotype as he lists the foods favoured by different nationalities: "Roots for the French-man a Pippin Pye for your Irishman, and a péece of cheese for the Cambro-Brittans".[39] John Page mocked the equally stereotypical Welsh obsession with tracing their genealogies: "our Cambro-Britanni can derive their descent from the Moon, but other Nations are not so happy".[40] And James Smith found a new rhyme for Cambro-Briton as he memorialised Alexander Gill, the notoriously brutal master of Paul's School:

> A Welch man once was whipt there,
> Untill be did beshit him,
> His Cuds-Pluttera Nail,
> Could not prevail,
> For he whipt the Cambro brittain.[41]

"Cuds-Pluttera Nail" (or "Cats Plutter a Nails") is the commonplace oath of the comic or stage Welshman in moments of exasperation. A little corporal punishment, Page suggests, is all it takes to bring out the Taffy hiding within the Cambro-Briton. The linguistic quirks of the stage Welshman are also on display in the Civil War newsletter *Mercurius Cambro-Britannus*, in which news of military action in Wales and the west is mingled with tales of Merlin and digressions on leeks and cheese, all delivered in a mock Welsh voice: "her swore to her to by Saint Taffy, that tere was create hope tat te Parliament forces was have pig successes, and tat her Garrison at Plimmouth have pravely defended temselves …".[42]

Such openly mocking references are the tip of an iceberg of subtler, sustained condescension. Awareness of the English reception and use of the term, combined with disappointment at the failure of other British nations to adopt comparable hyphenated identities, may have contributed to the marked decline in the use of Cambro-Briton among Welsh writers, especially as a self-designation, from around 1620. The few who still employed the term were usually interested in marking a relationship to writers of an earlier generation. Following the lead of Siôn Dafydd Rhys and Thomas Wiliems, John Davies of Mallwyd used the hyphenated *Cambro-Britannicae* in the title of his Welsh grammar (1621) and subsequent dictionary (1632).[43] In 1646, Roger Lort of Pembrokeshire nominated himself Cambro-Britannus in a book of epigrams, unmistakably modelling himself on John Owen. After this, there are few examples to be found beyond Alexander Griffith, the royalist clergyman who revived the old title of *Mercurius Cambro-Britannicus* to petition Parliament in 1652, and Thomas Jones who, as late as 1678 still hoped that the Scots and English might follow the Cambro-Britons' lead by identifying as Alban-Britons and Loegrian Britons.[44]

As employed by Humphrey Llwyd and a range of other Welsh authors writing in three languages, the terms Cambro-Britannus, Brytanaidd Gymro, and Cambro-Briton had sought to demonstrate the relationship between a core identity (that of Briton) and a more local, modifying identity (Welsh or Cambrian). English writers who used the term, whether they did so in mockery or simply declined to apply the equivalent hyphenated identity to their own nation, seem to have interpreted the phrase rather as a fusion of two versions of Welsh identity, and thus as an intensified expression of Welshness. Rather than functioning like "London Irish" or "African-American", in other words, Cambro-Briton as employed by the English more closely resembled "Anglo-American" or "Judeo-Christian", terms which by emphasising common traits and values within the group draw a powerful boundary between insiders and outsiders. The Cambro-Briton, in English eyes, was not a certain kind of Briton, but a true or absolute Briton. In other words, a real Welshman.

The English adoption and adaptation of "Cambro-Briton" in the seventeenth century, and the consequent abandonment of the term by almost all Welsh writers, marked the failure of a certain project. Though the hyphenated phrase lived on, by 1625 the age of the Cambro-Britons was over. Perhaps, however, we should only regard the period 1560–1625 as the First Age of the Cambro-Britons. The name would rise again, in and after the eighteenth century.[45] Early in the nineteenth century, the short-lived journal *The Cambro-Briton* (1819–22) proclaimed its aim "to diffuse amongst strangers a knowledge of the history, the manners, the genius of Wales, and to extend beyond her mountain barriers the fame of those literary treasure, which are now, as it were, covetously hoarded within them".[46] *The Cambro-Briton* thus sought to distinguish itself from other Welsh periodicals which, whether in Welsh or English, were addressed primarily to a native audience. The aim of diffusing knowledge amongst strangers is one that Humphrey Llwyd would have warmed to, but the shift in emphasis is unmistakable. To call oneself a Cambro-Briton in the sixteenth or early seventeenth century was to say, "I am British, but I am ready to share this title with others". To use the phrase in the eighteenth or (still more) the nineteenth century was to say, "I am Welsh, but my patriotism is not narrow; I wish to be recognised as British too". The early modern Cambro-Britons saw themselves as graciously offering inclusion to others under the mantle of Britishness. The Cambro-Britons of later centuries were struggling to ensure that their own Britishness was not forgotten, that they might be included themselves.

Notes

1. "EU Referendum 'How Did You Vote' Poll; Online Fieldwork: 21st-23 June 2016"; https://lordashcroftpolls.com/wp-content/uploads/2016/06/How-the-UK-voted-Full-tables-1.pdf. The pollster contacted 12,369 voters, including 10,468 in England, 1102 in Scotland, 629 in Wales, and 170 in Northern Ireland.
2. The polling question in Northern Ireland was slightly different, asking respondents to state which identities applied to them, but not requiring them to rank one over another. Those who identified themselves as either "Irish" or "Northern Irish" voted in majority to Remain, whilst those identifying as "British" or "British and Northern Irish" voted to Leave. By a small margin, a majority in Northern Ireland voted to Remain.
3. "Devolution: Trends in National Identity". See Langlands, "Britishness or Englishness?".
4. Langlands, "Britishness or Englishness?", 64. Langlands concludes that "there is not (and never has been) one single variant of Britishness" (64), although it has tended to be "constructed largely in English terms" (54).
5. The hallmarks of the Cambro-British identity and the careers of some notable Elizabethan and Jacobean Cambro-Britons have been explored previously in Jones, "The Welsh Gentry", and Roberts, "Tudor Wales". The present essay attempts to focus more narrowly, perhaps myopically, on the career of the hyphenated phrase itself.
6. Llwyd, *Commentarioli Britannicae descriptionis fragmentum*, 5^v.
7. Llwyd, *Breviary of Britain*, 56.
8. Llwyd, *Cronica Walliae*, 87, 89. Cf. Salesbury, *Briefe and a Playne Introduction*, sig. Bi^{r-v}; Salesbury, *Ban wedy i dynny*, sig. Aiii^r.
9. Llwyd's argument that the ancient Britons had inhabited the whole island, with the Scots, Picts, and Anglo-Saxons all being relative late-comers, particularly infuriated George Buchanan and later Scottish historians.
10. I am deeply grateful to Paul Bryant-Quinn for communicating his research on Denbighshire's intellectual networks, and for alerting me to Gruffudd Hiraethog's significance in this story, as well as to the use of "Cambro-Briton" by a number of Welsh Catholics on the continent, discussed below. Salesbury (c. 1520–1584), though he is not known to have exchanged his habitual "British or Welsh" for "Cambro-British", was the luminary and linchpin of this north Welsh intellectual community.
11. NLW MS Peniarth 155 includes a copy by Rhisiart Phylip of the 1561 compilation. On the manuscript, see Harper, *Music in Welsh Culture*, 33, 89–91. Harper translates *Brytanaidd Gymro* as "Welsh-speaking Welshman". See also Carr, "The Mostyns of Mostyn", 22.
12. Sidney to Hubert Languet, Padua, 11 February 1574, in *Correspondence of Philip Sidney*, 113. Sidney's father, Sir Henry, as Lord President of the Council in the Marches of Wales, would take an interest in Llwyd's work and support David Powel in revising Llwyd's *Cronica Walliae* for publication as *The Historie of Cambria* (1584). Whether Sir Henry's interest in Llwyd was established and known to his son as early as 1574 is unclear. See Schwyzer, "Happy Place".
13. Drayton, *Poly-Olbion*, A1^v.
14. Drayton, *Poly-Olbion*, A2^r.

15. Drayton, *Poly-Olbion*, 18, 148.
16. Robert Burton, *Anatomy of Melancholy*, 100; William Burton, *Commentary on Antoninus*, 89.
17. Enderbie, *Cambria Triumphans*, 3.
18. Speed, *History of Great Britaine*, 180.
19. Johnson, *Famous Historie*, sig. Aa3^v (part of the concluding section added to the 1616 edition of this frequently reprinted text).
20. Wood, *Athenae Oxonienses*, vol. 1, 612. I am grateful to Paul Bryant-Quinn for bringing the epitaphs for Owen Lewis and Hugh Owen (below) in the English College to my attention.
21. See Nice, *Sacred History and National Identity*, Ch. 6; Munday, *English Romayne Lyfe*, 56–67.
22. Champ, *Memorial Inscriptions*, 75–7; "Monumental Inscriptions at Rome", 130. The memorial plaque is now situated on the external wall of the English College.
23. Stradling, *Ioannis Stradlingi Epigrammatum libri quatuor*; on Owen: 159; Cambro-Britannus: 3, 72.
24. "Hugo Holland Cambro-Britannus" in Coryate, *Odcombian Banquet*, sig. G1^v. "I. D. Cambro-Britannus" in Henry Holland, *Heroologia Anglica*, 241.
25. Goodman, *Fall of Man*, sig. A6v. As earlier writers, including Llwyd, had observed, "Welsh" was not a native word, but a Germanic term descriptive of foreigners.
26. See "Owen, Hugh", *Dictionary of Welsh Biography*; "Llwyd, Humphrey", *Oxford Dictionary of National Biography*.
27. Owen, *Epigrammatum Libri Tres*, 64.
28. Stradling, *Ioannis Stradlingi Epigrammatum libri quatuor*, 176.
29. James Howell, *Angliae suspiria, & lachrymae ... Aut: Ia: Howell, Arm. Brit. Anglo* (1646). On Price, see Carver, *Protean Ass*, 347; Pennington, *Descriptive Catalogue*, 259, no. 1485.
30. Wood, *Athenae Oxonienses*, vol. 2, 269.
31. For Spelman and a handful of others, see Murdoch, *Network North*, 68–73. The Scottish situation is broadly similar; while a handful of Scottish writers identified themselves as Scoto-Britannus, they did so almost always in the context of the union question in the reign of James I, or where addressing a continental audience where clarity seemed vital; for examples see Murdoch, 64–67.
32. Weduwen, *Dutch and Flemish Newspapers*, 579–80; Murdoch, *Network North*, 71–72.
33. Sclater, *Briefe Exposition*, 298–99.
34. Parker, *Generall Junto*, 21.
35. *Cock-crowing at the approach of a free-parliament*, chorus.
36. Fitz-Geffrey, *Sir Francis Drake*, sig. E4^v.
37. Brooke, *Ghost of Richard III*, sig. K3^v.
38. See Schwyzer, "A Scum of Britons?".
39. Rowley, *A Search for Money*, 22.
40. Page, *Jus Fratrum*, 37. Note how the possessive pronoun rears its head again.
41. Smith, "On Doctor Gill, Master of Paul's School", in *Loves of Hero and Leander*, 55.
42. *Mercurius Cambro-Britannus ... from Friday November 11, till Munday the 20. 1643*, 5.
43. A subtle shift may be noted between the titles of Davies' *Antiquae linguae Britannicae, nunc communiter dictae Cambro-Britannicae .. rudimenta* (1621) and *Antiquae linguae Britannicae, nunc vulgò dictae Cambro-Britannicae...dictionarium duplex* (1632). The change from "communiter" to "vulgò" may indicate an intensified scepticism about the appropriateness of the term, though both words can mean "commonly".
44. Thomas Jones, *Of the Heart and its Right Soveraign*, 247. See also Edwards, *Hebraismorum Cambro-Britannicorum specimen*.
45. On self-declared Cambro-Britons in the eighteenth century, see Prescott, *Eighteenth-century Writing from Wales*; Jenkins, *Between Wales and England*.
46. "Introductory Address", 2.

Acknowledgments

I am grateful to Paul Bryant-Quinn, Daniel Cattell, and Ceri Davies for their vital suggestions and comments.

Disclosure statement

No potential conflict of interest was reported by the author.

Funding

This work was supported by two AHRC Research Grants: The Poly-Olbion Project [AH/K005073/1] and Inventor of Britain: The Works of Humphrey Llwyd [AH/P00704X/1].

ORCID

Philip Schwyzer ⓘ http://orcid.org/0000-0002-2381-4424

Bibliography

Brooke, C. *The Ghost of Richard III*. London, 1614.
Burton, R. *The Anatomy of Melancholy*. London, 1621.
Burton, W. *A Commentary on Antoninus, His Itinerary, Or, Journies of the Romane Empire*. London, 1658.
Carr, A. D. "The Mostyns of Mostyn, 1540-1642 (Part I)". *Journal of the Flintshire Historical Society* 28 (1978): 17–38.
Carver, R. H. F. *The Protean Ass: The Metamorphoses of Apuleius from Antiquity to the Renaissance*. Oxford: Oxford University Press, 2007.
Champ, J. *Memorial Inscriptions in the Venerable English College, Rome*. Rome: Il Venerabile Collegio Inglese, 2012.
The Cock-Crowing at the Approach of a Free-Parliament. 1659.
Coryate, T. *The Odcombian Banquet*. London, 1611.
Davies, J. *Antiquae linguae Britannicae, nunc communiter dictae Cambro-Britannicae .. rudimenta*. London, 1621.
Davies, J. *Antiquae linguae Britannicae, nunc vulgò dictae Cambro-Britannicae...dictionarium duplex*. London, 1632.
"Devolution: Trends in National Identity". *British Social Attitudes* 30 (2013). http://www.bsa.natcen.ac.uk/latest-report/british-social-attitudes-30/devolution/trends-in-national-identity.aspx
Drayton, M. *Poly-Olbion*. London, 1612.
Edwards, C. *Hebraismorum Cambro-Britannicorum specimen honorandis antiquae Brittanicae gentis primoribus*. London, 1675.
Enderbie, P. *Cambria Triumphans, Or, Brittain in Its Perfect Lustre*. London, 1661.
Fitz-Geffrey, C. *Sir Francis Drake His Honorable Lifes Commendation, and His Tragicall Deathes Lamentation*. London, 1596.
Goodman, G. *The Fall of Man, or the Corruption of Nature, Proved by the Light of Our Naturall Reason*. London, 1616.
Harper, S. *Music in Welsh Culture before 1650: A Study of the Principal Sources*. Abingdon: Routledge, 2016.
Holland, H. *Heroologia Anglica*. London, 1620.
Howell, J. *Angliae suspiria, & lachrymae ... Aut: Ia: Howell, Arm. Brit. Anglo.* 1646.
"Introductory Address". *The Cambro-Briton* 1, no. 1 (September 1819): 1–5.

Jenkins, B. M. *Between Wales and England: Anglophone Welsh Writing of the Eighteenth Century*. Cardiff: University of Wales Press, 2017.
Johnson, R. *The Famous Historie of the Seaven Champions of Christendome*. London, 1616.
Jones, J. G. "The Welsh Gentry and the Image of the 'Cambro-Briton', C. 1603-1625". *Welsh History Review* 20 (2001): 615–655.
Jones, T. *Of the Heart and Its Right Soveraign, and Rome No Mother-Church to England, Or, an Historical Account of the Title of Our British Church*. London, 1678.
Langlands, R. "Britishness or Englishness? the Historical Problem of National Identity in Britain". *Nations and Nationalism* 5 (1999): 53–69.
Llwyd, H. *The Breviary of Britain, with Selections from the History of Cambria*. Edited by Philip Schwyzer. London: MHRA, 2011.
Llwyd, H. *Commentarioli Britannicae descriptionis fragmentum*. Cologne, 1572.
Llwyd, H. *Cronica Walliae*. Edited by Ieuan M. Williams and J. Beverley Smith. Cardiff: University of Wales Press, 2002.
Mercurius Cambro-Britannus, the Brittish Mercury, Or, the Welch Diurnall ... from Friday November 11, till Munday the 20. 1643. London, 1643.
"Monumental Inscriptions at Rome". *Archaeologia Cambrensis* n.s. 4 (1853): 130–132.
Munday, A. *The English Romayne Lyfe*. London, 1582.
Murdoch, S. *Network North: Scottish Kin, Commercial and Covert Associations in Northern Europe, 1603-1746*. Leiden: Brill, 2006.
Nice, J. *Sacred History and National Identity: Comparisons between Early Modern Wales and Brittany*. Abingdon: Routledge, 2016.
Owen, J. *Epigrammatum Libri Tres*. London, 1606.
Page, J. *Jus Fratrum. The Law of Brethren*. London, 1657.
Parker, H. *The Generall Junto or the Councell of Union, Chosen Equally Out of England, Scotland, and Ireland, for the Better Compacting of Three Nations into One Monarchy*. London, 1642.
Pennington, R. *A Descriptive Catalogue of the Etched Work of Wenceslaus Hollar 1607-1677*. Cambridge: Cambridge University Press, 1992.
Prescott, S. *Eighteenth-Century Writing from Wales: Bards and Britons*. Cardiff: University of Wales Press, 2008.
Roberts, P. "Tudor Wales, National Identity, and the British Inheritance". In *British Consciousness and Identity: The Making of Britain, 1533–1707*, edited by B. Bradshaw and P. Roberts, 8–42. Cambridge: Cambridge University Press, 1998.
Rowley, W. *A Search for Money*. London, 1609.
Salesbury, W. *Ban wedy i dynny air yngair allan o ben gyfreith Howel [d]da*. London, 1550a.
Salesbury, W. *A Briefe and A Playne Introduction, Teachyng How to Pronounce the Letters of the British Tong, (Now Commenly Called Walsh)*. London, 1550b.
Schwyzer, P. "'A Happy Place of Government': Sir Henry Sidney, Wales, and *the Historie of Cambria* (1584)". *Sidney Journal* 29 (2011): 209–217.
Schwyzer, P. "A Scum of Britons? Richard III and the Celtic Reconquest". In *Celtic Shakespeare: The Bard and the Borderers*, edited by W. Maley and R. Loughnane, 25–34. Farnham: Ashgate, 2013.
Sclater, W. *A Briefe Exposition with Notes, upon the Second Epistle to the Thessalonians*. London, 1627.
Sidney, P. *The Correspondence of Philip Sidney*. Vol. 1. Edited by Roger Kuin. Oxford: Oxford University Press, 2012.
Smith, J. *The Loves of Hero and Leander*. London, 1653.
Speed, J. *The History of Great Britaine*. London, 1611.
Stradling, J. *Ioannis Stradlingi Epigrammatum libri quatuor*. London, 1607.
Weduwen, A. D. *Dutch and Flemish Newspapers of the Seventeenth Century*. Leiden: Brill, 2017.
Wood, A. À. *Athenae Oxonienses*. Vols. 1-2. London, 1691-2.

The religious geography of Marvell's "An Horatian Ode": popery, presbytery, and parti-coloured picts

Stewart Mottram

ABSTRACT
Marvell's "Ode" (1650) is an English poem about a British problem – a problem further problematized by religion. The "Ode" lauds Cromwell's Irish and Scottish campaigns, but English responses to these "colonial" wars were in reality complicated by protestant infighting among presbyterians, independents, and sectarians. Writers like Milton and Nedham rallied English support for Cromwell's Irish campaign by recycling Spenserian stereotypes of Irish catholic barbarity. But Milton and Nedham also undercut English protestant unity by flinging these same anti-catholic stereotypes at Scottish presbyterians in Belfast and Edinburgh. Departing from previous studies, this article argues that Marvell's "Ode" eschews Milton and Nedham's anti-Presbyterianism in ways calculated to elide, rather than divide, protestant communities. The article explores how the "Ode" presents Cromwell's Irish and Scottish campaigns as exclusively anti-catholic (rather than anti-presbyterian) crusades, comparing Marvell's presentation of Cromwell in the "Ode" with his identification of Cromwell as an anti-catholic crusader in "First Anniversary" (1655). Both poems anticipate in this respect Marvell's later anti-catholic, but pro-nonconformist, approach to Ireland in *Rehearsal transpros'd* (1672–1673). The article is therefore concerned to root Marvell's post-Restoration commitment to protestant tolerationism within the anti-catholic language of the "Ode".

Andrew Marvell's "An Horatian Ode upon Cromwell's Return from Ireland" is a centripetal poem, its central lines a meditation on that century's central event, the "memorable scene" of Charles I's execution on 30 January 1649.[1] The poem's sympathies for the king's performance on the "tragic scaffold" erected outside the Banqueting House at Whitehall – "He nothing common did, or mean", Marvell writes, "Nor called the Gods with vulgar spite" – contrasts with the implied vulgarity of the soldiers who with "bloody hands" applaud the unfurling tragedy on stage.[2] Whether the poem sees royalist tragedy or republican opportunity in the regicide is a question that not only continues to divide critics; it is also one that has historically detracted attention from the significance of the two "kingdoms" – Ireland and Scotland – inhabiting the poem's peripheries.[3] The poem's mid-point is occupied with Whitehall, yet it is from Ireland that Cromwell returns to Whitehall three quarters of the way through the "Ode", and "to the Commons' feet presents | A kingdom, for his first year's rents".[4] From these

Irish victories the poem foretells Cromwell's military success in Scotland, whence Cromwell "March[es] indefatigably on" at the poem's close.[5] For one seventeenth-century reader, the archipelagic arc of Cromwell's post-regicidal career was as central to the "Ode" as its central meditation on Cromwell's part in Charles I's tragedy. The poem, as printed in the two known un-cancelled copies of *Miscellaneous Poems* (1681), has Cromwell "cast the Kingdome old | Into another Mold", but the manuscript version in the Bodleian Library speaks of "kingdoms" in the plural.[6] It is an emendation that has animated more recent archipelagic interest in the poem's Celtic margins, in keeping with the archipelagic turn of early modern literary criticism more generally in recent decades.[7]

David J. Baker writes that Marvell's "'Ode' is a poem by an Englishman who glimpses the potential for more-than-Englishness that Cromwell's victories seem to imply". Yet the politics of British-Irish state-formation is not the only framework inflecting Marvell's representations of Ireland and Scotland in the "Ode". Also key is the question of Marvell's religion. This article develops on the archipelagic angle of Baker's and other recent approaches to the "Ode" to offer a more religiously inflected reading of Marvell's representation of these nations in the poem, one attuned to the potential for religious differences to divide as well as elide protestant communities across the British-Irish archipelago. David Coleman reminds us that national identities "more often than not include a religious component in their self-definition".[8] This was particularly true of mid-seventeenth century England, where identity was as much bound up with religious as with national allegiances, and thus was as open to permutation as the religious situation itself in commonwealth England, where Independency vied with Presbyterianism over questions of church government, and both faced challenges from the rise in religious sectarianism. As these religious divisions undercut national unity in England, they also complicated English perspectives on its Celtic neighbours, muddying support for Cromwell's Irish campaign in 1649–50 among English Levellers, and support for Cromwell's invasion of Scotland among English presbyterians, including Marvell's future patron Thomas, third lord Fairfax, who resigned as general of the parliamentary army in June 1650 in protest of Cromwell's impending invasion.[9]

In two key interventions into debates over Marvell's relative royalist versus republican sympathies, Blair Worden and David Norbrook argue that the poem makes its republicanism manifest through verbal and ideological parallels with republican writing by Milton and Nedham, among others.[10] Central to these arguments is the claim that Marvell shares Milton and Nedham's readiness to think of "Cromwell as a Machiavellian prince".[11] While I also want to acknowledge Marvell's familiarity with Milton and Nedham's Machiavellian language, in what follows I focus less on what Marvell borrows from these writers than on what he chooses to omit. Marvell's "Ode" may have been politically aligned with English republican writing, but I argue that the "Ode" departs significantly from Milton and Nedham's religious prejudices, airbrushing the anti-presbyterian rhetoric of Milton and Nedham's writings on Ireland and Scotland, to produce representations of the tamed Irish and "parti-coloured" Pict that are anti-catholic without being anti-presbyterian.[12] This, I suggest, is an attitude consistent with Marvell's later anti-catholic, but pro-nonconformist, approach to Ireland, in his two-part defence of nonconformity, *The Rehearsal transpros'd* (1672–1673), part one of which offers a damning assessment of John Bramhall's Irish career under Thomas

Wentworth, earl of Strafford, the Caroline lord deputy of Ireland (1633–41).[13] Marvell writes of how Bramhall's attack on "the Calvinian Doctrines" and insistence on Anglican uniformity had exacerbated existing divisions within Irish Protestantism, creating the conditions that had allowed "the Irish Rebellion and Massacre" of 1641 to occur.[14] Reading Marvell's later views on Ireland's religious landscape back into "An Horatian Ode", this article argues that Marvell was more selective in his reading of Milton and Nedham than has been previously recognised, and that Marvell's focus on catholic stereotypes of Scots and Irish in the "Ode" implies his refusal to entertain the barbed language of Milton and Nedham's anti-Presbyterianism.

Popery, presbytery and English republican writing: Milton's *Observations* and Nedham's *Mercurius Politicus*

If religion inflected English responses to Cromwell's Irish and Scottish campaigns, the same was true of Irish and Scottish responses to the religious politics of commonwealth England. "They say, wee are not all *England*", Milton writes, attacking what the Belfast presbytery – the "*Scottish* Inhabitants of the Province" – had written in *A Necessary Representation* against "the insolent and presumptuous practises of the Sectaries in *England*". But "we reply they are not all *Scotland*".[15] Milton published his animadversions on the Belfast *Representation* in May 1649 alongside his *Observations* attacking the peace articles brokered in Ireland between the royalist, protestant, lord lieutenant of Ireland, James Butler, marquess of Ormond, and the catholic confederation of Kilkenny. Milton's *Observations* deliberately muddies these religious differences between the English Commonwealth's various catholic and protestant enemies in Ireland, lumping English protestant royalists and Scottish presbyterians together, as "accomplices and assistants to the abhorred *Irish* Rebels".[16] Similar anti-presbyterian strategies punctuate early issues of Marchamont Nedham's republican newsbook, *Mercurius Politicus*. Published weekly from 13 June 1650 in the build up to Cromwell's Scottish campaign, *Politicus* turns Milton's tactic of identifying presbytery with popery in Ireland against the "high *Raunters* of Presbyterie" in Edinburgh.[17]

Milton's damning assessment of "the abhorred *Irish* Rebels" in *Observations* was in part informed by his reading of the first printed edition of Edmund Spenser's *A View of the State of Ireland*, prepared by James Ware and printed in Dublin in 1633. That Milton read Spenser's *View* in Ware's 1633 edition is clear from the several entries in Milton's commonplace book that reflect his admiration for Spenser's brutal solution to the problem of pacifying Ireland.[18] Spenser, through the person of Irenius, proposes to uproot rebellion through a policy of mass starvation, transforming "stout and obstinate rebells" into "anatomies of death".[19] Yet the suppression of rebellion is only one aspect of Spenser's plans for the "reformation of that realme", the success of which, he writes, will also be dependent on reforming the laws and offices of English colonial government, on "planting [...] religion", as well as crops, and on controlling access to the land itself.[20] Milton shows particular interest in these, Spenser's long-term proposals for colonial reform. Willy Maley's research highlights two relevant entries in Milton's commonplace book, the first concerning Spenser's discussion of "the wicked policies of divers deputies and governours", the second his "provision for souldiers after the warrs", "from p. 84. &c". of Ware's edition, Milton notes.[21] Spenser's discussion of 'some blame thereof in the "principall governours" roots his list of particular faults in one "chiefe evill" – that lord deputies exercise a partial and piecemeal authority, reliant on the English Privy Council's support, and subject to censure by "maligners" who "deprave and pull back what ever thing shall be begun or intended there".[22] These combined pressures create politic governors, who "will rather winke at some faults, and will suffer them unpunished".[23] Spenser's solution is to grant lord deputies a "more ample and absolute authority" through the appointment of a lord lieutenant, to whom alone the lord deputy would be answerable, and who would be "no discountenancing of the Lord Deputy, but rather a strengthening of all his doings".[24] In support of these measures, Spenser cites "Machiavel in his discourses upon Livie, where he commendeth the manner of the Romans government, in giving absolute power to all their Councellors and Governors, which if they abused, they should afterwards dearely answere".[25]

Maley argues that Milton's *Observations* "was evidently influenced by a close reading of Spenser's *View*", and Norbrook notes the possible influence of Spenser's Machiavellian reference on Milton's own praise of Cromwell's future Machiavellian leadership in *Observations*.[26] Commissioned in March, Milton's *Observations* was published "by Autority" in the same month – May 1649 – that Cromwell was named lord lieutenant of Ireland, and Jim Daems is among those to read Milton's attack on "those inhumane Rebels and Papists of *Ireland*" as "a preemptive justification of Cromwell's brutal Irish campaign".[27] The *Observations* also attacks the actions of the royalist lord lieutenant, the marquess of Ormond, who in a letter written in March 1649 to the parliamentarian governor of Dublin, Colonel Michael Jones, had accused England's Independent-led republican government of subverting "true religion" and establishing "Anarchy" under the Anabaptist, "*Crumwell*".[28] Milton responds with withering criticism of Ormond's own "*Irish* exploits", contrasting these with the "eminent and remarkable Deeds" that Cromwell "in few yeares" has achieved.[29] His "valour and high merit many enemies more noble then himself have both honour'd and feard, to assert his good name and reputation", Milton asserts of Cromwell, "of whose service the Common-wealth receaves so ample satisfaction".[30] Balancing praise of Cromwell's "valour" with assurances of his "service", Milton's language anticipates Marvell's own assessment of Cromwell's achievements in Ireland the following year. Marvell's "Ode" also speaks Miltonically of Cromwell as leader and servant – "How fit he is to sway", Marvell notes, "That can so well obey".[31] Marvell does not just repeat the language of *Observations*, however; his "Ode" adds weight to Milton's claim that even Cromwell's enemies can "assert his good name and reputation" by putting these words in the mouths of the "tam'd" Irish themselves:

> They can affirm his praises best,
> And have, though overcome, confest
>   How good he is, how just,
>   And fit for highest trust;
>
> Nor yet grown stiffer with command,
> But still in the republic's hand.[32]

Marvell's "Irish" here echo Milton's affirmation of Cromwell's fitness "for highest trust", while Milton himself may in turn have been echoing Spenser's Machiavellian assessment of the ideal Irish governor in *A View* – one who, Spenser writes, should "sway" and "obey" in equal measure, granted "absolute power", but answerable for abuses of power with their lives.

Marvell was not the only writer in the summer of 1650 to praise Cromwell in Miltonic terms, by the measure of his military "Deeds". Marvell's accent on Cromwell's "industrious valour", and his admiration for Cromwell having taken but "one year" to tame a nation that had troubled the English for a century or more, is also reflected in Nedham's account of Cromwell's return from Ireland, in the first issue of *Mercurius Politicus* (6–13 June 1650).[33] Nedham writes that "it is the wonder of our Neighbour Nations, that so much should be done in so little time", and that Cromwell's "Deeds" had earned him the title "*Novus Princeps*", a reference, Worden notes, to the new prince – *il nuovo principe* – who rules by might not birth right, and for whom Machiavelli had originally intended *The Prince*.[34] Nedham writes admiringly of Cromwell's military prowess – his "bare reputation", he notes, "is battery strong enough against the stoutest hearts, and most impregnable Castles" – even as his news from Ireland throughout June reveals the realities behind the rhetoric of conquest.[35] Cromwell's absence has emboldened the confederates, Nedham admits on 8 June, and while he assures readers that "one *Thunder-Clap* more will serve to clear all *Ireland* from infection", his report for 21 June brings news of "how the bold Rebels came 6000. in a body out of *Ulster*".[36] Cromwell's victory, as Michael Komorowski notes, was by no means assured on his return to London in early June.[37]

Nedham, like Marvell, however, speaks the language of conquest, even as the war in Ireland raged on. *Politicus* reports these confederate advances in muscular prose, revealing a sneering disregard for "those *Brutes* of the Nation", hunted "like *Deer* in a Forrest", and driven "into a Bogg, where they were pursued till they were lost all in a fogg".[38] The language is Spenserian, for *A View* also applies the epithets "brutish" and "barbarous" to the native Irish and Old English and characterises Irish rebels as "a flying enemie, hiding himselfe in woodes and bogges".[39] Patricia Coughlan writes that Spenser applied to the Irish "pre-formed notions about the incivility of those without a native urban culture" – notions Spenser adopted from classical sources such as Herodotus's description of the nomadic Scythians, whose savagery Herodotus deliberately contrasts with the civility of urban Athenian culture.[40] Spenser, as Richard McCabe writes, uses Herodotus to inform comparisons between Irish and "Scythian customes", his aim being not merely to suggest that the Irish were as savage as the Scythians but that the Irish were themselves originally Scythian.[41] So too were the Scots, Spenser maintains: for the Scythians had arrived "in the North parts of Ireland, where some of them after passed into the next coast of Albine, now called Scotland".[42] Spenser forges a history of ancestral relations between "the wilde Scotts" and "naturall Irish" and argues that this pan-Gaelic alliance continues to operate against New English interests in late Elizabethan Ireland.[43] Spenser was evidently writing with recent events in mind, for the summers of 1594–95 had seen armed rebellions by catholic earls, first in Scotland, under Huntly and Erroll, then in Ulster under the earl of Tyrone.[44]

A View therefore traces a geography of barbarity that extends from the "naturall Irish" to the "wilde Scotts", two nations as related by blood as by their "brutish" religion – for the Irish, as the Highland Scots, "be all Papists in their profession, but [...] blindly and brutishly informed".[45] Equally barbarous is the Old English catholic community in Ireland, who as Irenius asserts have "degenerated and growne almost mere Irish", taking on the "barbarous rudenes" of Irish language, customs, and religion.[46] Although twice noting that he has "little [...] to say of religion", Irenius nevertheless recommends that Catholicism be uprooted in Ireland through a two-pronged approach.[47] First, by cutting off the two-way traffic between Ireland and the catholic seminaries "beyond the sea", for the seminaries send Jesuits to Ireland, or make Jesuits of the sons of Old English families, who "doe more hurt and hinderance to religion with their private perswasions then all the others can doe good with their publique instructions".[48] Second, Irenius recommends measures to re-edify churches and increase church livings, as first steps towards re-establishing the established church in Ireland – for "godly teachers" can never work a reformation in Ireland unless adequately recompensed with "meete maintenance".[49]

Spenser's "rebarbatively negative" characterisation of the Irish was resurrected with vitriol in English responses to the 1641 Irish Rebellion.[50] Depositions reporting catholic violence against the New English in Ireland were quickly escalated in the London press, culminating in Sir John Temple's sensationalised *The Irish Rebellion* (1646), the "standard Protestant interpretation" of the uprising.[51] Temple cements two key "facts" about the Rebellion that had been circulating since at least the publication of Henry Jones' official enquiry into the causes of the Rebellion, commissioned by the Long Parliament, and published as *A Remonstrance* in March 1642: that the rebellion was the product of an international papist conspiracy, "intending the utter extirpation of the reformed Religion, and the professors of it", and that the "cruelties" and "depredations" of the rebels were such as would shame even "the most barbarous and heathenish Nations".[52] To the standard Spenserian stereotype of the bog dwelling papist brute, therefore, English protestant responses to the Irish rebellion brought the language of righteous outrage and religious retribution. As Nedham writes, Irish rebels must "drink the same measure of blood which they gave the *English*, in the rise of their *Rebellion*".[53] He and Milton both write of Cromwell's campaign in Ireland as an anti-catholic crusade – an opportunity to enact a Spenserian "reformation of that realme".[54]

It is with Spenser's plans for the "planting of religion" in mind, therefore, that Milton extends his praise of the Machiavellian governor to a consideration of the governor's role in the war against Irish Catholicism.[55] To Ormond's claim that independents in England's commonwealth government were "the Subverters of true Religion", Milton responds by contrasting Ormond's record in Ireland with the anti-catholic ordinances of the English parliament.[56] Ormond, Milton writes, has made peace with catholic confederates, and so "of all Protestants may be calld most justly the Subverter of true Religion". "Parlament", on the other hand, are "the maintainers and defenders of true Religion", for they have not "countenac'd Popery or Papists, but have every where brok'n their Temporall power, thrown down their public Superstitions", while "encourag[ing] all true Ministers of the Gospel".[57] Milton here directs his praise to the work of the parliament in England, not that of the lord lieutenant in Ireland. However the context of his remarks – an attack on Ormond's failings as lord lieutenant – implies the translatability of parliament's anti-catholic religious policy in England to the situation in Ireland under its new lord lieutenant, Cromwell. Framed through his description of the English parliament's achievements for "true Religion", the religious "reformation" that Milton encourages Cromwell to enact in Ireland is broadly Spenserian in its emphasis on stifling the "Temporall power" of "Popery" and "Papists", and on supporting "true Ministers of the Gospel" financially and through political protection. Milton's argument that the state should exercise minimal control over matters of conscience, departs from Spenser's own religious views. Recent research reveals Spenser to be a moderate, non-separating puritan whose writings attack Presbyterianism and insist on conformity to the established church, as Irenius' jibe at "some of our late too nice fooles" who criticise the "seemely forme, and comely order of the Church" reveals.[58] But Spenser and Milton find common ground in their identification of Irish papists as the common enemy of (New) English Protestantism, and their acknowledgement of the need for Machievallian leadership in Ireland, to uproot rebellion "by the sword", and plant "true Religion" in its stead.[59]

Spenser and Milton both attacked presbyterians, although both for very different reasons. For Spenser, presbyterians were separatists who threatened the uniformity of the established, episcopal, church. For Milton, writing in an era when the established church had been all but disestablished, it was now presbyterians who were insisting on national uniformity, and who in so doing were threatening the religious freedoms to which Milton was committed. It is not the ideological, so much as rhetorical differences between Spenser and Milton's approaches to Presbyterianism that I here want to emphasise, however. Irenius' attack on "too nice fooles" in *A View* comes in a passage recommending rebuilding ruinous Irish churches "in some better forme, according to the churches of England". Irenius argues that "the outward shew" of churches would "drawe the rude people to the reverencing and frequenting thereof", and that their "seemely forme" was thus a necessary first step in converting the Irish to Protestantism. "Godly teachers" would "bring them to the true understanding" of religion, but what good was preaching if you couldn't entice "the rude people" to the pulpit? Irenius' jibe at those who would make much of "outward shew" therefore makes clear that such "too nice", or overly fastidious, objections, by discouraging "the rude people" from attending church, detracts from the greater goal of converting "Papists" to Protestantism. But Irenius' accent on "*our* late too nice fooles" also acknowledges a place for these "fooles" within the wider protestant community; indeed, Irenius' language actively encourages their inclusion, the use of "our" rhetorically uniting factions whose ideological opposition to aspects of ecclesiastical "forme" tends otherwise to divide.[60] Spenser's point is that separating puritans and presbyterians make trouble for the church, dividing the protestant community in Ireland at a time when it should be uniting against Catholicism.

Milton also thinks of presbyterians as fools. His *Observations* pillories the Belfast presbytery as "blockish Presbyters" for their writing against "the Sectarian party in *England*", and it does so for reasons similar to Spenser's, arguing that their "unexampl'd virulence" against fellow protestants ultimately supports the cause of Irish Catholicism, making them "accomplices and assistants to the abhorred *Irish* Rebels" because colluding in their "war against the Parlament".[61] Milton, however, not only identifies the Belfast presbyterians with the catholic cause of "*Irish* Rebels". In *Observations*, Milton also aligns this particular presbytery, sitting "so haughtie in the Pontificall See of Belfast", with "Popery" more generally, arguing that their writing reveals them to be no better than papists in their claim to wield "an absolute and undepending Jurisdiction" over the state, as "the Pope hath for many Ages done".[62] And not only in Belfast are presbyterians guilty of popery; that presbyterians are no better than papists is a claim Milton also extends to Presbyterianism more generally, animadverting that "Presbyteriall government" is as "the Popish and Prelaticall Courts, or the *Spanish*

Inquisition.⁶³ Milton's elision of presbytery and popery may be rhetorical, a means to shame the Scots presbytery at Belfast to their senses, yet Milton's language nevertheless does something quite different to Spenser's jibe at "our fooles" in Ireland: Spenser encourages unity, Milton division. By lumping Scots presbytery, Anglican prelacy, and Irish popery together, the rhetoric of *Observations* divides "true Protestants" in England from those, like Ormond, or the Belfast presbyterians, who "would be thought a Protestant Assembly".⁶⁴ The *Observations* not only chides the "blockish Presbyters" of Belfast, therefore; it elides this Scots presbytery with the common catholic enemy of English protestants. In the process, it links animosity towards Presbyterianism with animosity towards Scotland in ways that would have implications for how the Commonwealth chose to conduct its propaganda war with Scotland in the summer of 1650.

Joad Raymond argues that Milton's anti-Presbyterianism was fuelled by "his suspicion of and antipathy to the Scots", and while Maley and Swann are right to note the more "nuanced" perspective on Scotland that Milton's respect for John Knox's Presbyterianism and republicanism reveals, in *Observations* Milton nevertheless connects Belfast presbyterians with "the Scottish inhabitants of that province" in ways calculated to combine religious with national prejudice.⁶⁵ Milton draws on Spenser's claims for the consanguinity between Highland Scots and Ulster Irish – for "doe we not all know", Irenius asks, "that those which now are called the North Irish, are indeed very Scottes"? – to argue in Spenserian terms that the Belfast presbyterians are no better than "High-land theevs and Red-shanks", a coinage Milton may well have borrowed directly from Spenser's *View*, which notes how the Ulster O'Neills have historically had "all succours of those Scottes and Redshankes".⁶⁶ Spenser himself borrowed "Redshank" from Holinshed's *Chronicles* (1587), where it is used with reference to the "Picts", whom Holinshed writes "were settled in this Ile long before the [...] coming of the Scots", and whom Mamertinus "calleth [...] Redshankes and Pictones".⁶⁷ Holinshed distinguishes Picts from Scots, whom he, like Spenser, describes as "a people mixed of the Scithian and Spanish blood", who "arrive[d] here out of Ireland". Holinshed also assumes "Scithian" origins for the Picts, however, who in any event had combined with the Scots "against the Britains [...] not long before the beginning of *Cesars* time".⁶⁸ Spenser also blurs distinctions between "Scottes and Redshankes", arguing that both "succour" the Ulster Irish in their campaigns against English colonial rule. Milton follows suit, flinging both epithets at the Belfast presbytery in ways again calculated to associate the presbyterians with papists, and here specifically with the Scottish catholic clans whose collusion with the Ulster Irish had so animated Spenser in the 1590s.

Milton's anti-presbyterian language therefore mines a seam of English anti-Scottish and anti-catholic prejudice that draws on Spenser's own "anti-Scottish" stereotypes.⁶⁹ A year later, the same jingoistic jibes against Scottish presbyterians – in Ulster, as well as Edinburgh – would reappear in Nedham's *Politicus*, the mouthpiece of the republican propaganda war against Scotland in summer 1650.⁷⁰ Nedham's first issues mingle stock parodies of Scottish poverty and proclivity for *"Mackerel"* eating with Miltonic parries at "the common cause of *Scotch Presbyterie*, and *Irish* Popery".⁷¹ In Ireland, he writes, "the bold *Rebels*" are "called *good Subjects*" by the future king, Charles II, "the bonny Lad of *Scotland*", while the same catholic rebels call on "the *Scotish* Priests" of the presbyteries to pray for their victory against the Cromwellian army.[72] The Scottish kirk, Nedham writes, is as "haughtie" in its handling of civil matters as Milton's Belfast presbytery (Nedham calls on readers to judge "whether the Kirk be not bravely inthroned in Scotland; when she destines whom she pleases to death"), and he argues that the kirk wears only a mask of royalism, its support for Charles II a means to "inthrone" itself "on this side *Berwick*", in England as well as Scotland.[73]

Milton inherits Spenser's language of Ireland: his anti-Catholicism, his horror of rebellion, and his suspicion that Scots and Redshanks were colluding with the Ulster Irish against the English. But it is Milton's application of this language to the Scots presbytery at Belfast that marks a shift in *Observations* from the religious geography of *A View*, a shift later replicated in *Politicus*. Similar claims appear in the English army pamphlets that were printed in July–August 1650 to justify the army's invasion of Scotland and parry the kirk's counterblasts against "the Sectaries of *England*".[74] The authors of *A Vindication of the Declaration of the Army of England*, for example, answer the General Assembly's *Short Reply* (reprinted in the same pamphlet) by returning to Milton's analogy between popery and presbytery, noting the Scottish kirk's "Spiritual Tyranny & outward Violence [...] not unlike that under the Inquisition".[75] No longer Spenser's English "fooles", by 1650 presbyterians had become England's Scottish enemies, aligned with the politics of Irish "rebel" confederates and the religion of Irish catholics. Milton's presbyterians were the new "Red-shanks" worrying the English commonwealth, their seat the General Assembly at Edinburgh, their aim to wage war "against the Britains", as their ancestors, the Scots and Picts of Caesar's day, had done.

The religious geography of Marvell's "A Horatian Ode"

Marvell's "Horatian Ode" also trades in the anti-Scottish propaganda of *Politicus* and other republican writing produced in the summer of 1650. With Cromwell "march[ing] indefatigably on" towards Berwick, Marvell writes,

> The Pict no shelter now shall find
> Within his parti-coloured mind;
> But from his valour sad
> Shrink underneath the plaid:
>
> Happy if in the tufted brake,
> The English hunter him mistake,
>   Nor lay his hounds in near
>   The Caledonian deer.[76]

"The Pict", as we have seen, is a synonym for Spenser and Milton's "Redshank", and Marvell follows both in assuming an alliance between "Highland" Scots and Pictish Redshanks, dressing his Pict in the "plaid", or tartan kilts, associated with Highland clans.[77] Marvell's Pict is thus a composite, "parti-coloured" Scotsman, woven, plaid-like, from the warp and weft of Scotland's history of Scots and Picts, and here combining into one negative stereotype – a figure who spans the Highland/Lowland divide, just as Spenser and Milton blur distinctions between "Scottes and Redshankes" when acknowledging their combined collusion with the Ulster Irish against English colonial rule. Marvell's Pict also emerges in the first stanza above in Spenserian guise, an embodiment of Spenser's "Scythian" stereotype of "the wilde Scotts" whom, as Irenius writes, "are indeed the very naturall Irish".[78] This stereotype Milton mobilises for his attack on catholic "Red-shanks" in the Belfast presbytery, and this in turn anticipates Nedham's conflation of popery with presbytery, in his jibes at "*Scotish* Priests" in Ireland and Edinburgh. It has been argued that Marvell also intended his Pict as an anti-presbyterian caricature, and indeed there is nothing in the first stanza above to oppose this reading.[79] Marvell's Pict is rooted in Spenser's anti-catholic stereotypes of Irish-Scottish savagery, yet like Milton, Marvell might have intended this stereotype as a snub at the presbyterian kirk, implying that the Scottish kirk was just as "blindly and brutishly informed" in its religion as Spenser's Irish papists, or Milton's Ulster presbyterians.

Perhaps; but if we turn from the first to the second stanza quoted above, the idea of Marvell's Pict as a vehicle for anti-kirk satire becomes more difficult to sustain. Here, the Pict is hunted like "the Caledonian deer" through terrain thick with "brake" or bracken, a description that, as John Kerrigan notes, places Marvell's Scotsman "beyond the Highland line, among the followers of Montrose".[80] James Graham, first marquess of Montrose, had been the enemy of the kirk since he had defected to the royalist cause in winter 1644–45, leading a combined troop of Highlanders and Irish to a string of victories against the covenanters in the Scottish Highlands. Returning to the Highlands from royalist exile in the Low Countries in 1649–50, Montrose tried to repeat his earlier military successes against Scotland's covenanting regime, this time fighting for the new king, Charles II, following the collapse of the king's discussions with the covenanters in May 1649. Montrose's campaign was doomed from the outset, however, for even Montrose recognised that he was merely a pawn in the king's plans to force the covenanters back to the negotiating table. Montrose's own endgame came soon after with defeat and capture at Carbisdale (April 1650), and then execution at Edinburgh on 21 May 1650.[81] In the early issues of *Politicus*, Nedham makes much of Montrose's decapitated head, displayed on the Edinburgh Tolbooth.[82] For Nedham, this head symbolised "the wicked partiality and Hypocrisie of the *Presbyterians*", who could condemn Montrose – the actor of this royalist uprising – in the same breath as they courted its author, the new king, one "more guilty than he".[83]

Marvell might have intended his "p-coloured" Pict as an anti-presbyterian reference, a jibe, with Nedham, at the "wicked partiality [...] of the *Presbyterians*". But, standing in the Highlands, the partiality of Marvell's Pict would seem more plausibly to echo Scottish presbyterian accusations against Montrose, who was himself accused at his trial of hypocrisy and partisanship, as a turncoat to the covenanting cause.[84] Had Marvell really intended his Pict to pillory Scottish Presbyterianism, the most sensible place to have located him, in a poem written over the summer of 1650, was not the Highlands, but Edinburgh, the backdrop to Nedham's presbyterian satire and scene of the kirk's executive power (and Montrose's execution). By choosing to set his Pict in the Highlands, therefore, Marvell, as Kerrigan suggests, actually "deflects hostility from Lowland Presbyterians".[85] In the process, Marvell signals his departure from the anti-presbyterian rhetoric of Milton and Nedham, suggesting that while the "Ode", as Worden and Norbrook argue, is a poem invested in the politics of English republicanism and its campaigns in Ireland and Scotland, it is less committed to the religious propaganda of republican writing and its attempts to blacken presbytery with the name of popery.[86]

Marvell's representation of the Irish also lacks anti-presbyterian bite, for like the Pict, the Irish stand in Marvell's poem as Spenserian stereotypes of Scythian barbarism – a barbarism that Cromwell's conquest has now "tamed". Marvell's language of "taming" likens the Irish to Nedham's "Brutes of the Nation", suggesting that the term "Irish" is used exclusively in the "Ode" of those actors in the rebellion of October 1641 – Milton's "inhumane Rebels and Papists of *Ireland*". Marvell does not extend his characterisation of these brutish rebels to a satire on those other "accomplices and assistants to the abhorred *Irish* Rebels" – the English royalists under Ormond and the Scots presbyterians at Belfast – that Milton attacks in *Observations*; neither does he emphasise, with Nedham, "the common cause of *Scotch Presbyterie*, and *Irish Popery*", or quip at the involvement of "*Scotish* Priests" in Ireland's confederate wars.[87] Milton and Nedham both flatten out the religious differences between Ireland's various "rebel" factions, lumping popery and presbytery together, yet they also acknowledge ethnic divisions between Scots and English on the one hand, and Irish "brutes" on the other, and while they imply that presbyterians are as "brutishly informed" as Irish papists, they never extend the Irish epithets of barbarity to the Scots and English themselves. The fact Marvell only trades in this language of Irish barbarity, therefore, leaves no nuance in his characterisation of the Irish for anything approaching Milton and Nedham's republican satire on the religious similitudes between "*Scotch Presbyterie*, and *Irish Popery*". Marvell reduces the plurality and complexity of Ireland's competing religious voices to a single, univocal "confession" of Cromwell's greatness. When the "Irish" speak in the poem to "affirm his praises best", therefore, it is only the voice of the "inhumane" Irish papists that we hear.

For all Marvell's republican admiration for Cromwell, therefore, the "Ode" is profoundly ambivalent about the religious dimensions of republican propaganda. The poem ends with Cromwell "March[ing] indefatigably on" towards Berwick, yet the nature of the enemy he will encounter in Scotland remains unclear. Readers of *Politicus* and the army pamphlets circulating in the summer of 1650 are left in no doubt that Cromwell's enemy is the spiritual tyranny of the Scottish kirk and its intention to impose Presbyterianism "on this side *Berwick*". Readers of the "Ode", on the other hand, are confronted, in Marvell's Pict, with a figure who frustrates these anti-presbyterian expectations. Standing in the Highlands, dressed in tartan plaid, Marvell's Pict dissolves into a parody of Spenser's "Scottes and Redshankes" – a plausible embodiment of Montrose's Highlanders and their alliance with the Irish in the Highland campaigns of 1644–45, and thus a reminder of Spenser's fears over the Celtic consanguinity and catholic collaboration between Irish and Highland clans. Marvell's "Irish" also evoke Spenserian fears of Irish catholic rebellion, the "Ode" in this sense echoing the Spenserian language of Milton's *Observations* and Nedham's *Politicus*, yet at the same time departing from both in the studied simplicity of Marvell's anti-catholic stereotype, which leaves no room for republican attacks on the "*Scotch Presbyterie*" in Ulster and its hostility towards English Independency and the English republican cause. Both Milton and Nedham engage in forms of protestant infighting, acknowledging "*Scotch Presbyterie*" alongside "*Irish Popery*" as the common enemy of English Protestantism. Marvell avoids these internecine battles, representing the English commonwealth's enemies as primitive stereotypes of Scythian barbarity and Celtic Catholicism – straw men of incivility, to be hunted like deer and tamed like beasts.

Such caricatures may simply reflect Marvell's prejudices towards the inhabitants of Britain's "Celtic fringe", but given what critics have noted about Marvell's engagement with the Machiavellian language of Milton and Nedham elsewhere in the "Ode", I would suggest that his deviation from their anti-presbyterian position on Scotland and the Ulster Scots seems less a reflection of Marvell's views on Scottish and Irish Catholicism than of his views on Milton and Nedham's anti-Presbyterianism. To read the "Ode" alongside Milton and Nedham's attacks on Presbyterianism in Scotland and Ireland is thus to reveal, if not Marvell's support for the Scottish presbyterian position (which may well, for Marvell, have seemed too "tyrannous" in its insistence on presbyterian conformity), then at least his belief that protestants should not make enemies of each other. Identifying a catholic, Celtic enemy helps heal internecine divisions between Britain's protestant communities; aligning Scottish presbytery with Irish popery serves only to aggravate these divisions.

Marvell's representation of the British-Irish archipelago's catholic, Celtic margins also has implications for our reading of "restless Cromwell", the figure at the centre of "An Horatian Ode".[88] Worden and Norbrook both read Marvell's Cromwell in a Machiavellian light, arguing that Marvell commends Cromwell's military ambition, his "industrious valour", at a time when the English republic, beset by enemies in Britain, Ireland, and mainland Europe, needed a *Novus Princeps* strong enough to stand up to the forces of royalism, and silence, with military might, the continued clamours of "the ancient rights".[89] However the recognition that Marvell trades in anti-catholic stereotypes of the Scots and Irish qualifies considerably Marvell's Machiavellian preparedness to applaud Cromwell's military muscle, implying as it does that Marvell frames Cromwell's campaigns in these countries as exclusively anti-catholic crusades – a significant departure from Milton and Nedham's more partisan concern to identify Presbyterianism, alongside popery, as the royalist enemy of English republicanism. Marvell places limits on the ascent of Cromwell's "active star", his poem urging military activity only insofar as this is directed outwards, not at protestant royalists in England, Ireland, and Scotland, but at the caricatures of Celtic, catholic incivility that people the margins of Marvell's "kingdoms old".[90] Cromwell's enemies in Britain and Ireland are in this sense of a piece with his catholic enemies abroad, the kingdom of France, and the kingdoms, duchies, and papal states of Italy whose emancipation Marvell briefly imagines in the "Ode":

> A Caesar he ere long to Gaul,
> To Italy an Hannibal,
>   And to all states not free
>   Shall climacteric be.[91]

Sandwiched directly between his poem's celebration of Cromwell's Irish conquest – "What may not others fear, | If thus he crowns each year?" – and its anticipation of Cromwell's military success over the plaid-wearing "Pict", the above lines invite readers to connect Cromwell's conquests in Britain and Ireland with his crusading efforts to emancipate other western European nations from their subservience to papal, as well as regal, power.[92] Blair Worden is among critics to read Cromwell's intended emancipation of France and Italy in a primarily political light, connecting the above lines with those of Marchamont Nedham, who in *The case of the commonwealth of England, stated* (May 1650), observes "how the Worm works in many parts of *Europe* to cast off the *Regall* yoke".[93] This conception of Cromwell's European campaigns as directed against "the *Regall* yoke" is itself implicit in Marvell's choice of similes: as a latter-day Julius Caesar, Cromwell's conquests abroad would help consolidate his – and the English republic's – "forcèd power", its *de facto* right to rule, just as Caesar's conquest of Gaul had strengthened both the Roman republic and his own political career within it.[94] Marvell's identification of the catholic powers of France and Italy as the particular battlegrounds of Cromwell's wars abroad also helps convey strong religious motivations for these European campaigns, however. These are crusading connotations to which Marvell returns four years later, in "The First Anniversary of the Government under His Highness the Lord Protector" (December 1654-January 1655). In this poem, "Angelic Cromwell" is depicted in an explicitly millenarian light, as one who

> [...] in dark nights, and in cold days alone
> Pursues the monster thorough every throne:
> Which shrinking to her Roman den impure,
> Gnashes her gory teeth; nor there secure.[95]

Cromwell's target here is less the "regal yoke" of western European princes as the papal "monster" who occupies "every throne", and who itself yokes these "Unhappy princes" to the ignorance and "error" of Roman doctrine: "Hence still they sing hosanna to the whore, | And her whom they should massacre adore".[96]

Writing of Marvell's "Angelic Cromwell", Derek Hirst positions the poem's millenarian language as Marvell's considered response to the particular threat posed by fifth monarchists to the stability of Cromwell's protectorate around the time of its first anniversary in December 1654.[97] Leading fifth monarchists like Christopher Feake and John Simpson, both mentioned by name in "First Anniversary" (l. 305), had taken advantage of the protectoral anniversary to preach against Cromwell and the protectorate, which Feake denounced as "another kind of Kingship" and a "NEW UNEXPECTED TYRANNY", no different from Antichrist's other "ten Horns, or Kings", and thus no more to be suffered, but rather shaken off and opposed.[98] Hirst argues that in "First Anniversary" Marvell plays the fifth monarchists at their own game, applying their millenarian language to construct Cromwell, not as a horn of Antichrist, but as "the great captain" whose pursuit of the "monster" – the beast of Revelation – would in fact help herald the dawn of the promised millennium.[99] Marvell's millenarian language is thus calculated to persuade fifth monarchists to drop their "apocalyptic onslaughts on Oliver", Hirst writes, this despite the fact that elsewhere Marvell's poem derides fifth monarchists as a "race most hypocritically strict! | Bent to reduce us to the ancient pict".[100] Marvell's reference to "the ancient pict" here recalls the occurrence of that figure in the "Ode", although with its accent on "ancient", the Pict in "First Anniversary" is far removed from the contemporary, Highland setting of the earlier poem. It is the Pict's proverbial nakedness, not his Highland plaid, that Marvell emphasises in "First Anniversary", as his subsequent allusion to sectaries "act[ing] the Adam and Eve" makes clear. Marvell's former jibes at Highland barbarity here morph into an "identification of radicalism and native primitivism", as Marvell's later poem responds to new instabilities in the English commonwealth by training its sights on new sectarian targets.[101] In "First Anniversary", sectaries who actively undermine Cromwell's protectorate are as unwelcome in commonwealth England as the catholic princes who "sing hosanna to the whore".

Yet there are also important differences between the treatment of papists and sectarian "picts" in "First Anniversary", for while fifth monarchists are the target of Marvell's satire, it is only the papist "monster" whom Marvell imagines Cromwell actively "pursu[ing]" in battle "thorough every throne". Unlike Milton and Nedham, who blur distinctions between "*Scotch Presbyterie*" and "*Irish* Popery" in ways calculated to identify both as legitimate targets of English swords, Marvell's verbal attack on fifth monarchists turns from swords to words. This is a poem which, rather than fan the flames of division, seeks to appease protestant radicals, and to reconcile them with "Angelic Cromwell" – a poem which envisions the architecture of a protectorate made stronger through "the resistance of opposèd minds".[102] Edward Holberton writes of "First Anniversary" that the poem "breaks with established monarchical and republican conceptions of the English constitution" to celebrate Cromwell as architect of a third way, an English protectorate of checks and balances, "structured vigilantly against internal and external dangers".[103] Holberton sketches a very different political terrain for this poem from the binaries of royalism versus republicanism that tend to animate critical approaches to "An Horatian Ode", and by highlighting Marvell's emphasis in "First Anniversary" on the novelty, as well as necessity, of the protectorate, Holberton also departs from conventional readings of "First Anniversary" as a republican "critique" of "the trend towards monarchy" exemplified in Edmund Waller's Augustan *Paneqyrick* to Cromwell (1655).[104] Yet whatever the politics of "First Anniversary" and its departures or otherwise from the republicanism of the "Ode", it should be emphasised that the respective religious geographies of these poems differ little from each other. Both poems pit an English republic founded on the principles of liberty of worship to all but "Popery or Prelacy", against the error and ignorance of catholic regions in Britain, Ireland and "all states not free".[105] In so doing, both poems accord a key role to Cromwell as a military leader – "the great captain" of the commonwealth. At the same time, however, both can only contemplate Cromwell with "sword erect" when this sword is directed, not inwards at presbyterians, fifth monarchists, or other protestant communities, but outwards, at the common, catholic enemy of them all.[106]

Marvell's catholic caricatures of Scots, Irishmen, and "Unhappy princes" in mainland Europe thus help deflect attention from unseemly infighting among protestant communities in Britain and Ireland – a careful avoidance of internecine strife that in this sense anticipates Marvell's later commitment to the cause of religious toleration for protestant beliefs and practices outside the established church. Marvell's tolerationism is particularly manifest in his controversial writings from the 1670s that attack the Anglican insistence on conformity to the established church, yet I would argue that these are attitudes nevertheless consistent with the religious geography of the "Ode" and Marvell's other Cromwellian poems from the 1650s.[107] When two decades later Marvell returns to Ireland in *The Rehearsal transpros'd*, it is to revisit the religious context behind the Irish Rebellion that Cromwell had "tamed" in the "Ode". In *Rehearsal*, Marvell disputes Samuel Parker's assessment of John Bramhall's Irish career, first under

Thomas Wentworth, later earl of Strafford, then, after the Restoration, as archbishop of Armagh. Where Parker writes that Bramhall had showed "*a mind large and active enough to have managed the Roman Empire*", Marvell counters that, at a time when "the Ecclesiastical Differences in our own Nations" were rife, Bramhall might have spent less time "managing the Roman Empire", more "the Peace of his own Province and Country".[108] Bramhall might, like the "good *Primate*" his metropolitan, James Ussher, have set out to "abate … our Episcopall *Grandeur*", Marvell continues, and "reduce the Ceremonious Discipline in these Nations to the Primitive Simplicity".[109] Bramhall, however, was an acolyte of Archbishop Laud, not Ussher, and like Laud "*a zealous and resolute Assertor of the Publick Rites and Solemnities of the Church*". In Marvell's eyes, Bramhall's zeal for "external neatness" had had only negative results, striking a blow for protestant unity by further exacerbating "Ecclesiastical Differences" among Irish protestants.[110] "What then was this that Bishop Bramhal did?", Marvell asks.

> Did he, like a Protestant Apostle, in one day convert thousands of the Irish Papists? The contrary is evident by the Irish Rebellion and Massacre, which, notwithstanding his *Publick Employment and great Abilities*, happened in his time.[111]

It was not just that Bramhall had misapplied his "*Publick Employment and great Abilities*" by channelling these energies towards the eradication of protestant nonconformity. It was that, by turning his antagonism inwards, against "the Calvinian Doctrines", Bramhall had turned his back on the common, catholic enemy, thus creating the conditions that had allowed the Irish Rebellion of 1641 to ignite.

Marvell's religious position in *Rehearsal* is, then, a recapitulation of what we might infer of Marvell's earlier position on the anti-Presbyterianism of English republican writing in the "Ode", insofar as the "Ode", like *Rehearsal*, also refocuses its readers' attention on "the Irish Papists" that it was left for Cromwell to conquer, because Bramhall had neglected to convert. Milton, too, was guilty of diverting his protestant zeal away from "Irish Papists", for the rhetoric of *Observations* incites as much anti-catholic animosity towards the "blockish Presbyters" of Belfast as towards "the abhorred *Irish* Rebels" themselves. The "Ode" writes from the perspective of the "Protestant Apostle" that Marvell would later chide John Bramhall for failing to be, a perspective that attacks the kirk-baiting of Milton and Nedham in 1649–50 just as much as it pillories "the Irish Bishops Tyranny" over protestant nonconformists some two decades later. Cromwell's soldiers wrote of their march to Scotland in summer 1650 that they went to battle "with the Covenant on the tops of our Pikes".[112] Marvell, significantly, removes kirk and covenant from the religious geography of "An Horatian Ode". The final lines of the "Ode" call on Cromwell to "keep thy sword erect", but the poem elsewhere directs Cromwell's sword at "brutish" papists – the barbarous Irish and kilted Pict – not at presbyterians, however "popish" Milton and Nedham claim them to be. Although the execution of Charles I is the most "memorable scene" of Marvell's poem, the poem also draws attention to its – and the English commonwealth's – Celtic margins. Marvell's generation of readers must have found plenty to reflect on here; so too, I would suggest, might we.

Notes

1. "An Horatian Ode", in Smith, ed., *Poems of Marvell*, 267-79 (l. 58); hereafter cited as 'Marvell, "Ode"'. As an occasional poem marking 'Cromwell's return from Ireland', and anticipating his military successes in Scotland, there is broad critical agreement that the "Ode" was composed between Cromwell's return to London on 1 June, and his crossing into Scotland at the head of the parliamentary army on 22 July 1650. See Smith, ed., *Poems of Marvell*, 267.
2. Marvell, "Ode", ll. 57 and 61. 'The contrast between Charles's own conduct and that of his killers' at this mid-point in the poem is particularly emphasized by Worden, *Literature and Politics*, 86.
3. Criticism of Marvell's "Ode" was divided in the second half of the twentieth century between those, like Coolidge ("Marvell and Horace") and Everett ("Shooting of the Bears"), who admire Marvell's 'Horatian' balance between the competing claims of Cromwell and Charles I, and those, like Mazzeo ("Cromwell as Machiavellian Prince"), Wallace ("Destiny his Choice"), Worden ("Politics of Horatian Ode" and its fuller development in *Literature and Politics*, chapter 5), and Norbrook ("Politics of Genre"), who argue that the poem sides with Cromwell, signalling a switch in Marvell's political allegiance from the royalism of the pre-1650 poems to the pragmatic 'loyalism' of his republican phase.
4. Marvell, "Ode", ll. 85-6.
5. Marvell, "Ode", l. 114.
6. Marvell, *Miscellaneous Poems*, 116; cf. Marvell, "Ode", ll. 35-6. Nigel Smith, like other of the poem's modern editors, accepts the manuscript reading. The additions to Bodleian Library, Oxford, MS Eng. Poet. d. 49 – a copy of the printed 1681 *Miscellaneous Poems* containing MS corrections and interleaved transcriptions of the cancelled Cromwell poems – have been persuasively (although inconclusively) attributed to Marvell's nephew, Will Popple. See Patterson, "Lady State's Two Sittings", 396-402. The change from 'Kingdome' to 'kingdoms' is one of several variations in the Bodleian manuscript from the printed text of "An Horatian Ode" in the two known un-cancelled copies (British Library C.59.i.8 and Huntington Library 79660). See von Maltzahn, *An Andrew Marvell Chronology*, 224-25.
7. See Baker, *Between Nations*, 124-68; and Kerrigan, *Archipelagic English*, 233-34 *passim*. For a recent review of the aims and achievements, as well as limitations, of archipelagic criticism, see Baker, "Britain Redux".
8. Baker, *Between Nations*, 135; Coleman, ed., *Region, Religion*, 8.
9. For the Levellers, see Wilding, *Dragons Teeth*, chapter 5, and Norbrook, "Politics of Genre", 156-7. For Fairfax's objections, see Wilson, *Fairfax*, 159-60, and Fairfax's later account of his resignation, in *Short Memorials*, 126-7.
10. Worden, "Politics of Horatian Ode", and *Literature and Politics*, chapter 5; Norbrook, "Politics of Genre".
11. Worden, "Politics of Horatian Ode", 536.
12. Marvell, "Ode", l. 106.
13. Dzelzainis, ed., *Rehearsal Transpros'd*, 62.
14. Ibid.
15. Milton, *Articles of Peace: Observations*, 247, 242, 228, 247; hereafter cited as *Observations*. For the text of *A Necessary Representation* (dated 15 February 1649/50), see ibid., 228-31. For Milton's response, ibid., 239-49.
16. *Observations*, 232.
17. *Mercurius Politicus*, 1-2. Ibid., 59, 56.
18. Horwood, *Common-place book of Milton*; Maley, "How Milton read Spenser".
19. Spenser, *View*, ed. Hadfield and Maley, 101. Hereafter cited as 'Spenser, *View*'.
20. Ibid., 11, 153.
21. Cited in Maley, *Salvaging Spenser*, 121, 123.

22. Spenser, *View*, 89 and 159; cf. Spenser, *View of Ireland*, in Huntington 28118, 63 and 118. *View of Ireland* is paginated separately from other works in Huntington 28118.
23. Spenser, *View*, 89
24. Spenser, *View*, 159.
25. Ibid., 160.
26. Maley, 'How Milton read Spenser', 202, 195. Norbrook, "Politics of Genre", 152.
27. Milton, *Observations*, 232. The claim to 'Autority' comes on the title page to *Observations*, reproduced in ibid., 188. Daems, "Dividing Conjunctions", 52. See also Corns, "Milton's *Observations*", both cited in Maley and Swann, "Milton on the Margins", 140.
28. Milton, *Observations*, 224.
29. Ibid., 238.
30. Ibid., 237.
31. Marvell, "Ode", ll. 83-4.
32. Ibid., ll. 74, 77-82.
33. Ibid., ll. 33, 74. *Mercurius Politicus*, 17-32.
34. *Mercurius Politicus*, 29. Worden, "Politics of Horatian Ode", 536.
35. *Mercurius Politicus*, 21.
36. *Mercurius Politicus*, 22, 53.
37. Komorowski, "Public Verse and Property", 323-4.
38. *Mercurius Politicus*, 43, 23.
39. Spenser, *View*, 96.
40. Coughlan, "'Cheap and Common Animals'", 207.
41. McCabe, *Spenser's Monstrous Regiment*, 148. Spenser, *View*, 59.
42. Ibid., 45.
43. Ibid., 63; Maley, *Salvaging Spenser*, 138-42; McCabe, *Monstrous Regiment*, 142-64.
44. Spenser, *View*, 110-11. See Grant, "George Gordon"; MacDonald, *The Jacobean Kirk*, 57-60.
45. Spenser, *View*, 85.
46. Ibid., 54.
47. Ibid., 84, 153.
48. Ibid., 154.
49. Ibid., 155.
50. Coughlan, "'Cheap and Common Animals'", 208.
51. Canny, *Making Ireland British*, 463.
52. *A Remonstrance*, B1r-v.
53. *Mercurius Politicus*, 23.
54. Spenser, *View*, 11.
55. Ibid., 153.
56. Milton, *Observations*, 236.
57. Ibid., 236.
58. Spenser, *View*, 155. King, "Was Spenser a Puritan?"; King, "Spenser's Religion". See also Mottram, "'With guiltles blood'".
59. Spenser, *View*, 93.
60. Ibid., 155.
61. Milton, *Observations*, 246, 232, 242.
62. Ibid., 248, 241.
63. Ibid., 244, 245.
64. Ibid., 232.
65. Raymond, "Complications of Interest", 334, cited in Maley and Swann, "Milton on the margins", 141. Ibid., 142.
66. Spenser, *View*, 110. Milton, *Observations*, 248. For Milton's probable borrowing from Spenser, see ibid., 622, n. 171.
67. Holinshed, *Chronicles*, 6.

68. Ibid., 5. For more on the 'Scithian' origins of Scots and Picts, see McCabe, *Spenser's Monstrous Regiment*, 143.
69. Here I am thinking not only of Spenser's *View*, but of Spenser's identification of Mary Queen of Scots with the catholic queen Duessa in *Faerie Queene* V – an identification that caused 'great offence' to Mary's son, James VI of Scotland, as the diplomatic correspondence reveals. See McCabe, "Masks of Duessa"; Hadfield, *Matter of Britain*, 122-36; Maley, *Salvaging Spenser*. For the correspondence, see Bowes to Burghley, 1 November 1596 and 12 November 1596, calendared in Guiseppi, ed., *CSP: Scotland*, XII: nos. 288 and 291.
70. For the impact of *Politicus*, see Worden, *Literature and Politics*, 21-23.
71. *Mercurius Politicus*, 17, 59.
72. Ibid., 21, 23, 59.
73. Ibid., 36, 124.
74. Ibid., 124.
75. *A Vindication*, D3r; for discussion, see Gribben, "Cromwellian Invasion", 9.
76. Marvell, "Ode", ll. 105-112.
77. "Plaid, n.1 (2a)", in *OED Online*. Oxford: Oxford University Press, 2017. http://www.oed.com/view/Entry/144969?rskey=5ZqKMN&result=1&isAdvanced=false (accessed 30 October 2017).
78. Spenser, *View*, 63.
79. See the discussion in Smith, ed., *Poems of Andrew Marvell*, 278 (note to line 106).
80. Kerrigan, *Archipelagic English*, 233.
81. Stevenson, "Graham, James".
82. *Mercurius Politicus*, 19.
83. Ibid., 40.
84. Stevenson, "Graham, James".
85. Kerrigan, *Archipelagic English*, 233.
86. Worden, "Politics of Horatian Ode"; Norbrook, "Politics of Genre".
87. *Mercurius Politicus*, 59.
88. Marvell, "Ode", l. 9.
89. Worden, "Politics of Horatian Ode"; Norbrook, "Politics of Genre". Marvell, "Ode", ll. 33, 38.
90. Ibid., ll. 12, 35.
91. Ibid., ll. 101-4.
92. Ibid., ll., 99-100, 105.
93. Nedham, *Case of the common-wealth*, B3r, cited in Worden, "Politics of Horatian Ode", 535.
94. Marvell, "Ode", l. 66.
95. In Smith, ed., *Poems of Marvell*, 281-98 (ll. 126, 128-30); hereafter cited as 'Marvell, "First Anniversary"'.
96. Ibid, ll. 117, 118, 113-14.
97. Hirst, "'That Sober Liberty'".
98. Marvell, "First Anniversary", l. 305; Feake, *The oppressed close prisoner*, G4v, H1r.
99. Marvell, "First Anniversary", l. 321.
100. Hirst, "'That Sober Liberty'", 43. Marvell, "First Anniversary", ll. 317-18.
101. Marvell, "First Anniversary", l. 319. Holberton, *Poetry and the Cromwellian Protectorate*, 112.
102. Marvell, "First Anniversary", l. 95.
103. Holberton, *Poetry and the Cromwellian Protectorate*, 118.
104. Norbrook, *Writing the English Republic*, 340, 299.
105. Cromwell, *Government of the Common-wealth*, L2r.
106. Marvell, "Ode", l. 116.
107. Dzelzainis, ed., *Rehearsal Transpros'd*, 4-20.
108. Ibid., 60.
109. Ibid., 57.

110. Ibid., 62.
111. Ibid., 57.
112. *Declaration of the Army*, 40-1, cited in Gribben, "Cromwellian Invasion," 8.

Disclosure statement

No potential conflict of interest was reported by the author.

ORCID

Stewart Mottram http://orcid.org/0000-0003-3110-3777

Bibliography

Anon. *A Short Reply Unto A Declaration Entitled the Declaration Entitled, the Declaration of the Army of England upon Their March into Scotland. Together with A Vindication of the Declaration of the Army of England upon Their March into Scotland*. London: John Field for Francis Tyton, 16 August, 1650.
Baker, D. J. *Between Nations: Shakespeare, Spenser, Marvell, and the Question of Britain*. Stanford, CA: Stanford University Press, 1997.
Baker, D. J. "Britain Redux". *Spenser Studies* 29 (2014): 21–36. doi:10.7756/spst.029.002.21-36.
Canny, N. *Making Ireland British, 1580-1650*. Oxford: Oxford University Press, 2001.
Coleman, D. "Introduction: Regional Religions and Archipelagic Aesthetics". In *Region, Religion and English Renaissance Literature*, edited by D. Coleman, 1–11. Aldershot: Ashgate, 2013.
Coolidge, J. S. "Marvell and Horace". *Modern Philology* 63 (1965): 111–120. doi:10.1086/389746.
Corns, T. N. "Milton's *Observations upon the Articles of Peace*: Ireland under English Eyes". In *Politics, Poetics, and Hermeneutics in Milton's Prose*, edited by D. Loewenstein and J. Grantham Turner, 123–134. Cambridge: Cambridge University Press, 1990.
Coughlan, P. "'Cheap and Common Animals': The English Anatomy of Ireland in the Seventeenth Century". In *Literature and the English Civil War*, edited by T. Healy and J. Sawday, 205–223. Cambridge: Cambridge University Press, 1990.
Cromwell, O. *The Government of the Common-Wealth of England, Scotland, & Ireland* ['The Instrument of Government']. London: William du-Gard and Henry Hills, 1653.
Daems, J. "Dividing Conjunctions: Milton's Observations upon the Articles of Peace". *Milton Quarterly* 33, no. 2 (1999): 51–55. doi:10.1111/j.1094-348X.1999.tb00885.x.
Darcy, E. *The Irish Rebellion of 1641 and the Wars of the Three Kingdoms*. Woodbridge: Boydell, 2013.
Dzelzainis, M., ed. "The Rehearsal Transpros'd". In *Prose Works of Andrew Marvell*. edited by M. Dzelzainis and A. Patterson, Vol. 1, 1–203. New Haven: Yale University Press, 2003.
Everett, B. "The Shooting of the Bears: Poetry and Politics in Andrew Marvell". In *Andrew Marvell: Essays on the Tercentenary of His Death*, edited by R. L. Brett, 62–103. Oxford: Oxford University Press, 1978.
Fairfax, T. *Short Memorials of Thomas Lord Fairfax. Written by Himself*. edited by Brian Fairfax. London: for Ri[chard] Chiswell, 1699.
Feake, C. *The Oppressed Close Prisoner in Windsor-Castle*. London: L. Chapman, 1655 [i.e. 1654].
Grant, R. "George Gordon, sixth Earl of Huntly, and the politics of the Counter-Reformation in Scotland, 1581-1595." Ph.D. diss., University of Edinburgh, 2010.
Gribben, C. "Polemic and Apocalyptic in the Cromwellian Invasion of Scotland". *Literature & History* 23, no. 1 (2014): 1–18. doi:10.7227/LH.23.1.1.
Guiseppi, M. S., ed. *Calendar of the State Papers Relating to Scotland and Mary, Queen of Scots, 1547-1603*, Vol. XII, 1595–1597. London: HMSO, 1952.

Hadfield, A. *Shakespeare, Spenser and the Matter of Britain*. Basingstoke: Palgrave Macmillan, 2004.

Hirst, D. "'That Sober Liberty': Marvell's Cromwell in 1654". In *The Golden and the Brazen World: Papers in Literature and History, 1650-1800*, edited by J. M. Wallace, 17–53. Berkeley: University of California Press, 1985.

Holberton, E. *Poetry and the Cromwellian Protectorate: Culture, Politics, and Institutions*. Oxford: Oxford University Press, 2008.

Holinshed, R. *The First and Second Volumes of Chronicles*. rev ed. London: John Hooker, Alias Vowell, 1587.

Horwood, A. J., ed. *A Common-Place Book of John Milton: And A Latin Essay and Latin Verses Presumed to Be by Milton*. Camden Society Publications, n.s. 16. London: Camden Society, 1878.

Jones, H. *A Remonstrance of Divers Remarkeable Passages Concerning the Church and Kingdome of Ireland*. London: for Godfrey Emerson and William Bladen, 1642.

Kerrigan, J. *Archipelagic English: Literature, History, and Politics 1603-1707*. Oxford: Oxford University Press, 2008.

King, J. N. "Was Spenser a Puritan?" *Spenser Studies* 6 (1985): 1–31.

King, J. N. "Spenser's Religion". In *The Cambridge Companion to Spenser*, edited by A. Hadfield, 200–216. Cambridge: Cambridge University Press, 2001.

Komorowski, M. "Public Verse and Property: Marvell's 'Horatian Ode' and the Ownership of Politics". *ELH* 79 (2012): 315–340. doi:10.1353/elh.2012.0017.

MacDonald, A. R. *The Jacobean Kirk, 1567-1625: Sovereignty, Polity, and Liturgy*. Aldershot: Ashgate, 1998.

Maley, W. "How Milton and Some Contemporaries Read Spenser's *View*". In *Representing Ireland: Literature and the Origins of Conflict, 1534-1660*, edited by B. Bradshaw, A. Hadfield, and W. Maley, 191–208. Cambridge: Cambridge University Press, 1993.

Maley, W. *Salvaging Spenser: Colonialism, Culture and Identity*. Houndmills: Palgrave Macmillan, 1997.

Maley, W., and A. Swann. "'Is This the Region . . . that We Must Change for Heav'n?': Milton on the Margins". In *Region, Religion and English Renaissance Literature*, edited by D. Coleman, 139–152. Aldershot: Ashgate, 2013.

von Maltzahn, N. *An Andrew Marvell Chronology*. Basingstoke: Palgrave Macmillan, 2005.

Marvell, A. *Miscellaneous Poems*. London: Robert Boulter, 1681.

Mazzeo, J. A. "Cromwell as Machiavellian Prince in Marvell's 'An Horatian Ode'". *Journal of the History of Ideas* 21 (1960): 1–17. doi:10.2307/2707996.

McCabe, R. A. "The Masks of Duessa: Spenser, Mary Queen of Scots, and James VI". *ELR* 17 (1987): 224–242.

McCabe, R. A. *Spenser's Monstrous Regiment: Elizabethan Ireland and the Poetics of Difference*. Oxford: Oxford University Press, 2002.

Milton, J. "Articles of Peace, Made and Concluded with the Irish Rebels, and Papists [...] and A Representation of the Scotch Presbytery at Belfast in Ireland. Upon All Which are Added Observations". In *The Complete Works of John Milton, Volume VI: Vernacular Regicide and Republican Writings*, edited by N. H. Keeble and M. Nicholas, 187–249. Oxford: Oxford University Press, 2013.

Mottram, S. "'With Guiltles Blood Oft Stained': Spenser's *Ruines of Time* and the Saints of St Albans". *Spenser Studies* 31/32 (2016/2017): 533–556. doi:10.1086/694442.

Nedham, M. *The Case of the Common-Wealth of England, Stated*. London: E. Blackmore and R. Lowndes, 1650.

Nedham, M. *Mercurius Politicus 1650*. Facsimile reprint with notes by Peter Thomas. The English Revolution III: Newsbooks 5, Volume 1. London: Cornmarket Press, 1971.

Norbrook, D. "Marvell's *Horatian Ode* and the Politics of Genre". In *Literature and the English Civil War*, edited by T. Healy and J. Sawday, 147–169. Cambridge: Cambridge University Press, 1990.

Norbrook, D. *Writing the English Republic: Poetry, Rhetoric, and Politics, 1627-1660*. Cambridge: Cambridge University Press, 1998.

Patterson, A. "Lady State's First Two Sittings: Marvell's Satiric Canon". *Studies in English Literature* 40.3 (2000): 395–411. doi:10.2307/1556253.

Raymond, J. "Complications of Interest: Milton, Scotland, Ireland, and National Identity in 1649". *Review of English Studies* 55 (2004): 315–345. doi:10.1093/res/55.220.315.

Smith, N., ed. *The Poems of Andrew Marvell*. rev ed. London: Routledge, 2013.

Spenser, E. *A View of the State of Ireland: From the First Printed Edition (1633)*. Edited by A. Hadfield and W. Maley. Oxford: Blackwell, 1997.

Spenser, E. "A View of the State of Ireland, Written Dialogue-Wise Betweene Eudoxus and Irenaeus". In *The Historie of Ireland, Collected by Three Learned Authors*, edited by J. Ware. Dublin: Society of Stationers, 1633. Huntington Library, California: Rare Books 28118.

Stevenson, D. "Graham, James, First Marquess of Montrose (1612-1650)". In *Oxford Dictionary of National Biography*, edited by H. C. G. Matthew and B. Harrison, Vol. 60. XXIII: 189–195. Oxford: Oxford University Press, 2004.

Temple, J. *The Irish Rebellion [...] Together with the Barbarous Cruelties and Bloody Massacres Which Ensued Thereupon*. London: R. White for Samuel Gellibrand, 1646.

Wallace, J. *Destiny His Choice: The Loyalism of Andrew Marvell*. Cambridge: Cambridge University Press, 1968.

Ware, J., ed. *The Historie of Ireland, Collected by Three Learned Avthors*. Dublin: Society of Stationers, 1633. Huntington Library, California: Rare Books 28118.

Wilding, M. *Dragons Teeth: Literature in the English Revolution*. Oxford: Clarendon, 1987.

Wilson, J. *Fairfax: A Life of Thomas, Lord Fairfax*. London: John Murray, 1985.

Worden, B. "The Politics of Marvell's Horatian Ode". *Historical Journal* 27, no. 3 (1984): 525–547. doi:10.1017/S0018246X00017969.

Worden, B. *Literature and Politics in Cromwellian England: John Milton, Andrew Marvell, Marchamont Nedham*. Oxford and New York: Oxford University Press, 2007.

"Neptune to the Common-wealth of England" (1652): the "Republican Britannia" and the continuity of interests

Willy Maley

ABSTRACT
In the seventeenth century, John Kerrigan reminds us, "models of empire did not always turn on monarchy". In this essay, I trace a vision of "Neptune's empire" shared by royalists and republicans, binding English national interest to British overseas expansion. I take as my text a poem entitled "Neptune to the Common-wealth of England", prefixed to Marchamont Nedham's 1652 English translation of *Mare Clausum* (1635), John Selden's response to *Mare Liberum* (1609) by Hugo Grotius. This minor work is read alongside some equally obscure and more familiar texts in order to point up the ways in which it speaks to persistent cultural and political interests. I trace the afterlife of this verse, its critical reception and its unique status as a fragment that exemplifies the crossover between colonial republic and imperial monarchy at a crucial moment in British history, a moment that, with Brexit, remains resonant.

In the seventeenth century, John Kerrigan reminds us, "models of empire did not always turn on monarchy".[1] In what follows, I trace a vision of "Neptune's empire" shared by royalists and republicans, binding English national interest to British expansion.[2] I take as my text a poem entitled "Neptune to the Common-wealth of England", prefixed to Marchamont Nedham's 1652 English translation of *Mare Clausum* (1635), John Selden's response to *Mare Liberum* (1609) by Hugo Grotius.

In an era of fake news and claims to be taking the country back and making it great again – an era much like our own – Nedham stands out as a writer who typifies the spirit of the times.[3] Notoriously shifty, he is consistently inconsistent. Nedham remained committed to the cause of England – monarchy and republic – through turbulent regime change. If Milton's reputation was for unwavering consistency – 'In the face of near-universal backsliding, he stands as a one-man remnant'[4] – by contrast, Nedham was as slippery, if not as subtle, as Andrew Marvell. Benjamin Woodford observes: "Finding consistency in [Nedham's] labyrinth of allegiances and writings can be challenging".[5] For Philip Knachen, "his several shifts of political allegiance [...] badly

---

Some of the work for this article was undertaken during a research fellowship from the Leverhulme Trust for which I am most grateful. I am also grateful to John Kerrigan and to the anonymous reader for sharp observations and suggestions.

compromised his intellectual integrity".[6] Convert to the Commonwealth, traitor to his royalist friends – Blair Worden calls him 'the serial turncoat of the Puritan Revolution'[7] – Nedham acknowledged his own capacity for metamorphosis:

> Perhaps thou art of an Opinion contrary to what is here written: I confess, that for a Time I my Self was so too, till some Causes made me to reflect with an impartiall eye upon the Affairs of this *new Government*.[8]

A flighty side-switcher, Nedham was a pivotal figure as a servant of the new republic and influential editor and publisher, an outsider-turned-insider who knew his enemies as well as his allies. As Jason Peacey notes, "one of the hallmarks of Nedham's newspapers [was] his almost unrivalled ability to secure detailed intelligence from within Westminster".[9] Nedham's changing partisanship damaged his reputation, but paradoxically his inconsistency reveals the continuity at the heart of radical change, reminding us that those upon whom we too readily confer consistency have their own contradictions – the anti-imperialist Milton's charged advocacy of Irish colonisation being one example.[10] Homing in on a short text attributed to Nedham I argue that it mattered little in the end whether the goal of global conquest was achieved through imperial monarchy or colonial republic.[11]

The 2016 EU Referendum and the United Kingdom's decision to quit the European Union dredge up old arguments around sovereignty.[12] We are urged to look to the Reformation for the submerged origins of the current crisis.[13] An exception is Mark Royce, for whom a strand of the "critique of governance at the European level ultimately derives from the revolutionary theology of the English Civil War".[14] Mid-seventeenth century politics offers an excellent starting-point in our efforts to understand how we arrived at breakpoint for the British state, but only if we look beyond Anglocentric narratives and attend to archipelagic dimensions. The UK vote to exit the EU entailed a "Leave" campaign supported by radicals and reactionaries alike. Strangers to the seventeenth century might puzzle over an anti-European movement supported both by progressives and conservatives, radical Left and extreme Right – hence "Lexit" (Left-wing Brexit). Scholars of the seventeenth century will have no such problem.[15] According to Stefan Collignon, "The political map of [the] Brexit vote resembles the regional distribution of support for the King, Court and Tories against Parliament, Merchants and liberal Whigs".[16] But this "regional distribution" overlooks national differences.

When it comes to "Taking our country back", one-nation conservatism reigns. But what is this "nation"? An imperial monarchy that blanks its own history, forgets Ireland and Scotland, never remembers Wales, and confuses its Left and its Right? That the Irish Border became news in 2017 is evidence of the amnesia afflicting British state formation.[17] As for England "itself", it may well secure what it sought in the 1530s, namely independence.[18] The problem goes back to the moment when a colonial republic that deemed itself more capable of pursuing a successful foreign policy supplanted an imperial monarchy.[19] What emerged was a common commitment to the British imperial project, an anti-European enterprise from its inception, not because it excluded intra-European activity – Ulster and Gibraltar, both at issue because of Brexit, testify to the contrary – but because it sought an imperial power base that went beyond Europe and challenged continental colonial powers. Nedham is an exemplary figure for understanding this crossroads in Anglo-British history.

On 28 March 1649, Cromwell's Council of State asked "Milton [...] to make some observations upon the Complicacon of interests [...] amongst the severall designers against the peace of the Commonwealth".[20] Milton took up the gauntlet and in *Observations upon the Articles of Peace with the Irish Rebels* duly exposed what he chose to depict as the underlying complicity between Irish Catholic royalists and Ulster Presbyterians, united in opposition to English hegemony. The *Observations*, now viewed as key to Milton's archipelagic interests, has attracted considerable attention in recent years.[21] The complication of interests it identifies is really a complicity of opponents that conceals a broader entanglement in the period between royalist and republican imperial ambitions. In accepting this commission Milton declined another closer to home. Cromwell's Council also sought a riposte to Leveller demands for more radical change, and it has been speculated that Milton was reluctant to accept due to some residual Leveller sympathies.[22] Two days before the Irish commission, Milton was asked to "make some observations upon a paper lately printed called old & new Chaines". According to Martin Dzelzainis, "The 'paper' [...] actually comprised two incendiary Leveller pamphlets by John Lilburne".[23] This commission may have passed to another respondent, and possible takers have been identified.[24]

One contemporary who could have taken on the task Milton declined is Marchamont Nedham.[25] In 1650 Nedham published *The case of the Commonwealth of England, stated*, with a section addressed explicitly to the Levellers, even using the same phrase – "complication of Interests" – employed by the Council of State to unpick the tangled knots and expose the underlying ties of the "opposite parties".[26] One biographer calls it "Nedham's most unified, most thoughtful, and most persuasive work".[27] Joad Raymond considers it "a hybrid pamphlet, made up of different languages and perspectives: [...] stimulating and user-friendly, a little like a newspaper".[28] Seldom cited in discussions of Milton's *Observations*, Nedham's text has other intriguing echoes.[29] It confronts four key groups that challenge the authority of the new regime, denouncing "the Designes of the severall Parties claiming an Interest in this Nation; Viz: {ROYALISTS. SCOTS. PRESBYTERIANS. LEVELLERS; as they stand in opposition to the present Government, and would each of Them introduce a New *Form* of their owne".[30] Nedham was well placed to handle the topic of "interest" – he practically invented it. As John Gunn observes, "His tract, *Interest Will Not Lie*, firmly established the maxim in English thought".[31]

David Norbrook suggests that in converting to the commonwealth cause Nedham had a mentor: "Milton [...] one of those charged with hunting him down [...] became licenser to [Nedham's] journal [and] may have had something to do with the change".[32] Norbrook sees Nedham's sudden switch of allegiance as "explicable within the terms of interest politics", and thus strategic rather than merely opportunistic: "In the spring of 1650, Charles II was moving closer [...] to an alliance with Nedham's arch-enemies, the Scottish Presbyterians, and to return to Parliament's side was to campaign against them".[33] Here, "interest politics" is the politics of "national interest", an English nationalism that maps in equal measure onto imperial monarchy or colonial republic. For Nedham, as for Milton, England's interest is paramount. Charles I's Irish-Scottish machinations threaten England's integrity and entitlement to dominance within the three kingdoms. Norbrook's reluctance to discuss the archipelagic and imperialist implications of Nedham's position allows him to flit all too easily between Britain and England:

If he [...] first voiced British patriotism against the court (*Mercurius Britanicus*), his royalist phase could be seen as a merely tactical adjustment (*Mercurius Pragmaticus*), from which he emerged not just as a nationalist but a republican (*Mercurius Politicus*). He had chosen this title [...] because the new government was a true *politeia* as opposed to a despotism. He thus aligned himself with Milton in linking the English republic with the Greek *polis*.[34]

This slippage from British patriotism to English nationalism and republicanism is evident in Norbrook's reading of the title-page image of Nedham's translation of Selden's *Mare Clausum*: "It was specifically as an image of the English republic, treading down the Stuart crown, that Britannia made an early appearance as the symbol of an emergent naval empire".[35] That image of "Britannia", treading down Ireland and Scotland, bears the inscription "ANGLIÆ RESPUB".[36] According to David Armitage:

> This was the first time the image of Britannia had been used in the context of extending British dominion and, though the origins of this embodiment of expansionism should surprise no-one familiar with the radical strains in later British patriotism, the knowledge of this republican Britannia seems to have been lost along with the Cromwellian moment itself.[37]

The "republican Britannia" complicates our image of nation in the seventeenth century. Nedham's epistle laments of Selden's work "that so rare a Jewel as this [...] should lie so long lockt up in a Language unknown to the greatest part of that Nation whom it most concern's [sic]".[38] This locked aspect goes beyond language. Selden's Latin work, dedicated to Charles I, "defined British territorial waters as part of the new British Empire".[39] Nedham's translation, in the wake of the 1651 Navigation Act, was dedicated to the Commonwealth.[40]

In cutting Selden's dedication, Nedham added something new, his translation book-ended by the Neptune poem (facing the title-page) and some supplementary tracts. Marc Shell homes in on Nedham's Neptune, which poses a powerful rhetorical question:

> What then should great *Britannia* pleas,
> But rule as Ladie o're all the seas...
> Here was the overt claim to rule the world's main (ocean) and, by implication, to rule also the world's main(lands).[41]

"Neptune to the Common-wealth of England" is a little tugboat pulling Selden's great ship of state. It is a rousing verse – "Go on (great STATE!) and make it known / Thou never wilt forsake thine own".[42] Verse 5 renders regal a republican claim to Empire:

> For Sea-Dominion may as well bee gain'd
> By new acquests, as by descent maintain'd.

The phrase "new acquests" – acquisitions, or possessions, rather than conquests – anticipates, or echoes, Milton's *Samson Agonistes*: "His servants he with new acquist", &c.[43] Andrew Zurcher fastens onto this lexical choice: "Milton reaches for a technical legal term [...] 'acquist', attested most frequently, in this period, by lawyers and political philosophers in their efforts to describe the way in which political sovereignty can be gained over land through conquest, purchase, or treaty".[44] In a footnote, Zurcher links "acquist" in the closing Chorus of *Samson Agonistes* with Nedham's translation of Selden:

'Acquest' or 'acquist' is a key term in John Selden's 1636 [*sic*] work on English rights to dominion over the sea [...] Marchamont Nedham's 1654 [*sic*] English translation [...] is fronted by an English poem, 'Neptune to the Common-wealth of *England*', the fifth stanza of which spells out the lawyer's traditional distinction between rights acquired by inheritance and acquest.[45]

Zurcher gets his dates wrong, but is astute in refusing to assume Nedham wrote these verses – there remains some dubiety around the poem's provenance – and in linking *Samson* and Selden, Zurcher reminds us that Milton's text may have been written around 1647–53.[46]

Two earlier occurrences of the phrase "new acquests" argue against fresh imperial acquisitions. In 1640, James Howell – later a polemical opponent of Nedham – wrote: "A true maxime it is [...] *that state which goeth out of the lists of mediocrity, passeth also the limits of safety*: there is a cloud of examples to this purpose: while *Sparta* kept her selfe within those boundaries that *Lycurgus* prescrib'd unto her, she was both safe and flourishing; but attempting to enlarge her territories by new acquests of other Cities in *Greece* and *Asia*, shee went every day declining".[47] Two years later, Richard Baker's translation of Virgilio Malvezzi's *Discourses upon Cornelius Tacitus* sounded the same cautionary note: "But if the Prince have no ayme at augmentation by new acquests and stands not so much in feare of externall enemies, as of friends at home, he then ought to let the people enjoy a negotious ease, of buildings, and playes, and such like things. And [...] *Augustus* [...] aymed not at all, at any amplifying of his Empire".[48] A later treatise by William de Britaine pursues the same line: "Consider, the *East-India* Company by reason of their exceeding Charges in enlarging their Dominions there, and the vast expences which must necessarily attend the keeping of them, cannot be rich. *For all Countries of new acquest, till they be setled, are matters rather of burthen, then of profit*".[49]

Milton's use of Neptune, from *Comus* – 'Neptune besides the sway / Of every salt Flood, and each ebbing Stream, / Took in by lot 'twixt high, and neather *Jove* / Imperial rule of all the Sea-girt Iles'[50] – to *The History of Britain*, where he recounts with characteristic scepticism – "perhaps as wide from truth" – the tale of "*Albion* a Giant, Son of *Neptune*: who call'd the Iland after his own name, and rul'd it 44 years", only to add "Sure enough we are, that *Britan* hath bin anciently term'd *Albion*, both by the *Greeks* and *Romans*", suggests that the sea-god, Empire, and Britain were tethered in his thought.[51]

Neptune was a nodal point for imperial narratives in the period. Michael Drayton's great archipelagic poem, *Poly-Olbion*, with historical notes by Selden, features Neptune in various guises, including father of Albion, "from whom that first name of this *Britaine* was supposed".[52] It opens with an invocation heralding Prince Henry's future rule as Henry IX:

He like great Neptune *on three Seas shall rove,*
And rule three Realms, with triple power, like Jove.[53]

In Ben Jonson's masque for James I, *Neptune's Triumph* (1624), the poet announces:

The mightie Neptune, *mightie in his styles,*
And large command of waters, and of Isles,
Not, as the Lord and Soveraigne of the Seas,
But, Chiefe in the art of riding, late did please

To send his *Albion* forth, the most his owne,
Upon discovery, to themselves best knowne,
Through *Celtiberia*.[54]

"Celtiberia", or "Celtiberian", a term freighted with colonial ballast, was used by Nedham, who alludes to the "*Celtiberians* in *Spain*" in a passage on the dissolution of the Roman Empire, "rent in pieces" by a multi-pronged process of self-determination of its former colonies:

> The *Scots* and *English* shook off the imperiall yoke in *Britain*. The *Burgundians* and *Franks* seized part of *France*. The *Gothes* another part of it, and part of *Italy*, the Country of *Aquitain*, with the seats of the ancient *Cantabrians* and *Celtiberians* in *Spain* [...] By which means, the *Emperors* had no certain power in the *West*.[55]

Milton depicted Comus "ripe and frolic of his full grown age, Roving the *Celtic* and *Iberian* fields" (ll. 59–60), and Nedham's geography maps onto Jonson's and Milton's.[56]

In Dryden's *Annus mirabilis* (1667), Neptune is invoked as the scourge of the Dutch:

> It seemd as there the *British Neptune* stood,
> With all his host of waters at command,
> Beneath them to submit th'officious floud:
> And, with his Trident, shov'd them off the sand.[57]

Invocations of Neptune from Drayton to Dryden, and from Campion's hymn to Nedham's naval anthem, reflect the archipelagic and imperial history of an expansionist England reliant on naval power to extend its frontiers. Although Nedham's Neptune poem is seldom cited, its patriotic potential did not go unnoticed. It may have had a lyrical source, since the line "Thou never wilt forsake thine Owne" appears in George Sandys' 1638 paraphrase of Psalm 9.[58] It certainly had a musical afterlife, for in 1794 Willoughby Bertie, fourth earl of Abingdon, commissioned the Austrian composer Joseph Haydn to set Nedham's muse to music. As one commentator notes, "the 17th-century verses, which petulantly criticize an earlier generation for allowing Spanish colonization of the Indies, must have appeared rather odd in late 18th-century England".[59] Haydn's biographer speculates that the commission was unfulfilled "because the text [...] was of poor quality".[60] Quality aside, "Neptune to the Common-wealth of England" repays attention. The petulant passage in the Spain stanza cited by Arthur Searle arguably anticipates Cromwell's 1655 declaration of war against that country, a declaration laced with the language of colonial resentment:[61]

> Thy great endeavors to encreas
> The Marine power, do confess
> thou act'st som great design.
> Which had Seventh *Henrie* don, before
> *Columbus* lanch'd from Spanish shore,
> the *Indies* had been thine.
> Yet do thy Seas those Indian Mines excell
> In riches far: the *Belgians* know it well.

Armitage cites the Haydn commission without mentioning its patron or unfinished state: "This poem contributed to the burgeoning maritime mythology of the eighteenth century in various musical settings, including a truncated one by Haydn from 1794, but without acknowledgement of its republican roots".[62] In the English commonwealth republican roots are intertwined with empire, and it was as naval ballad rather than classical composition that Nedham's Neptune survived.

Armitage astutely identifies the acceleration of Empire under the commonwealth as key to understanding Nedham's prefatory poem:

> This was not merely a poetaster's idle epigram. The English crown had been slow to take up the imperial gauntlet and had proceeded by colonies planted under charter by private individuals and companies. The Navigation Ordinance of 1651 tied Britain and its overseas possessions for the first time into a single transatlantic trading unit [...] The turn to a non-dynastic foreign policy [...] left the commonwealth and Protectorate open to take an aggressive attitude towards the dominions of competing powers.[63]

For Armitage, "Selden's work provided the foundation for later claims to dominion over the seas in the name of a 'British Empire'".[64] More pointedly, Armitage notes "the commingling of regal and republican claims".[65]

This confluence of commonwealth and crown around empire made the various editions of Selden – 1635, 1652, 1663 – consistent with the times. In 1636, in the backwash of its first appearance in Latin, a pirated edition was proscribed by Charles I, the language of dominion applying to books as well as boats:

> Whereas there was heretofore by Our expresse command published in print a Booke, intituled *Mare Clausum* [...] manifesting of the right and dominion of Us and Our Royall Progenitors, in the Seas which incompasse these Our Realmes and Dominions of great *Brittaine* and *Ireland*: [...] since the publishing thereof, some persons [...] have caused the same Booke to be printed in some place beyond the Seas, and to the same impression have added some other things, as if they were parts of that which was first printed here by Our Command [...] From henceforth no person or persons [...] shall at any time import, publish, put to sale, or in any kinde buy, sell, exchange or disperse, in any of Our Realmes or Dominions any Bookes or Copies of any Edition of the said Booke.[66]

In *Areopagitica* Milton compared the blockading of books implicit in licensing to the restriction of trade, "more then if som enemy at sea should stop up all our hav'ns and ports, and creeks, it hinders and retards the importation of our richest Marchandize, Truth".[67] Charles's proclamation turns Selden's flagship defence of freedom of the seas into a pirate vessel.

Sebastian Sobecki notes that Nedham's "Neptune encourages England to adopt an imperialist policy, grounded in its naval strength" and goes on to suggest that "Edgar's alleged possession of the four seas becomes the foundation myth of maritime Englishness as well as the vindication for the Protectorate's archipelagic empire".[68] Sobecki sees Nedham pushing out the boat on Selden's claims to sovereignty of the seas: "Equipped with Neptune's ode and the triumphalist allegory of a demonstrably English Britannia, Nedham's authoritative translation elevates Selden's riposte to Grotius to the level of a national epic".[69] Sobecki's richly detailed reading of Nedham's cover image makes Norbrook's use of it for *Writing the English Republic* (1999) appear anomalous:

> Its iconography makes it the companion piece to Neptune's ode: Britannia is shown holding an English shield, and under her feet piles up the loot of her conquests, marked by the flags of subdued Scotland, Ireland, and Wales [...] Next to each other on the ground, the crowns and sceptres of Scotland and Ireland (territories which were occupied by the Protectorate at the time) make her an empress. To mark the historical continuity of

the Republic's claim to the archipelago, Britannia is dressed in a Roman centurion's armour and sandals as she sits on the insular rock of the English Commonwealth (*Angliae respvb.*), washed by the English sea.[70]

"English sea" aside, this is astute. As Derek Hirst, always alert to the imperial undertow of the English republic, observes, Nedham's "frontispiece trumpeted Cromwell's first, British, conquests on which Britannia's rule of the seas was to be based".[71] Nedham's contemporary, Michael Hawke, urged Cromwell's "acceptation of the empire", praising "our Prince, a *Caesar* for valour, *Augustus* for fortune [...] By whose valourous vertue *England* was quieted, *Ireland* settled, and *Scotland* subdued and brought under subjection".[72]

According to Mark Somos, "The English colonial advantage of secularising law" allowed it to pursue its imperial aims with a clear conscience.[73] Indeed, the claim in the 1533 Act in Restraint of Appeals "that this realm of England is an empire" suggests that the roots of this quest for colonial advantage lay in the Reformation.[74] The Reformation itself was partly a response to the pope's donation of the "New World" to Portugal and Spain, and partly a declaration of England's intention to secure the borderlands of the Tudor state.[75] This is a grievance laid out explicitly in Cromwell's 1655 declaration of war against Spain, sometimes thought to have been authored by Milton.[76] Colonial commonwealth blurs into British Empire. Selden's work is crucial because it served the continuity of interests from 1635 to 1663, the year James Howell, recently appointed first historiographer royal, reissued Nedham's edition of *Mare Clausum* with the original dedication to Charles I restored and a prefatory "Advertisement" castigating its English translator as one who "gave himself the licence to foist in the name of a Commonwealth, instead of the Kings of England".[77]

Nedham was steeped in the sovereignty of the seas. According to Robert Batchelor, "Two other English pamphlets most likely by Nedham also supported the Parliamentary cause: *Additional Evidences Concerning the Right of Soveraignite and Dominion of England in the Sea* (London: William Du Gard, 1652); and *Dominium Maris: or the Dominion of the Sea ... translated out of Italian* (London: William Du Gard, 1652)".[78] To complicate matters further, David Padwa notes that Nedham tacks onto his translation without acknowledgment the concluding section of another maritime treatise.[79] Nor is Nedham's role as translator secure, for Batchelor notes that "William Watts made a translation in 1636 that may have been the basis for Nedham's edition".[80]

In Selden's text, according to Edward Cavanagh, "the case for a public law relationship between *praescriptio* and *imperium* was developed and Anglicized: the Italians had used prescription for their *civitates*, the Spaniards had used it for their own *supremum potestatem*, and now came the turn of Anglia, Scotia, and Hibernia".[81] But rather than "rule three Realms, with triple power", Selden, and later Nedham, envisaged Anglia trampling Scotia and Hibernia. Another critic describes *Mare Clausum* as a "treatise in defense of exclusive fishing rights in English waters", and a "celebrated vindication of exclusive fishing rights in the North Sea", which underestimates the text's significance, and rebrands Scottish waters as English.[82] Cromwell's interest in angling rights – and Anglo rights – extended beyond the archipelago.[83]

Selden's case for a three-kingdom British Empire under Stuart sovereignty differs from Nedham's dismissive attitude to Ireland and Scotland in his commonwealth writings. They are not oceans apart, but there's a shift from an archipelagic to an Anglocentric perspective. Chapters 30–32 of Nedham's translation show that Selden set out to subsume the three kingdoms into one: "Of the Dominion of the King of Great Britain in the Irish and Western Sea" (433–443), "Touching the Dominion of the King of Great Britain in the Scotish Sea" (443–447), and "Touching that Right which belong's [sic] to the King of Great Britain, in the main and open Sea of the North" (447–459). Since *Mare Clausum* is a response to Hugo Grotius' *Mare Liberum* (1609), Selden cleverly cites Grotius' panegyric to James I on his accession, to hoist his Dutch counterpart by his own petard, before concluding:

> that the very Shores or Ports of the Neighbor-Princes beyond-Sea, are Bounds of the Sea-Territorie of the *British* Empire to the Southward and Eastward; but that in the open and vast Ocean of the North and West, they are to bee placed at the utmost extent of those most spacious Seas, which are possest by the *English, Scots,* and *Irish.*[84]

A Restoration pamphlet poem against the Dutch rehearsed the Grotius-Selden debate:

> The *Dutch* no sooner thriv'd, no sooner grew,
> But slighted us, as if no duty due
> As when their *Grotius*, forward by their Pride,
> Did undertake their Title should reside
> On these our Seas; as if their Fleet was come,
> To challenge Right be'ng *Mare Liberum*.
> And though by arguing Selden overcame
> His strongest Reasons, they were still the same;
> Their courage not abated, till we us'd
> Expelling force to Right us be'ng abus'd.[85]

By 1689, the diplomat Philip Meadows, who in 1653 had served as assistant to Milton as Latin translator, could praise Selden as an imperial monarchist without mentioning Nedham or the commonwealth: "Mr. Selden has excellently well deserv'd of the Publick, by heightning the Sea-Sovereignty of the Crown of England, in his Learned Book, entituled, *Mare Clausum*; a Treatise so comprehensive of what can be said on that Argument, that he, who should now write of the same, would certainly incur the old Censure, of writing an Iliad after *Homer*".[86]

John Kerrigan observes how "stringently and classically republican was the language used in 1651-2, by [...] Nedham, to justify the English Commonwealth's policy towards Scotland".[87] In a section "Concerning the Scots" in *The case of the Commonwealth of England, stated*, Nedham is unequivocal about the hierarchy of nations in the new republic, saying of Scotland, "I am sorry I must waste Paper upon this Nation".[88] Many modern "British" historians have refused to waste paper on Scotland, whose subordinate status, alongside that of Ireland and Wales, is the key to the colonial commonwealth, as it is to the British Empire. This is "the plural history of a group of cultures situated along an Anglo-Celtic frontier and marked by an increasing English political and cultural domination" identified by John Pocock.[89] Here I must make a brief digression on Pocock's plea, and in doing so double back to my opening gambit on Brexit.

Often read as the founding statement of the new British history, Pocock's essay is actually a recapitulation of the anti-European history of the seventeenth century, as the passage that follows on from the familiar sentence just cited makes clear:

> The history of Scotland in relation to England in the seventeenth century, like that of the United Kingdom in relation to Europe in the twentieth, is that of the progressive absorption of one political culture by a neighboring culture complex whose conflicts it fails to dominate; but Scotland is no more English than Britain is European. The fact of a hegemony does not alter the fact of a plurality, any more than the history of a frontier amounts to denial that there is history beyond the advancing frontier.[90]

Pocock's analogy between English hegemony within the early modern British imperial monarchy and the status of Britain in the context of post-war European Union is striking, for in each case Anglo-British sovereignty is at stake. Pocock was quite explicit about his aim:

> Within very recent memory, the English have been increasingly willing to declare that neither empire nor commonwealth ever meant much in their consciousness, and that they were at heart Europeans all the time. [...] With communal war resumed in Ireland and a steady cost in lives being paid for the desire of one of the 'British' peoples to remain 'British' as they understand the term, it is not inconceivable that future historians may find themselves writing of a 'Unionist' or even a 'British' period in the history of the peoples inhabiting the Atlantic archipelago, and locating it between a date in the thirteenth, the seventeenth, or the nineteenth century and a date in the twentieth or the twenty-first.[91]

Here, British history – "neither empire nor commonwealth" – is imperilled by an encroaching European union. But what "historically based identities" are maintained by being subsumed within British history, old or new, especially one "marked by an increasing English political and cultural domination"? The new British history, it transpires, is the old "English political and cultural domination" writ large. Conversely, for Murray Pittock, "if Britishness depended on the British Empire, it is doomed; and moreover, if so it is by its nature in part colonial, a demanding appropriation which denies variety".[92] A fuller examination of early modern Irish and Scottish relations with Europe would act as a reminder that there was a world beyond the Anglo-British project.[93]

The strange paradox of the seventeenth-century press identified by Joad Raymond applies to politics more generally: "early newspapers are, importantly, national phenomena; yet they are also transnational".[94] Likewise, English political theory, including, perhaps even especially republican theory, is transnational. Moreover, in an archipelagic context – and beyond – it is colonial. Yet in his essay on early modern media management, Raymond frames the nation as "Britain" in a way that is problematic precisely because it depicts the four nations of the Anglo-Celtic frontier as a single political entity to be set against, or alongside, Europe, apparently unaware that this challenge to archipelagic history is also a restoration of the Anglocentric model that critics from Pocock to Pittock ostensibly sought to displace:

> Though following a popular format and [...] written in English, *Politicus* crossed linguistic and national boundaries. It used the vernacular in an era when Britain's second language was Latin, the language of pan-European communication, and Latin may have served as a conduit between one vernacular and another [...] But a paradox nonetheless emerges from

this account of a vernacular form and a nationalist historiography versus a trans- and inter-national life and it needs unravelling. And to do this we need to go much further than the archipelagic perspective that currently informs early-modern history and criticism.[95]

Before we go beyond the archipelagic perspective we need to address the residual Anglocentric perspective that underpins purportedly European and global perspectives. Raymond shows how Nedham balanced his role as news editor with that of state employee, and his commitment to offering an international perspective with his championing of the English Commonwealth, surrounded by foreign enemies.[96] Raymond speaks of Nedham's complex role as author-editor-journalist-pamphleteer, and calls his collected articles, *The Excellencie of a Free State* (1656), "a key text in British republicanism".[97] But just how "British" was Nedham's republicanism? According to Blair Worden, "Milton and Nedham [...] are in at the birth of English republicanism".[98] They were certainly in at the birth of a short-lived colonial republic, and as champions of English hegemony and English imperialism they are in at the death of any levelling aspirations. This is not to suggest that the imperial monarchy that supplanted the colonial republic would establish business as usual. Rather, there was colonial continuity within constitutional change. Worden recognises this when he identifies Nedham's "ambitious initiatives in foreign policy" in the early 1650s:

> Following Machiavelli's advice about colonization, and invoking classical examples, he recommends the 'incorporation' of Scotland, which Cromwell has conquered, into England and the award of parliamentary representation to the Scots – a policy carried out by the Rump in 1652, if in terms less bold than those for which Nedham may have hoped. Nedham wants England to become, in Machiavelli's language, a commonwealth for expansion.[99]

That commonwealth for expansion gave way to an imperial monarchy for expansion, and in time the word "commonwealth" itself would lose its roots in appeals to a more equitable society and come to describe the subjugated former colonies of the British Empire.

Other English republicans found ways to reconcile liberty and land grabs. In *Oceana* (1656), James Harrington observed: "Empire is of two kinds, *Domestick* and *National*, or *Forrain* and *Provinciall*".[100] Harrington distinguishes between three types of national empire: "absolute *Monarchy*", "mixed *Monarchy*", and "*Common-wealth*".[101] With foreign empire things get complicated: "A man may as well say that it is unlawfull for him who hath made a fair and honest purchase to have tenants, as for a Government that hath made a just progresse, and inlargement of it self, to have Provinces".[102] This prompts a discussion around establishing provinces and their relationship to the colonizing nation. Harrington insists that Empire begins at home, and Scotland and Ireland – in his allegory, Marpesia and Panopea to England's Oceana – "will be of greater Revenue unto you, then if you had the *Indies*; for whereas heretofore She hath brought you forth nothing but her native Thistle: ploughing out the ranknesse of her *Aristocracy* by your *Agrarian*, you will find her an inexhaustible Magazine of Men".[103] Harrington suggests that combining Celtic forces under English rule "may adde unto a Parliamentary Army an equall number of *Marpesians*, or *Panopeans*, as that Colony shall hereafter be able to supply you".[104] Later, Algernon Sidney, in his refutation of Robert Filmer's *Patriarcha* (1680) asks ironically "whether the intire conquest of *Scotland* and *Ireland*, the Victories obtained against the *Hollanders* when they were in the height of their Power, and the reputation to which *England* did rise in less than five years after 1648. be good marks of the instability, disorder, and weakness of free Nations".[105] The free – and freely conquering – nation in this case being England.

Lenin's marginal note on the dramatic increase in shipbuilding in the 1650s reads "the republic and imperialism!!!!"[106] Marx made the link earlier, declaring that "the English republic under Cromwell met shipwreck in – Ireland".[107] By this Marx meant that the social revolution was supplanted by overseas expansion.[108] Colonialism displaced class.[109] More broadly, Empire-building wrecked the republic.[110] While Empire, and the triumphalism and racism that accompanies it, may prove popular, it does not lead to social equality at home. But if "republican Britannia" sank, the refitted imperial monarchic version sails on.[111] As Milton declares in his last-ditch effort to save the republic: "The ship of the Commonwealth is alwaies under sail".[112] That ship steered a steady course, and the fortunes of Nedham's Neptune poem suggest that the short-lived republic – a Republican Britannia that harboured Empire at its heart – speeded up rather than slowed down its imperial progress.

Notes

1. Kerrigan, *Archipelagic English*, 51. For a sidelight on this see, Sawday, "Marvell's 'Bermudas'".
2. The phrase, Horatio's in *Hamlet* (1.1.122), rippled through the Restoration. See Ross, *The Second Punick war*, 406; Canning, *Gesta Grayorum*, 58; and Warren, *Geologia*, 249. Canning's allusion, an account of Gray's Inn revels for 1594-5, predates *Hamlet*, with a poem, 'Of Neptune's Empire let us sing', attributed to Thomas Campion in Francis Davison's 'The Masque of Proteus' (1594). See Albright, "Gray's Inn Revels", 500.
3. This is not to equate two civil wars, regicide and constitutional collapse with more recent uncivil wars and efforts at regime change abroad, but I would maintain that the seeds of the current crisis were sown in the battlefields of the seventeenth century.
4. Holstun, *Puritan Utopias*, 262.
5. Woodford, "Nedham's Representation", 20.
6. Knachel, "Introduction", ix.
7. Worden, *Literature and Politics*, 14
8. Nedham, *Case of the Common-Wealth*, A2^r.
9. Peacey, "Marchamont Nedham", 26.
10. Only by overlooking Ireland can we view Milton as anti-colonial. See Armitage, "Poet Against Empire".
11. As Victor Kiernan observed of the English bourgeoisie: 'The solution they really aimed at (as became apparent under Cromwell) was a programme of militant imperialism' (Parker, ed., *Ideology, Absolutism*, 98).
12. See my 'Spenser and Europe'.
13. The current crisis being Britain's relationship with Europe and the future of Britain itself, as the Irish Border, crucial to the maintenance of the British state even when all too conveniently forgotten, once again becomes key to British identity. Meanwhile the question of Scottish independence, seemingly put to bed by the outcome of the 2014 Referendum, resurfaces as a determination to remain within or rejoin Europe post-Brexit.
14. Royce, "Protestant Supranationalism", 248.
15. On the unionist anti-European project see Maley, "'Another Britain?'", esp. 10.
16. Collignon, "Brexit". I do not share Collignon's analysis, only his recognition of the shaping force of the 1640s and 1650s.
17. On the complication of interests in Ireland after Brexit, see Gormley-Heenan and Aughey, "Northern Ireland and Brexit"; Holder, "Good Friday Agreement"; and Stevenson, "Peace in Northern Ireland?".
18. See O'Toole, "Brexit".

19. The imperialism of the Protectorate was implicit in the early policies of the Republic. See Worden, "Marvell's Horatian Ode", 534-5. I am grateful to John Kerrigan for this point.
20. French, ed., *Life Records*, 240.
21. Milton, *Articles of Peace*. See Raymond, "Complications of Interest".
22. The Levellers were certainly sympathetic to Milton, or at least willing to use him as a conduit to the Council of State. Lilburne's mention of Milton is more than a passing reference, for Lilburne cites – and translates – the conclusion of Milton's *Defence*. Lilburne, *As You Were*, 16-17, citing Milton, *Defence*, 245-6.
23. Dzelzainis, "History and Ideology", 274.
24. Dzelzainis lists some likely candidates, including John Canne, John Hall and Walter Frost.
25. On relations between these two major republican thinkers, see Worden, "Milton and Marchamont Nedham". On Nedham and the Levellers see Worden, "'Wit in a Roundhead".
26. Nedham, *Case of the Common-Wealth*, 37.
27. Frank, *Cromwell's Press Agent*, 75.
28. Raymond, "Marchamont Nedham", 384.
29. There is a brief but incisive discussion in McDowell, *Poetry and Allegiance*, 222-3, 232-3, and 237. McDowell expands the familiar focus on the Engagement Controversy (Part 1, Chapter 5, 25-32) to home in on Nedham's treatment of the Presbyterians but doesn't compare Nedham's text to Milton's *Observations*, stress its archipelagic dimension, or suggest it may be Milton's unfulfilled commission.
30. Nedham, *Case of the Common-Wealth*, 33.
31. Gunn, "'Interest Will Not Lie'", 557, 558.
32. David Norbrook, *Writing and the English Republic*, 222.
33. Ibid.
34. Ibid., 223.
35. Ibid., 294. Norbrook uses this imperialist image as his own cover.
36. Selden, *Ownership, of the sea*.
37. Armitage, "Cromwellian Protectorate", 534.
38. Selden, *Ownership, of the Sea*, A2^v.
39. Levack, "Britain's First Global Century", 107.
40. A feature corrected by the 1663 reprint which kept the translation but dropped Nedham's name and dedication. See Padwa, "English Translation".
41. Shell, *Islandology: Geography, Rhetoric, Politics*, 184-5. The 1652 text reads 'o're all seas'. In the British Library copy, owned by Oswald Allen Moore – Wing / 294:01 – the poem faces the image of 'ANGLIÆ RESPUB', while in the Harvard copy of Francis Hargreave – Wing / S2432 – it faces the title page and the image is omitted.
42. Norbrook speculates that the Greek letters with which the poem is signed – which phonetically appear to spell out 'Klareamont' – may be an anagram of 'Thomas Chaloner' (1595-1660), a key figure with naval experience who played a part in the production of the accompanying engraving of Britannia. See Norbrook, *Writing and the English Republic*, 294, n. 146. Norbrook's suggestion holds water. Chaloner wrote a dedicatory poem along similar lines for Thomas Gage's *The English-American, his travail by sea and land, or, A new survey of the West-India's* (1648). See Scott, "Chaloner, Thomas (1595-1660)".
43. Milton, *Samson Agonistes*, l. 1755.
44. Zurcher, "Milton on Tragedy", 185.
45. Ibid., 201-2, n. 8. The word appears again in the text of Nedham's translation (425), and Zurcher appears to attribute this to Selden rather than Nedham.
46. The debate is rehearsed in Dzelzainis, "Dating and Meaning".
47. Howell, *Dendrologia*, 29. Nedham's *The Excellencie of a Free State* (1656) was in part an answer to Howell's *Som sober inspections made into the cariage and consults of the late-long Parlement* (1655).
48. Malvezzi, *Discourses upon Cornelius Tacitus*.

49. De Britaine, *Interest of England*, 22-3; emphasis in original.
50. Milton, *Comus*, ll. 18-21.
51. Milton, *History of Britain*, 4.
52. Drayton, *Poly-Olbion*, 19. See Spenser, *Faerie Queene*, 4.16.1: 'For *Albion*, the son of *Neptune* was'. See also Pease, "Son of Neptune".
53. Drayton, *Poly-Olbion*, 35. On Selden's archipelagic annotations, see Hadfield, "Question of Britain", 593-4. See also Prescott, "Marginal Discourse": 'Selden undoes *Poly-Olbion*'s mythology from its margins like acid eating a book from the edges' (309). Selden was averse to wordplay: 'Take largest etymologicall liberty, and you may have it from *Ellan-ban, the white Isle*, in Scottish, as they call their *Albanie*; and to fit all together, the name of *Britaine* from *Brith-inis, the coloured Isle* in Welsh [...] But this is to play with syllables, and abuse precious time' (Drayton, *Poly-Olbion*, 20).
54. Jonson, *Neptunes Triumph*, A[r]. In Anthony Munday's Jacobean pageant, Britannia, hitherto known as Albion, 'After the name of *Neptunes* valiant Sonne: / *Albion* the Gyant', is now renamed after Brute, who, coming 'from *Albania*' has made conquest of '*Britania*' (Munday, *Re-United Britania*, B2[v]). Neptune as imperial theme was exploited by other colonial powers. See Welch, "Performing a New France". In a restoration royalist panegyric, Neptune would address not 'great STATE', but 'GREAT SIR!' See Tatham, *Neptunes Address*, 6.
55. Nedham, *Case of the Common-Wealth*, 3.
56. See Maley, "Peninsula Lost".
57. Dryden, *Annus mirabilis*, 47. This recalls *Cymbeline*'s wicked Queen commending to the King the capacity of his country to repel borders: 'The natural bravery of your isle, which stands / As Neptune's park, ribb'd and pal'd in / With rocks unscaleable and roaring waters, / With sands that will not bear your enemies' boats, / But suck them up to th'topmast' (3.1.19-23).
58. Sandys, *Paraphrase*, 10. Sandys' dedication is to Charles I, 'LORD OF THE FOUURE SEAS'.
59. Searle, "Haydn Autographs".
60. Jones, "Haydn, (Franz) Joseph (1732-1809)". One sign that something survived from Haydn's commission or that the poem proved popular is the fact that three verses (1, 5 and 6) were published as "Neptune to England" in Halliwell-Phillipps, ed., *Early Naval Ballads*, 68. As the editor observes, 'the triumphs of our marine powers cannot be too frequently recalled to our memories' (viii). C. H. Firth reprinted the same three verses in 1908, dating them from the time of Selden's *Mare Clausum* and the strengthening of the navy under Charles I in the mid-1630s, suggesting the poem 'was probably derived from some masque played at Court during these years' (Firth, ed., *Naval Songs and Ballads*, xxv). The poem appears on page 36. Two twelfth night masques by Ben Jonson might lie behind Firth's suggestion, the already mentioned *Neptunes Triumph* (1624), and *The fortunate isles and their union Celebrated in a masque design'd for the court, on the Twelfth night. 1624* (1625). Abingdon was a slippery character himself, as his biographer indicates. Echoing Leveller opposition to Cromwell's Irish campaign, in his best-known work, *Thoughts on the letter of Edmund Burke, esq. to the sheriffs of Bristol on the affairs of America* (1777), Abingdon declared: 'The dagger uplifted against the breast of America, is meant for the heart of Old England' (cited in Lowe, "Bertie, Willoughby, fourth earl of Abingdon (1740-1799)".
61. Cromwell, *Declaration of His Highnes*.
62. Armitage, *Ideological Origins*, 119.
63. Armitage, "Cromwellian Protectorate", 535.
64. Armitage, *Ideological Origins*, 119. See also Armitage, "Empire and Liberty": 'At the heart of the shared European heritage of republicanism lay a tension between the competing demands of two overwhelmingly desirable but ultimately irreconcilable goals: liberty and greatness' (29). For later developments in colonial republican ideology, see Horsman, "Expansion and Republicanism".

65. Armitage, *Ideological Origins*, 120.
66. Charles I, *Proclamation*.
67. Milton, *Areopagitica*, 29.
68. Sobecki, "Introduction", 4, 5.
69. Ibid., 7.
70. Ibid., 5.
71. Hirst, "English Republic", 467. For Hirst: 'There can be little doubt of the imperialist fervor engendered during the period of the Western Design, or of the dreams spawned then of imperial status for Cromwell' (467, n. 70).
72. Hawke, *Right of Dominion*, 86-7. Hawke is cited – but not quoted – in Hirst, "English Republic", 467, n. 69. On the colonial commonwealth, see also Smyth, "Empire-Building".
73. Somos, "Selden's *Mare Clausum*", 290. While Grotius 'essentially argued that the sea was international territory and that all nations should be free to use it for seafaring trade [...] Selden developed the opposing doctrine of *mare clausum*, amounting to a division of the sea into national spheres of interest to the exclusion of third states' (Ratter, "Geopolitics of Small Islands", 108).
74. Cited in MacLachlan, "Arthur, Legend of", 66.
75. For a beautifully textured treatment of the colonial roots and routes of the 1530s, see Conlan, "Homespun Origins". For fascinating sidelights, see Potter, "French Intrigue", and White, "Henry VIII's Irish Kerne".
76. For the attribution to Milton, see Milton, *Manifesto of the Lord Protector*. Here within the bounds of a single publication is the 'republican Britannia'.
77. Selden, *Mare clausum*, (d). The story of Samuel Pepys' restoration struggle with Nedham's republican text has been well told. See, for example, Brook, *Selden's Map of China*, 38: 'Samuel Pepys, secretary to the Navy board and therefore concerned with such matters, spent his evenings in the winter of 1661-2 reading the two books [i.e. Selden and Grotius] side by side. He read Selden in the English translation of 1652 by Marchamont Nedham, in which the original dedication to Charles I was replaced by a paean to Parliament's "right of Soveraigntie over the Seas". On 17 April 1663, with Britain once again under a monarch, Pepys had his copy rebound with a new title page dedicated to the king, "because I am ashamed to have the other seen dedicated to the Commonwealth". Four days later he wrote in his diary: "Up betimes and to my office, where first I ruled with red ink my English 'Mare Clausum,' which, with the new orthodox title, makes it now very handsome"'.
78. Batchelor, *The Selden Map*, 285, n. 82. Both are appended to Nedham's 1652 translation as part of its '*additional evidences and discourses*'.
79. Sir John Borough's *The Sovereignty of the British Seas* (1651); Padwa, "English Translation", 158. In Nedham's translation, 484-99 map onto 108-65 of Borough's text.
80. Batchelor, *The Selden Map*, 287, n. 100. On Watts, who translated Augustine's *Confessions* in 1631 and later served as chaplain with the English army in Scotland and Ireland, see McElligott, "Watts, William (c. 1590-1649)".
81. Cavanagh, "Prescription and Empire", 292.
82. Vieira, "Selden's Debate", 362, 377.
83. Cromwell, *Proclamation*. The transition from monarchy to republic and back again saw England angling for fishing rights, and other resources, far and wide. See Smith, *A True Narration*; Smith, *Trade & Fishing*; and Codrington, *His Majesties Propriety*. See also Bratspies, "Finessing King Neptune". The finessing doesn't extend to archipelagic nuance, as we're told Selden 'claimed, on behalf of King James I of England [sic], all the seas "inseparably and perpetually appurtenant to the British Empire"' (220, n. 34).
84. Selden, *Ownership, of the Sea*, 459.
85. Settle, *Mare clausum*, 4. The two texts were spoofed earlier in Gayton, *The Lawyer's Duel* (1655). For the early development of Dutch maritime policy, see Sicking, *Neptune and the Netherlands*.
86. Meadows, *Observations concerning the Dominion*, A^v.

87. Kerrigan, *Archipelagic English*, 51. Alluding to 'decades of English royalist and republican antagonism towards the Scots', Kerrigan cites 'the ease with which the versatile Marchamont Nedham could recycle hostile material from the chapter "Concerning the Scots" in his apology for the Republic, *The Case of the Common-wealth of England, Stated* (London, 1650), Pt II, ch. 2, to a royalist-phase *True Character of a Rigid Presbyter: With a Narrative of the Dangerous Designes of the English and Scotish Covenanters, as they have Tended to the Ruine of our Church and Kingdom* (London, 1661), 13-24' (276, 510, n. 43).
88. Nedham, *Case of the Common-Wealth*, 56.
89. Pocock, "British History", 606.
90. Ibid., 605-6.
91. Ibid., 602-3.
92. Pittock, *Celtic Identity*, 102. Pittock's characteristically trenchant comment on the British Empire and the complexity of Scottish complicity is astute: '"Britons never never shall be slaves" is a historic sentiment of imperial Protestant identity which functioned externally in ruling the waves, not internally through understanding each other. Less than ten years after the Scot, James Thomson, wrote these lines, his compatriots were being sold into slavery in the American colonies for bearing arms in the cause of "Prosperity to Scotland and no Union", the badge on their Jacobite blades' (144).
93. For the deep roots of Franco-Scottish relations, see Bonner, "Scotland's 'Auld Alliance'". On sixteenth-century Irish-Spanish relations, see Fuchs, "Spanish Lessons". For Fuchs, 'Ireland functions as a key site for analyzing England's tortuous relationship to Spain as both model and rival' (43).
94. Raymond, "Newspapers", 249.
95. Ibid., 256. The claim that Britain's second language was Latin would have to be looked at in light of the fortunes of the Celtic languages under English expansion, since at the outset of the early modern period, 'The archipelago was still predominantly Celtic-speaking – at least when measured in terms of geographical area' (Ellis and Maginn, *Making of the British Isles*, 4).
96. Raymond, "Monopoly and Censorship", 8-9.
97. Raymond, "Nedham, Marchamont (bap. 1620, d. 1678)".
98. Worden, "Milton and Marchamont Nedham", 166.
99. Ibid., 173.
100. Harrington, *The Common-wealth of Oceana*, 4. In Richard Flecknoe's opera *The Marriage of Oceanus and Brittania* (1659) the mariners are urged 'Brittania to please, / Queen of all Iles, and Empress of the Seas' (11).
101. Harrington, *The Common-wealth of Oceana*, 4.
102. Ibid., 8.
103. Ibid., 233.
104. Ibid.
105. Sidney, *Discourses concerning Government*, 112.
106. Lenin, *Collected Works*, vol. 39, 446. On Cromwell's shipbuilding strategy, see Scott, *When the Waves Ruled*, 75: 'the republic patrolled the channel, Mediterranean and Caribbean simultaneously'.
107. Marx to Ludwig Kugelmann, 4 December 1869. Marx and Engels, *Irish Question*, 379.
108. In his 'Confidential Communication on Bakunin' of 28 March 1870, Marx declared: 'England today is seeing a repetition of what happened on a gigantic scale in ancient Rome. A nation that enslaves another forges its own chains' (Marx, *On the First International*, 174).
109. Studies of the period that fail to take on board Marx's perspective remain flawed. See, for example, Holstun's magisterial *Ehud's Dagger*.
110. Empire helped the British state navigate a later revolutionary tempest: 'When it was announced that a convict ship, the Neptune, was on its way to the Cape with 288 prisoners on board, many of them Irishmen convicted during the agrarian agitation of 1848, a petitioning campaign against the Colonial Office began, coordinated by the newly formed Anti-Convict Association' (Taylor, "1848 Revolutions", 168).

111. See Weber, "Could Brexit", and Frizzell, "Use Lottery Money".
112. Milton, *Readie and Easie Way*, 46. On this passage, see Scott, *When the Waves Ruled*, 90. Milton's work is awash with maritime metaphors. In the same treatise he feared liberty of conscience, rather than pursuit of colonies, might prove 'the rock wheron they ship wrack themselves', and urged parliament 'to keep thir due channell' (92, 108).

Disclosure statement

No potential conflict of interest was reported by the author.

Bibliography

Albright, E. M. "*The Faerie Queene* in Masque at the Gray's Inn Revels". *PMLA* 41, no. 3 (1926): 497–516.
Armitage, D. "The Cromwellian Protectorate and the Languages of Empire". *The Historical Journal* 35, no. 3 (1992): 531–555.
Armitage, D. "John Milton: Poet Against Empire". In *Milton and Republicanism*, edited by D. Armitage, A. Himy, and Q. Skinner, 206–225. Cambridge: Cambridge University Press, 1995.
Armitage, D. *The Ideological Origins of the British Empire*. Cambridge: Cambridge University Press, 2000.
Armitage, D. "Empire and Liberty: A Republican Dilemma". In *Republicanism: A Shared European Heritage, Volume 2, the Values of Republicanism in Early Modern Europe*, edited by M. van Gelderen and Q. Skinner, 29–46. Cambridge: Cambridge University Press, 2002.
Batchelor, R. K. *London: The Selden Map and the Making of a Global City, 1549-1689*. Chicago: University of Chicago Press, 2014.
Bonner, E. "Scotland's 'Auld Alliance' with France, 1295-1560". *History* 84, no. 273 (1999): 5–30.
Borough, S. J. *The Sovereignty of the British Seas*. London: Printed for Humphrey Moseley, 1651.
Bratspies, R. "Finessing King Neptune: Fisheries Management and the Limits of International Law". *Harvard Environmental Law Review* 25 (2001): 213–258.
Brook, T. *Mr. Selden's Map of China: Decoding the Secrets of a Vanished Cartographer*. London and Berlin: Profile Books, 2013.
Canning, W. *Gesta Grayorum*. London, 1688.
Cavanagh, E. "Prescription and Empire from Justinian to Grotius". *The Historical Journal* 60, no. 2 (2017): 273–299.
Charles, I. *A Proclamation to Forbid the Importing, Buying, Selling, or Publishing Any Forraine Edition of A Booke Lately Printed at London by His Maiesties Command, Intituled Mare Clausum*. London, 1636.
Codrington, R. *His Majesties Propriety and Dominion on the Brittish Seas Asserted Together with a True Account of the Neatherlanders Insupportable Insolencies and Injuries They Have Committed, and the Inestimable Benefits They Have Gained in Their Fishing on the English Seas*. London, 1665.
Collignon, S. "Brexit has the Semblance of a New English Civil War". Accessed March 9, 2018. http://blogs.lse.ac.uk/brexit/2018/03/09/brexit-has-the-semblance-of-a-new-english-civil-war/
Conlan, J. P. "'[Who] Hath Covered the Naked with a Garment': The Homespun Origins of the English Reformation". *Reformation* 9, no. 1 (2004): 49–66.
Cromwell, O. *A Declaration of His Highnes, by the Advice of His Council Setting Forth, on the Behalf of This Commonwealth, the Justice of Their Cause against Spain*. London, 1655.
Cromwell, O. *A Proclamation Declaring the Right of the Fellowship and Company of English Merchants for Discovering of New Trades (Commonly Called the Muscovia Company) to the Sole Fishing for Whales upon the Coasts of Green-Land and Chery-Island, and for Restraining and Prohibiting of All Others*. [i.e. 1658]. London, 1657.
De Britaine, W. *The Interest of England in the Present War with Holland by the Author of the Dutch Usurpation*. London, 1672.

Drayton, M. *Poly-Olbion*. London, 1612.
Dryden, J. *Annus Mirabilis, the Year of Wonders, 1666 an Historical Poem Containing the Progress and Various Successes of Our Naval War with Holland, under the Conduct of His Highness Prince Rupert, and His Grace the Duke of Albemarl: And Describing the Fire of London*. London: Printed for Henry Herringman, 1667.
Dzelzainis, M. "History and Ideology: Milton, the Levellers, and the Council of State in 1649". *Huntington Library Quarterly* 68, no. 1&2 (2005): 269–287.
Dzelzainis, M. "Dating and Meaning: *Samson Agonistes* and the 'Digression' to Milton's *History of Britain*". *Milton Studies* 48 (2008): 160–177.
Ellis, S. G., and C. Maginn. *The Making of the British Isles: The State of Britain and Ireland, 1450-1660*. London: Routledge, 2013.
Firth, C. H., ed. *Naval Songs and Ballads*. Navy Records Society, vol. 33, 1908.
Bertie, W. *Thoughts on the Letter of Edmund Burke, Esq. To the Sheriffs of Bristol on the Affairs of America*. 1777.
Flecknoe, R. *The Marriage of Oceanus and Brittania an Allegoricall Fiction, Really Declaring Englands Riches, Glory, and Puissance by Sea: To Be Represented in Musick, Dances, and Proper Scenes*. London: s.n., 1659.
Frank, J. *Cromwell's Press Agent: A Critical Biography of Marchamont Nedham, 1620-1678*. Lanham, MD: University Press of America, 1980.
Milton, F. J., ed. *The Life Records of John Milton, Volume II, 1639-1651*. New Brunswick, NJ: Rutgers University Press, 1950.
Frizzell, N. 2017. "Use Lottery Money to Pay for a Royal Yacht? OK – Under These Conditions". *The Guardian*, December 29. Accessed December 31, 2017. https://www.theguardian.com/commentisfree/2017/dec/29/royal-yacht-lottery-brittania-monarchy-queen-timeshare
Fuchs, B. "Spanish Lessons: Spenser and the Irish Moriscos". *Studies in English* 42, no. 1 (2002): 43–62. Literature *1500-1900*.
Gage, T. *The English-American, His Travail by Sea and Land, Or, A New Survey of the West-India's*. London, 1648.
Gayton, E. *The Lawyer's Duel, or Two Sonnets Composed on Grotius's Mare Liberum. And Selden's Mare Clausum*. London: s.n., 1655.
Gormley-Heenan, C., and A. Aughey. "Northern Ireland and Brexit: Three Effects on 'The Border in the Mind'". *The British Journal of Politics and International Relations* 19, no. 3 (2017): 497–511.
Gunn, J. A. W. "'Interest Will Not Lie': A Seventeenth-Century Political Maxim". *Journal of the History of Ideas* 29, no. 4 (1968): 551–564.
Hadfield, A. "Spenser, Drayton, and the Question of Britain". *Review of English Studies* 51, no. 204 (2000): 582–599.
Halliwell-Phillipps, J. O., ed. *The Early Naval Ballads of England*. London: The Percy Society, 1841.
Harrington, J. *The Common-Wealth of Oceana*. London: Printed by J. Streater for Livewell Chapman, 1656.
Hawke, M. *The Right of Dominion, and Property of Liberty, whether Natural, Civil, or Religious*. London, 1655.
Hirst, D. "The English Republic and the Meaning of Britain". *Journal of Modern History* 66, no. 3 (1994): 451–486.
Holder, D. "Neither Hard nor Soft but Racist? the Good Friday Agreement and the Irish Border after Brexit". *Race & Class* 59, no. 2 (2017): 90–101.
Holstun, J. *A Rational Millenium: Puritan Utopias of Seventeenth-Century England and America*. New York: Oxford University Press, 1987.
Holstun, J. *Ehud's Dagger: Class Struggle in the English Revolution*. London: Verso, 2000.
Horsman, R. "The Dimensions of an "Empire for Liberty": Expansion and Republicanism, 1775-1825". *Journal of the Early Republic* 9, no. 1 (1989): 1–20.
Howell, J. *Dendrologia Dodona's Grove, Or, the Vocall Forrest*. London, 1640.
Howell, J. *Som Sober Inspections Made into the Cariage and Consults of the Late-Long Parlement*. London, 1655.

Jones, D. W. "Haydn, (Franz) Joseph (1732–1809), Composer". In *Oxford Dictionary of National Biography*. Oxford University Press, May 26, 2005. Accessed December 22, 2017.

Jonson, B. *Neptunes Triumph for the Returne of Albion Celebrated in a Masque at the Court on the Twelfth Night 1623*. London: s.n., 1624.

Jonson, B. *The Fortunate Isles and Their Union Celebrated in a Masque Design'd for the Court, on the Twelfth Night. 1624*. London: s.n., 1625.

Kerrigan, J. *Archipelagic English: Literature, History, and Politics 1603-1707*. Oxford: Oxford University Press, 2008.

Knachel, P. A. "Introduction". In *The Case of the Commonwealth of England, Stated*, edited by M. Nedham. Charlottesville: University of Virginia Press, 1969.

Lenin, V. I. *Collected Works, Vol. 39, Notebooks on Imperialism*. Translated by Clemens Dutt. Edited by M. S. Levin. Moscow: Progress Publishers, 1968 [1974].

Levack, B. P. "Britain"S First Global Century: England, Scotland and Empire, 1603-1707". *Britain and the World* 6, no. 1 (2013): 101–118.

Lilburne, J. *As You Were, Or, the Lord General Cromwel and the Grand Officers of the Armie Their Remembrancer Wherein as in a Glass They May See the Faces of Their Soules Spotted with Apostacy, Ambitious Breach of Promise, and Hocus-Pocus-Juggleing with the Honest Soldiers and the Rest of the Free-People of England*. Amsterdam: s.n., 1652.

Lowe, W. C. 2017. "Bertie, Willoughby, Fourth Earl of Abingdon (1740–1799), Politician". *Oxford Dictionary of National Biography*, Accessed December 26, 2017.

MacLachlan, H. "Arthur, Legend Of". In *A Spenser Encyclopedia*, edited by A. C. Hamilton, 64–66. London and Toronto: Routledge, 1990.

McDowell, N. *Poetry and Allegiance in the English Civil Wars*. Oxford: Oxford University Press, 2008.

McElligott, J. 2017. "Watts, William (C. 1590-1649), Church of England Clergyman and Author". *Oxford Dictionary of National Biography*, Accessed December 31, 2017.

Maley, W. 2017. "Spenser and Europe: Britomart after Brexit". *Spenser Review* 47.3.42. http://www.english.cam.ac.uk/spenseronline/review/item/47.3.42

Maley, W. "'Another Britain?': Bacon's *Certain Considerations Touching the Plantation in Ireland* (1606)". *Prose Studies: History, Theory, Criticism* 18, no. 1 (1995): 1–18.

Maley, W. "Peninsula Lost: Mapping Milton's Celtiberian Cartographies". *SEDERI Yearbook* 24 (2014): 69–93.

Malvezzi, V. *Discourses upon Cornelius Tacitus Written in Italian by the Learned Marquesse Virgilio Malvezzi [...] Translated into English by Sir Richard Baker*. London, 1642.

Marx, K. *On the First International*. Edited by Saul K. Padover. London: McGraw-Hill, 1973.

Marx, K., and F. Engels. *Ireland and the Irish Question*. Edited by L. I. Golman and V. E. Kunina. Moscow: Progress Publishers, 1986.

Meadows, P. *Observations Concerning the Dominion and Sovereignty of the Seas Being an Abstract of the Marine Affairs of England*. London, 1689.

Milton, J. *Areopagitica*. London, 1644.

Milton, J. *Articles of Peace Made and Concluded with the Irish Rebels*. London: Printed by Matthew Simmons, 1649.

Milton, J. "Comus". In *Complete English Poems*, edited by G. Campbell. London: Everyman, 1992.

Milton, J. *A Defence of the People of England by John Milton; in Answer to Salmasius's Defence of the King*. Amsterdam: s.n., 1692.

Milton, J. *The Readie and Easie Way to Establish a Free Commonwealth*. 2nd ed. London, 1660.

Milton, J. *The History of Britain, that Part Especially Now Call'd England from the First Traditional Beginning, Continu'd to the Norman Conquest*. London, 1670.

Milton, J. *A Manifesto of the Lord Protector of the Commonwealth of England, Scotland, Ireland, &C. Published by Consent and Advice of His Council. Wherein Is Shewn the Reasonableness of the Cause of This Republic against the Depredations of the Spaniards. Written in Latin by John Milton, and First Printed in 1655, Now Translated into English ... The Second Edition. To Which Is Added, Britannia, A Poem; by Mr. Thomson: First Published in 1727*. London, 1738.

Milton, J. "Samson Agonistes". In *Complete English Poems*, edited by G. Campbell. London: Everyman, 1992.

Munday, A. *The Triumphes of Re-United Britania*. London, 1605.

Nedham, M. *The Case of the Common-Wealth of England, Stated*. 2nd ed. London, 1650.

Norbrook, D. *Writing and the English Republic: Poetry, Rhetoric, and Politics, 1627-1660*. Cambridge: Cambridge University Press, 1998.

O'Toole, F. 2016. "Brexit Is Being Driven by English Nationalism. And It Will End in Self-Rule". *The Guardian*, June 18. Accessed December 5, 2017. https://www.theguardian.com/commentisfree/2016/jun/18/england-eu-referendum-brexit

Padwa, D. J. "On the English Translation of John Selden's *Mare Clausum*". *American Journal of International Law* 54, no. 1 (1960): 156–159.

Parker, D., ed. *Ideology, Absolutism and the English Revolution: Debates of the British Communist Historians 1940-1956*. London: Lawrence & Wishart, 2008.

Peacey, J. "Marchamont Nedham and the Lawrans Letters". *Bodleian Library Record* 17, no. 1 (2000): 24–35.

Pease, A. S. "The Son of Neptune". *Harvard Studies in Classical Philology* 54 (1943): 69–82.

Pittock, M. *Celtic Identity and the British Image*. Manchester: Manchester University Press, 1999.

Pocock, J. G. A. "British History: A Plea for A New Subject". *Journal of Modern History* 47, no. 4 (1975): 601–628.

Potter, D. "French Intrigue in Ireland during the Reign of Henri II, 1547-1559". *International History Review* 5 (1983): 159–180.

Prescott, A. L. "Marginal Discourse: Drayton's Muse and Selden's 'Story'". *Studies in Philology* 88, no. 3 (1991): 307–328.

Ratter, B. M. W. "Geopolitics of Small Islands". In *Geography of Small Islands: Outposts of Globalisation*, 93–131. Cham: Springer, 2018.

Raymond, J. "'A Mercury with a Winged Conscience': Marchamont Nedham, Monopoly and Censorship". *Media History* 4, no. 1 (1998): 7–18.

Raymond, J. "Complications of Interest: Milton, Scotland, Ireland, and National Identity in 1649". *Review of English Studies* 55, no. 220 (2004): 315–345.

Raymond, J. "Nedham, Marchamont (Bap. 1620, D. 1678)". In *Oxford Dictionary of National Biography*. online edition, September 2015 ed. Oxford University Press. 2004. Accessed March 12, 2016.

Raymond, J. "Marchamont Nedham". In *The Oxford Handbook of Literature and the English Revolution*, edited by L. L. Knoppers, 375–393. Oxford: Oxford University Press, 2012.

Raymond, J. "Newspapers: A National or International Phenomenon?" *Media History* 18, no. 3–4 (2012): 249–257.

Ross, T. trans *The Second Punick War*. London, 1661.

Royce, M. R. "The Protestant Supranationalism of Britain". In *The Political Theology of European Integration: Comparing the Influence of Religious Histories on European Policies*, 207–259. London: Palgrave Macmillan, 2017.

Sandys, G. *A Paraphrase upon the Divine Poems*. London, 1638.

Sawday, J. "Marvell's 'Bermudas' and the History of the Eleutherian Republic". *English Literary Renaissance* 48, no. 1 (2018): 60–97.

Scott, D. 2017. "Chaloner, Thomas (1595–1660), Politician and Regicide". *Oxford Dictionary of National Biography*, Accessed December 26, 2017.

Scott, J. *When the Waves Ruled Britannia: Geography and Political Identities, 1500-1800*. Cambridge: Cambridge University Press, 2011.

Searle, A. "Haydn Autographs and 'Authentic' Manuscript Copies in the British Library". *Early Music* 10, no. 4 (1982): 496–497.

Selden, J. *Of the Dominion, or Ownership, of the Sea Two Books: [...] Translated into English, and Set Forth with Som[E] Additional Evidences and Discourses by Marchamont Nedham*. London: Printed by William Du-Gard, 1652.

Selden, J. *Mare Clausum the Right and Dominion of the Sea in Two Books [...] Formerly Translated into English, and Now Perfected and Restored by J.H., Gent*. London, 1663.

Settle, E. *Mare Clausum: Or A Ransack for the Dutch May 23. 1666.* London: Peter Lillicrap, for John Million, 1666.
Shakespeare, W. "Cymbeline". In *The Arden Shakespeare Complete Works*, edited by R. Proudfoot, A. Thompson, and D. S. Kastan, 253–290. London: Arden Shakespeare, 2001.
Shakespeare, W. "Hamlet". In *The Arden Shakespeare Complete Works*, edited by R. Proudfoot, A. Thompson, and D. S. Kastan, 291–332. London: Arden Shakespeare, 2001.
Shell, M. *Islandology: Geography, Rhetoric, Politics*. Stanford, CA: Stanford University Press, 2014.
Sicking, L. *Neptune and the Netherlands: State, Economy, and War at Sea in the Renaissance*. Leiden: Brill, 2004.
Smith, J. *The Trade & Fishing of Great-Britain Displayed with a Description of the Islands of Orkney and Shotland [i.e. Shetland]*. London, 1661.
Smith, S. *A True Narration of the Royall Fishings of Great Brittaine and Ireland*. London, 1641.
Smyth, J. "Empire-Building: The English Republic, Scotland and Ireland". In *Varieties of Seventeenth- and Early Eighteenth-Century English Radicalism in Context*, edited by D. Finnegan and A. Hessayon, 129–144. London: Routledge, 2011.
Sidney, A. *Discourses Concerning Government*. London, 1698.
Sobecki, S. I. "Introduction". In *The Sea and Englishness in the Middle Ages: Maritime Narratives, Identity and Culture*, edited by S. I. Sobecki. Cambridge: D. S. Brewer, 2011.
Somos, M. "Selden's *Mare Clausum*: The Secularisation of International Law and the Rise of Soft Imperialism". *Journal of the History of International Law* 14 (2012): 287–330.
Stevenson, J. "Does Brexit Threaten Peace in Northern Ireland?" *Survival* 59, no. 3 (2017): 111–128.
Spenser, E. *The Faerie Queene*. Edited by A. C. Hamilton, with Hiroshi Yamashita, and Toshiyuki Suzuki. Revised 2nd ed. London: Routledge, 2007.
Tatham, J. *Neptunes Address to His Most Sacred Majesty Charls the Second: King of England, Scotland, France and Ireland, &C. Congratulating His Happy Coronation Celebrated the 22th. Day of Aprill, 1661. In Several Designements and Shews Npon [Sic] the Water, before White-Hall, at His Majesties Return from the Land-Triumphs*. London: William Godbid for Edward Powel, 1661.
Taylor, M. "The 1848 Revolutions and the British Empire". *Past & Present* 166 (2000): 146–180.
Vieira, M. B. "Mare Liberum Vs. Mare Clausum: Grotius, Freitas, and Selden's Debate on Dominion over the Seas". *Journal of the History of Ideas* 64, no. 3 (2003): 361–377.
Warren, E. *Geologia, Or, A Discourse Concerning the Earth before the Deluge*. London, 1690.
Weber, E. 2016. "Could Brexit Bring Back the Royal Yacht?" *BBC News*, September 27. Accessed December 31, 2017. http://www.bbc.co.uk/news/uk-politics-37428864
Welch, E. R. "Performing a New France, Making Colonial History in Marc Lescarbot's *Théâtre De Neptune* (1606)". *Modern Language Quarterly* 72, no. 4 (2011): 439–460.
White, D. G. "Henry VIII's Irish Kerne in France and Scotland". *The Irish Sword* 3, no. 1957-58: 213–225.
Woodford, B. "From Tyrant to Unfit Monarch: Marchamont Nedham's Representation of Charles Stuart and Royalists during the Interregnum". *History* 100, no. 339 (2015): 1–20.
Worden, B. *Literature and Politics in Cromwellian England: John Milton, Andrew Marvell, Marchamont Nedham*. Oxford: Oxford University Press, 2009.
Worden, B. "Milton and Marchamont Nedham". In *Milton and Republicanism*, edited by D. Armitage, A. Himy, and Q. Skinner, 156–180. Cambridge: Cambridge University Press, 1995.
Worden, B. "The Politics of Marvell's Horatian Ode". *The Historical Journal* 27, no. 3 (1984): 525–547.
Worden, B. "'Wit in a Roundhead': The Dilemma of Marchamont Nedham". In *Political Culture and Cultural Politics in Early Modern England*, edited by S. Asmussen and M. Kishlansky, 301–337. Manchester: Manchester University Press, 1995.
Zurcher, A. "Milton on Tragedy: Law, Hypallage, and Participation". In *Young Milton: The Emerging Author, 1620-1642*, edited by E. Jones, 182–205. Oxford: Oxford University Press, 2013.

The archipelagic turn: nationhood, nationalism and early modern studies, 1997–2017

Patrick J. Murray

In a memorable scene in the 2001 satire *Mike Bassett: England Manager*, the historic tensions of the Atlantic archipelago are played for darkly comic effect. The England football team, spying Scotland's representatives walking through the arrivals lounge before an international tournament, initiate the encounter. "Hey look lads, it's the Jocks", announces one of the party. After some exchanges, the Irish team arrive on the scene. Again, their arrival is proclaimed with a belittling epithet: "Here come the Paddies – give it up for the England B team". A quick conversation between an Irishman and Englishman ensues, with the latter questioning the legitimacy of the former's Irish accent, resulting in the Irishman declaring with scornful reference to his adversary's religious bent, "Shut your mouth, ya Proddy bollocks". A member of the Scottish party (still present, observing) overhears and takes exception, retorting, "Who you calling a Proddy bollocks, you Fenian twat?". Suddenly, religious tension agglomerates national confrontation – another of the Scottish team squares up to his erstwhile team-mate, asking belligerently, "Hey, I'm a Fenian, who you fucking speaking to?". Pushing and shoving follows, before a mass brawl concludes the scene.

National rivalry, which often finds its focal point in sporting endeavour, is the most obvious characteristic of the engagement. Casual racism and denigration are in evidence too. Yet the fraught interchanges all revolve around identity and its problematic conceptualisations. A Gaelicised Englishman is confronted on the authenticity of his Irishness, while the religious aspect of the historical relationship between Catholic Ireland and Protestant England is referenced. The interjection of the Scots, with their own intra-national sectarian tensions, foregrounds how the identities of all three parties are often refracted through their neighbours, and brings the scene to a heady and confrontational denouement. Meanwhile, the Welsh remain silent, their absence reminding us that the national, cultural and social texture of the islands always retains a crucial as-yet-uncovered stratum.

For scholars of the early modern period, the clearest parallel to this scene is Shakespearean. Or rather – keeping in mind the multivalent nationalities central to this essay's theme – present in the Englishman William Shakespeare's heavily-fictionalised chronicles of the life and times of a Welsh-born king of England with Norman lineage, namely Henry V. For the English, Irish and Scottish football teams in a modern airport, read English, Scottish, Irish and Welsh army captains on a battlefield in France. The comedic interlude between Gower (English), Fluellen (Welsh), Macmorris (Irish) and Jamy (Scottish) in Act 3 depicts a symbolic portrayal of archipelagic interaction, staging a conversation between all four main identities of the islands culminating in a squabble over national and ethnic stereotypes. Moreover, the figure of Macmorris, an amalgam of disingenuous early modern English notions about the Irish – hot-tempered, querulous and speaking with an unusual accent – exemplifies a study in the negotiations of nationhood within the framework of a heterogenous yet seemingly-singular identity. All four characters are fighting on behalf of an English king. Nonetheless Macmorris responds to the insinuations of the Welsh Fluellen's sly accusation, "Captain Macmorris, I think, look you, under your correction, there is not many of your nation", with an interrogative of his own: "Of my nation? What ish my nation? Ish a villain and a bastard and a knave and a rascal. What ish my nation? Who talks of my nation?"[1]

The impulse in Macmorris's response – an examination (ironic or otherwise) of national identity and its perceptions within the context of the convolutions of Britain and its respective components – are reciprocated in another literary exploration of early modern British nationhood, Michael Drayton's *Poly-Olbion*. Ostensibly a poetic journey through the topography of the British Isles, it also addresses questions germane to the constitution of the British nation, for example the state of the Anglo-Scots Union, and Britain's cultural and governmental relationship to the European continent.[2] Such texts retain a contemporary piquancy. In the last twenty years the archipelago of Ireland, Scotland, Wales and England has been regularly troubled by questions of identity, and experienced a series of tumultuous shifts regarding what exactly constitutes nationhood within an entity characterised by ethnic, social, cultural and religious difference. Quite apart from the long-standing complexities of partitioned Ireland, the islands have witnessed increased devolution of political power to its margins in the establishment of a Scottish Parliament, Welsh and Northern Irish Assemblies, each provoking their own fractures. Yet while such political manoeuvrings might have signalled a clear demonstration of the Yeatsian axiom that the centre cannot hold, the defeat of the independence movement in Scotland in 2014, alongside the protracted process of withdrawal from the European union following the referendum of 2016 appear to throw into question once more the constitution of British identity.

Fittingly, within this climate of interrogation of what constitutes nationhood in a political aggregation of nations, scholars of the early modern period have been drawn to re-examine the foundations of the discussion. This takes full advantage of the fact that the focus of their studies coincides with a period of centralising of political power within the British nation state. The long-standing debates of nationalism theory – between modernists who argue that the nation state emerged from the economic imperatives of bourgeoning capitalist societies to the primordialists who, taking a wider historical outlook on the development of human societies, emphasise a more fundamental narrative regarding the emergence of nationalities – have empowered scholars to consider what constitutes the basis of the archipelago's varied character. Yet, with this empowering there has understandably emerged disagreement. As John Breuilly writes in an examination of the origins not just of nationalism as a political ideology but also as a subject of intellectual investigation:

> Different authors have different views on nationalism. Some consider 'nations' as realities distinct from nationalism that in turn conditions that nationalism; others see nationalism as preceding, even constructing nations; yet others are sceptical as to whether 'nation' has

meaning beyond its use by nationalists. Some historians emphasize the destructive and irrational features of nationalism; others its contribution to promoting cultural diversity and autonomy; whereas for yet others it is always Janus-faced. Some historians regard nationalism as an analytic concept rather than a force in the world with moral qualities, be they good or bad or both. In part such disagreements relate to the types of nationalism about which different historians write, in part to the concepts and methods they bring to bear, in part to their moral perspective.[3]

For early modern scholars, such intricacies regarding nationalism, its origins and character are magnified by a period that represents the crucible for the British state. The enhancement of post-colonial awareness in social sciences following the seminal work of Fanon, Said and Bhabha in the middle of the twentieth century has further augmented approaches to nationhood, and seen an appreciable and appreciated increase in focus on the verges of the archipelago. As Andrew Hadfield writes in his important essay "Vanishing Primordialism: Literature, History, and the Public", the confluence of "nation, nationalism, literature and the public sphere" means that the study of literature is bound up with the study of nationhood. "Literature", Hadfield asserts, "does not reflect debates about nation and national identity: it invariably predicts and establishes them in periods before the creation of political institutions that have defined the contours of a nation" (54).

Literary scholars sensitive to this relationship between nation, literature and identity have sought to interrogate not just the meaning of texts, but also the socio-historical environment in which they were produced. According to Willy Maley, a figure at the centre of the new historiography of British identities, the discourses of nationhood and culture were symbiotic in the sixteenth and seventeenth century:

> English is a colonising culture, and its investment in empire is first and foremost bound up with the invention of Britain, a creative enterprise in which [...] writers [...] played a double part, as advocates and cross-examiners, witnesses for the defence and for the prosecution. It is for the reader to judge whether they should continue to be viewed as straightforwardly 'English' Renaissance writers, or whether they ought to be reinscribed, together with their contemporaries with a problematic British context (6).

The sense of what Maley describes as a "problematic British context" is understood if we consider the narrative of royal lineage from the mid-sixteenth century onwards. From the accession of Henry VIII – where an English-born man with a Welsh name became king of England, Ireland and Wales – to the reign of William III – a supplanting Netherlandish nobleman, nominally Protestant yet sponsored by the Catholic pope who would die "King of England, Scotland, France and Ireland, Stadholther of the Republic of the Seven United Netherlands, Prince of Orange, Count of Nassau [and] Defender of the Faith" – a kaleidoscopic interchange of identities suffused the Three Kingdoms. The recognition of Britain as a conglomeration of often messy and occasionally contradictory narratives from the top down characterises what may be termed the archipelagic turn in early modern studies of nationhood and identity. As John Kerrigan notes in the Preface to his seminal work *Archipelagic English*, "Historians increasingly recognise that early modern England, Scotland, Ireland, and Wales were in different degrees and for a variety of reasons, but sometimes to crucial effect, interactive entities" (vii).

Kerrigan's usage of the word "archipelagic" denotes not just a focus on the islands that sit to the northwest of the European landmass, but also emphasises the fractile though interconnected nature of that entity. As Kerrigan writes:

> This term [archipelago], as used by the historians, and redeployed in my title, does three related things: it designates a geopolitical unit or zone, stretching from the Channel Islands to the Shetlands, from the Wash to Galway Bay, with ties to North America and down to the Caribbean; it does so neutrally (avoiding the assumptions loaded into 'the British Isles'); and it implies a devolved, interconnected account of what went on around the islands (vii).

This "devolved, interconnected account of what went on around the islands" is an estimable piece of scholarship. Its central argument, namely how differences between the multiplicity of nations on the archipelago proved fertile ground for the production of outstanding culture, is advanced convincingly. Kerrigan's study ranges authoritatively across the archipelago, taking in depictions of Roman rule in Welsh and Jacobean drama; Ireland's religious tumults under Charles I and II; the work of the "gifted litterateur and lawyer" (271) George Mackenzie, whose *Aretina: Or, the Serious Romance* (published in 1660) presents a "thinly-veiled account of seventeenth-century Scottish history" (270); Roger Boyle, 1st Earl of Orrery and social satirist of post-Restoration Ireland; and the later figures of Daniel Defoe and Walter Scott, two writers fundamental to post-Union conceptions of British and (in the latter case in particular) Scottish identities.

Such a variety of primary literature, augmented by the standard touchstones of early modern scholarship (Shakespeare, Milton and Spenser) testifies to the truly archipelagic outlook of Kerrigan's work. In addition to the forensic nature of its literary criticism, *Archipelagic English* exhibits a historian's sensitivity to the convoluted historical narratives of the period. For example, there is a deft handling of the labyrinthine controversies of the Covenanters in mid-seventeenth century Scotland, a period where the contrasting tensions of religious loyalty, parliamentary rule and royal prerogative regularly coalesced into bloody warfare: as Kerrigan writes, "the determination of the English bishops to restrict the worship of Scottish Presbyterians, and the threat posed to archipelagic security by the rebellious Covenanters in the west of Scotland, guaranteed cross-border conflict" (269). Similarly, the author interweaves analysis of the literature of early modern Wales with examination of the discourses surrounding millenarian puritanism, and considers how the work of Milton and Marvell "figure in the larger design" (227) of Anglo-Scottish and Anglo-Dutch conflicts of the 1650s. Kerrigan's scholarship is exemplary, and with footnotes running to nearly one hundred and fifty pages and a primary bibliography of twenty-five pages, it will stand as both a supremely-argued thesis and an abundant resource of information for scholars for many years to come.

The archipelagic turn in early modern studies of nationalism is manifest in a variety of adroit studies of seminal sixteenth- and seventeenth-century thinkers and writers. Archetypal is the "Archipelagic Holinshed" section in *The Oxford Handbook of Holinshed's Chronicles* published by Oxford University Press. Holinshed is popularly known as a key source of Shakespeare, but his work as a chronicler of the island nations of the North Atlantic represents an important addition to the historiography of Britain in its many guises. As the editors Ian W. Archer, Felicity Heal and Paulina Kewes observe, Holinshed's twice-published work entitled *Chronicles of England, Scotland, and Ireland* (1577, 1587) stands as a "unique contribution to the perception of these islands in the sixteenth century" (xxxvii). Appropriately, Holinshed's work was a multi-authored text with a diversity of sources, incorporating the work of the Protestant English clergyman William Harrison (*Description of Britain*), Irish natural philosopher Richard Stanihurst ("a playne and perfecte description" of Ireland, and a *History of Ireland during the reign of Henry VIII*), alongside contributions from the Roman Catholic priest and English historian Edmund Campion. The editors continue, highlighting the interactions, imbrications and occasionally belligerent intersections of "British" history typified in the composite work:

> The *Chronicles* were, of course, unusual for their attention to space as well as time, and for their concern with the story of the component parts of the British archipelago. Harrison's *Description of Britain* has long been recognised as a significant moment in the development of chorography from Leland to Camden; and historians of Ireland have long valued Stanihurst's description, and Campion's history, of the country. [...] Although the descriptions are parallel rather than comparative, they often bear witness to the painful process of interweaving national identities, and to contested understanding of how the past might point to a different set of future political arrangements (xxxvii).

The citation of "a different set of future political arrangements" is a consciously politic phrase, suggesting a degree of anaesthetised engagement. Yet it is important to retain not only an awareness of the implications of freighted words in any dispute regarding nations and nationalisms on the Atlantic archipelago, but also the consequences of striving for apolitical or purportedly "neutral" assignations. This is particularly evident in toponymy. Where the subject is a conglomeration of nations and identities, the topic of nationhood and what denotes a singular entity becomes an especially heated debate. In the twenty-first century, with the political body of the United Kingdom of Great Britain and Northern Ireland riven with internal contrarieties – the majority of the English electorate, ostensibly the stronghold and centre of unionism, displaying apathy to potential Scottish secession; Irish identities in the partitioned northern enclave cleaving both to Britain and also to a broader principle of interchange with its southern neighbour; and the Welsh socio-political landscape marked by rejection of the sort of European communalism displayed by its Celtic counterparts – the act of describing exactly what the geographic area constitutes is itself a political act. When compounded by the day-to-day anxieties and contingencies of political and social administration, the process of identification is loaded with complexity.

For scholars whose eyes are trained on the early modern period, such debates are merely a continuation of a long-standing struggle between individuation and communal expression on the islands. According to Philip Schwyzer's excellent commentary on Holinshed and his roots in the archipelagic historiography of nationhood, the waters were perpetually muddy:

> In the late medieval and early Tudor chronicle tradition, 'Britain' had been an ambiguous and surprisingly mobile geographic term, as indeed was 'England'. At times the two names seem interchangeable, either because both are taken as terms for the whole island, or because both are taken to refer only to the southern part of it (as in *Polychronicon*'s assertion that Scotland is 'departed in the south side of Britain with arms of the sea'). At

times Britain is understood to be a larger entity, the whole of which England is a part; occasionally the terms are apparently reversed, as in [Robert] Fabyan's baffling reference to the 'Isle of Britain' as 'middle England'. One would indeed be forgiven for thinking on this basis that Britain was a muddy concept indeed (598).

In this brief passage, Schwyzer highlights how assignations retained an astonishing fluidity in a period of national self-determination. Indeed, it is telling that Fabyan's own phrase to describe the "Isle of Britain" has in our own time become synonymous with a description of a particularly insular, exclusivist strain of English conservatism.[4]

If Kerrigan's work draws attention to more liminal figures operating on the violable edges of the archipelago, several important recent studies have also sought to probe the role of nationhood and nationalism in more canonical figures. In *Early Modern Nationalism and Milton's England*, a collection of scholars including Andrew Hadfield, Achsah Guibbory and Mary Nyquist attempt to track a path through Milton's ideas regarding what constituted English identity. As the book's editors observe:

> At times Milton's nationalism is intensely ethnic, rooted in a sense of the native vitality of the English language [...] [while] [a]t other times, it is intensely religious, not a matter of nature but of divine election that contributes to Milton's sense of England's exceptionalism, his vision of her as a Protestant nation set apart and singled out by God with a special role to play in history (3-4).

Of note in the volume is Thomas Corns' essay on Milton's attunement to broader Protestant discourses. A sensitive biographer of the poet and pamphleteer, Corns argues against viewing Milton as a nationalist with a nuanced awareness of the significances of internationalism. Citing "On the Late Massacre in Piedmont" and its transnational perspective for example, Corns writes: "Milton's Protestantism often had a pronounced internationalism. Milton's treatment of Italy illustrates particularly well the conflicted nature of his appeals of notions of national identity". (209).

As with the complex deliberations around nomenclature, Milton's nationhood was informed by a complex interplay between religion, ethnicity and ideology. Elizabeth Sauer's seminal work on Milton, entitled *Milton, Toleration, and Nationhood*, is an informed analysis of the role of the nation state in the work of one of the period's most incisive thinkers. For Sauer, Milton stands at a key moment of English national identity, when a range of competing discourses fed into a composite – and often convulsive – notion of what it meant to be English, both on an individual and collective scale. Religion was key. As Sauer observes, "For Puritans like Milton, the elect status of England – often used interchangeably with 'Britain' – was associated with the progress of the Reformation and with the restoration of the church to its original form, one predating medieval Catholicism" (22). Debates about national identity in a period of deep familiarity with biblical texts understandably become inflected through biblical narratives of (in particular) Jewish statehood. According to Sauer:

> Although it certainly has universal applications, the scriptural paradigm of a chosen people as applied by Milton is specifically designed to reflect the conditions of English nationhood. Monitoring the character of the English, Milton constantly adjusted the concept of elect nationalism, which gave way to a history of moral vicissitudes and intolerance that called for the reworking of the paradigm. England-Israel identifications as correlative and

antithetical correspond most directly with England's fluctuating commitments to Christian liberty (23).

For Sauer, "the conditional concept of peculiar status informed Milton's reading of Reformation England" (23). She cites the 1641 tract *Animadversions upon the Remonstrants Defence against Smectymnuus* where Milton's concept of English nationhood as analogous with a Calvinist-inflected understanding of Jewishness is articulated: "Brittains God [….] pittying us the first before of all other Nations, after he had decreed to purifie and renew his Church that lay wallowing in Idolatorus pollutions" (Milton cited in Sauer, 23). However, any claim to England's socio-cultural prevalence is underpinned by a problematic assumption of consanguinity between religious and national identities, a dilemma of which Milton himself was painfully aware. The poet and pamphleteer would develop open disdain for those who purported to maintain and propagate the ideals of sixteenth-century Reformation martyrs into the seventeenth century in the name of a unitary vision of their England. In his philippic "On the New Forcers of Conscience under the Long Parliament" Milton would denounce those drawing up the rules of ordination by the classic presbyteries with the withering putdown "New Presbyter is but old Priest writ large". In the context of debates surrounding what constitutes national identity, the telling point is the criticism of religious pronouncement assuming the function of polity: Parliament, the articulation of national collectivism, is the locus of theological decree.

Sauer's study has a keen understanding of Milton within the fractile framework of the islands. In particular, she is careful to consider Milton's attitude towards Ireland and his role as propagandist for the bloody Cromwellian reconquests of the 1650s. For Sauer, Milton's output in this role reveals much about Milton's own attitudes towards English nationhood. As she observes:

> Inextricably entangled with domestic affairs of England, the incursion into and reduction of Ireland involved the English at the most basic level as a Protestant colonial master in a Britain only symbolically unified. A study of English-Irish relations and the debates over Irish transplantation exposes the 'complication of interest' implicit in the acts and expressions of civilizing, toleration, planting, and nation formation. For Milton, the writing of the nation becomes an exercise in the justification of expansionism and exclusionism and, by extension, in the negotiation of toleration and rhetorical management of internal difference (72-3).

What Sauer aptly terms "the rhetorical management of internal difference" is a reminder of the struggle to reconcile the diversity of nationhoods within the archipelago. When warfare breaks out, as it does frequently in the early modern period between Ireland, England and Scotland in particular, the rhetoric of identity has bloody implications. If Kerrigan's work stands as the pre-eminent survey of the early modern archipelagic landscape, several other important studies have zeroed in on the minutiae of specific interactions. In doing so, they have confronted the tensions between historical nationhoods and the emergent British identity materialising under the rule of the Tudors and Stuarts. Early modern Ireland, as Sauer's study of Milton in part shows, embodies this striking, co-existing binary. At once at the often viciously contested threshold of "British identity" and also at the centre of the British imperial project from its outset, Ireland in many ways holds the key to understanding the functioning of British nationhood.

Many the most important studies of nationhood in the early modern period produced in the last twenty years have come from scholars displaying a keen interest in Ireland's role in the makeup of the archipelago at a time of foundational change.[5] A noteworthy addition to this canon is Patricia Palmer's *The Severed Head and the Grafted Tongue: Literature, Translation and Violence in Early Modern Ireland* (2014). Palmer's thesis is a lucid addition to the study of the language, literature and history of the archipelago's most troubled geographic region. From its plangent opening sentence – "*The Severed Head and the Grafted Tongue* tackles one of the most disconcerting conjunctions in human culture by examining what happens when violence and art collide" (1) – to its concluding discussion of "Elegy and Afterlives", Palmer's study concerns the intersection of literature and bloody deed. The range of literature examined is diverse, from translations of Virgillian epics to Spenserian poetry to Gaelic lyric. Running through each work examined is the striking motif of the decapitated head and its historical and cultural significance. As Palmer writes, the study:

> focuses on that baleful manifestation of extreme violence – the severed head. Bouncing, winking, cursing, crying out, such heads haunt the extraordinary range of literary works that have emerged from the Elizabethan conquest of Ireland. The book's principal concern is less with fictional violence per se than with the real way violence bleeds into literary descriptions of warfare and decapitation (1).

Palmer's study, focusing on Anglo-Irish interactions in the early modern period, is just one of many recent studies to explore what the English presence in Ireland from the mid-fifteenth century onwards meant for the national consciousness of both entities. Christopher Highley's *Catholics Writing the Nation in Early Modern Britain and Ireland* (2008) and Ian Campbell's *Renaissance Humanism and Ethnicity Before Race: The Irish and the English in the Seventeenth Century* (2015) both examine how conflict in Ireland became a staging ground for conflicting ideas regarding English and British identities.

Similarly, three studies published by Ashgate – *Shakespeare and Wales: From the Marches to the Assembly*, edited by Willy Maley and Philip Schwyzer (2010); *This England, That Shakespeare: New Angles on Englishness and the Bard*, edited by Maley and Margaret Tudeau-Clayton (2010); and *Celtic Shakespeare: The Bard and the Borderers*, edited by Rory Loughnane and Maley (2013) – have helped to consolidate and advance the decentralizing impulses of studies of nationhood within the archipelago. In particular, *Shakespeare and Wales* focuses attention on the vital role Wales plays within the cohering of the British imperial state. It explores what the presence of Wales in the Shakespearean canon reveals about the varying boundaries – imaginative, cartographic, ideological – between Welsh and English identities in the late-sixteenth and early-seventeenth centuries. The history plays in particular prove fecund – as Maley and Schwyzer remind us, "In the drama of the period, and in Shakespeare's histories in particular, Welsh characters greatly outnumber representatives of England's other neighbor nations". Such pre-eminence, suggest the editors, has important consequences: "The Welsh were intimately more familiar to the English than were the Scots or the Irish – or any other people for that matter – and thus perhaps more apt to trouble emergent conceptions of

Englishness" (4). Amidst a range of thought provoking studies, Christopher Ivic's essay "'bastard Normans, Norman bastards': Anomalous Identities in *The Life of Henry the Fift*" is notable for its sensitivity to the emergent cartographic consciousness during Shakespeare's lifetime. While the archipelagic turn in scholarly discussions of "British" nationhood has manifested an increasing focus on writers and thinkers at the fringes of the canon as well as works on the fringes of canonical writers, the interdisciplinarity of the approach is indicated by the investigation of less straightforward "literary" works. This is demonstrated by the burgeoning scholarship on cartographic works from the period, such as Christopher Saxton's *Atlas* (1579) and John Speed's *Theatre of the Empire of Great Britaine* (1611–1612), as well as sundry cartographically-inflected chorographies by the likes of William Lambarde and William Camden. Ivic's essay notes how Speed's work presents Welsh nationhood in different ways to its English, Scottish and Irish counterparts, and asks how such national characterisations can be read in relation to Shakespeare's presentations of Welsh identity. His investigation proposes a tantalizing notion – the forgoing of the usual supplements to national maps in *The Theatre* (for example pictographs of the various strata of society for each country) as well as the "disruptive presence of Wales and Welshness" in *Henry V* indicates that "Welshness was viewed as more ancient, true and unmixed than English" (90).

If Ivic pays close attention to how cartography was used as a means of realising nationhood, other scholars have focused on how early modern archipelagic identities were enriched by localized, chorographic discourses. In John M. Adrian's *Local Negotiations of English Nationhood, 1570–1680* (2011) the author endeavours to "explore the vitality of early modern local consciousness [...] examin[ing] how early modern writers invoke local places, traditions, and ways of thinking to respond to the larger political, religious, and cultural changes of the sixteenth and seventeenth centuries" (2–3). Adrian's focus on the microcosm and what it reveals about the macrocosm pays rich dividends as a consideration of nationhood and its consciousness in the period. He draws attention to the centralizing forces of political imperatives latent in the work of describers of the countryside such as Lambarde. Moreover, it examines how a seemingly straightforward "fishing manual" like Izaak Walton's *The Compleat Angler* (1653) also addresses the multifaceted politics of Commonwealth England and the question of ownership of the land in a developing capitalist economy. "In chapter after chapter", Adrian writes:

> *The Compleat Angler* offers the image of a patient fisherman carefully consulting local conditions – an image that must have been appealing to a Royalist audience in enforced retirement in localities throughout the realm. [...] By limiting himself to a careful consideration of whatever local situation the angler finds himself in, he can make an informed and effective choice and exercise deliberate control over his environment (132).

If Adrian draws attention to chorogaphy as an important literary medium for interrogating national identities, Anna Suranyi's *The Genius of the English Nation: Travel Writing and National Identity in Early Modern England* (2008) shows how authors utilized the genre of travel writing to exhibit "positive English qualities" (37). "[B]y describing the characteristics of other countries", writes Suranyi, "the English strove to find a middle ground (inhabited by England) that was exemplified not by the extremes of tyranny and disorder, but by individual liberty, order, and freedom from oppression" (37). One of the most interesting aspects of Suranyi's volume is its discussion of how exoticized illustrations of foreign women by the likes of George Sandys, Fynes Moryson and William Lithgow were part of a more expansive "complex discourse that extended beyond human characteristics" (138) to incorporate the interplay of power relations between nationhoods and national identities. "As in the representation of other aspects of national identities", notes Suranyi astutely, "their observations were influenced by their awareness of current power relations between countries" (137). Ultimately, her study shows that while the writer of the travel narrative was ostensibly outward-looking in their gaze, they were fundamentally concerned with projections of English nationhood: "what to emulate, what to reject, how to be English" (168).

The archipelagic turn in early modern studies in the last twenty years has enhanced our understanding of nationhood on the archipelago immensely. It has broadened the access to non-canonical texts, as well as offering fresh insight into canonical writers of the period. More importantly, it has engaged with the knotty strands of nationhood and identity during a period characterized by fluctuating cross-national alliance and enmity. Ultimately, it has shown that in the crucible of the British Empire, what it meant to be British and what it meant to be one of its constituent parts was a subject of vigorous, antagonistic and often bloody dispute.

Notes

1. Shakespeare, *Henry the Fifth*, 3.3.52–6.
2. The ongoing *Poly-Olbion* digital project, led by Andrew McRae, Philip Schwyzer, Daniel Cattell, and Sjoerd Levelt, explores how this textured work delineates the central concerns of early-seventeenth century British nationhood, whilst also speaking to a twenty-first century audience (http://poly-olbion.exeter.ac.uk/: accessed 14 February 2018).
3. Breuilly, "Introduction: Concepts, Approaches, Theories", 13.
4. The term is regularly used by one of the largest-selling newspapers in the country, the right-wing *Daily Mail*. Frequently propagating a reactionary view of modern British life, it champions "Middle England" as a model of conscientious conservative values set against the interventionist forces of socialism. See for example "Middle England's £623million bailout for the NHS: Families are forced into debt to pay for vital surgery as the waiting list hits four million" (http://www.dailymail.co.uk/health/article-4937418/Middle-England-s-623million-bailout-NHS.html: accessed 14 February 2018); "This was Your victory: How Middle England rose up to humiliate pollsters and save the nation from Red Ed" (http://www.dailymail.co.uk/news/article-3074115/How-Middle-England-rose-save-nation-Red-Ed.html: accessed 14 February 2018); and "How Middle England took a meat cleaver to political correctness: The butcher forced to remove his window display tells Robert Hardman that he's putting it back up" (http://www.dailymail.co.uk/news/article-2568028/How-Middle-England-took-meat-cleaver-political-correctness.html: accessed 14 February 2018).
5. A emblematic, but by no means comprehensive, survey of these studies includes Christopher Highley, *Shakespeare, Spenser, and the Crisis in Ireland* (Cambridge, 1997); Nicholas Canny, *Making Ireland British, 1580–1650* (Oxford, 2001); Patricia Palmer, *Language and Conquest in Early Modern Ireland: English Renaissance Literature and Elizabeth Imperial Expansion* (Cambridge, 2001); Andrew Hadfield, *Shakespeare, Spenser and the Matter of Britain* (New York, 2004); and Willy Maley, *Salvaging Spenser: Colonialism, Culture and Identity* (Basingstoke, 1997).

Disclosure statement

No potential conflict of interest was reported by the author.

Bibliography

Breuilly, J. "Introduction: Concepts, Approaches, Theories". In *The Oxford Handbook of the History of Nationalism*, edited by J. Breuilly, 1–20. Oxford: Oxford University Press, 2013.
Shakespeare, W. "The Life of Henry the Fifth". In *The New Oxford Shakespeare: Modern Critical Edition*, edited by G. Taylor, J. Jowett, T. Bourus, and G. Egan, 1529–1606. Oxford: Oxford University Press, 2016.

Works Reviewed

Adrian, J. M. *Local Negotiations of English Nationhood, 1570-1680*. London: Palgrave Macmillan, 2011.
Campbell, I. *Renaissance Humanism and Ethnicity before Race: The Irish and the English in the Seventeenth Century*. Manchester: Manchester University Press, 2015.
Hadfield, A. "Vanishing Primordialism: Literature, History, and the Public". In *The Roots of Nationalism: National Identity Formation in Early Modern Europe*, edited by L. Jensen, 47–66. Amsterdam: Amsterdam University Press, 2016.
Highley, C. *Catholics Writing the Nation in Early Modern Britain and Ireland*. Oxford: Oxford University Press, 2008.
Kerrigan, J. *Archipelagic English: Literature, History, and Politics 1603-1707*. Oxford: Oxford University Press, 2008.
Kewes, P., I. W. Archer, and F. Heal, eds. *The Oxford Handbook of Holinshed's Chronicles*. Oxford: Oxford University Press, 2012.
Loewenstein, D., and P. Stevens. *Early Modern Nationalism and Milton's England*. Toronto: University of Toronto Press, 2008.
Maley, W. *Nation, State and Empire in English Renaissance Literature*. London: Palgrave Macmillan, 2003.
Maley, W., and P. Schwyzer, eds. *Shakespeare and Wales: From the Marches to the Assembly*. Aldershot: Ashgate, 2010.
Maley, W., and M. Tudeau-Clayton, eds. *This England, that Shakespeare: New Angles on Englishness and the Bard*. Farnham: Ashgate, 2010.
Maley, W., and R. Loughnane, eds. *Celtic Shakespeare: The Bard and the Borderers*. Farnham: Ashgate, 2013.
Palmer, P. *The Severed Head and the Grafted Tongue: Literature, Translation and Violence in Early Modern Ireland*. Cambridge: Cambridge University Press, 2014.
Sauer, E. *Milton, Toleration, and Nationhood*. Cambridge: Cambridge University Press, 2013.
Schwyzer, P. "Archipelagic History". In *The Oxford Handbook of Holinshed's Chronicles*, edited by P. Kewes, I. W. Archer, and F. Heal, 593–608. Oxford: Oxford University Press, 2012.
Suranyi, A. *The Genius of the English Nation: Travel Writing and National Identity in Early Modern England*. Newark: University of Delaware Press, 2008.

Index

Note: Page numbers followed by 'n' refer to end notes

Adrian, J. M. 112
The Anatomy of Melancholy (Burton) 52
Anglo-British history 84
Anglo-British project 92
Anglo-British sovereignty 92
Anglo-Celtic frontier 91, 92
Anglo-Saxon heritage 3
Anglo-Scottish border 8
Anglo-Scottish union 6, 8, 55, 105
Anglo-Welsh boundary celebrates 8
Annus mirabilis (Dryden) 88
anti-catholic prejudice 69
anti-catholic religious policy 67
anti-catholic stereotype 72
Anti-Convict Association 98n110
anti-European history 92
anti-European movement 84
anti-presbyterian 10, 63, 64, 69, 71–73, 76
Antiquities of Nottinghamshire (Thoroton) 4
Antiquities of Warwickshire (Dugdale) 4
anti-Scottish prejudice 69
Archer, I. W. 107, 108
Archipelagic English 98n87, 106, 107
Archipelagic Holinshed 107
Atlas (Saxton) 112

Baker, D. J. 17, 63
Baker, R. 87
Bakhtin, M. 21
Barnes, D. G. 29
Batchelor, R. K. 90
Belfast presbyterians 68, 69
Bertie, W. 96n60
Bevis of Hampton (Llwyd) 2
Birkmann, J. 50
Blome, R. 4
bloody warfare 107
Boyle, R. 107
Bramhall, J. 63, 64, 75–76
Bramhall's attack 64
Breuilly, J. 105

Breviary of Britain (Llwyd) 3, 50, 51
The Breviary of Britayne (Llwyd) 3, 12n38, 50, 51
Briefe and True Report of the New Found Land of Virginia (Hariot) 6
Britain (Camden) 4
de Britaine, W. 87
Britain's territorial purview 33
Britannia, or a Geographical Description of the Kingdom of England, Scotland and Ireland (Blome) 4
Britannia's Pastorals (Browne) 4
British imperial project 84, 110
British territorial waters 86
Brooke, C. 28, 56
Browne, W. 4, 28
Brown, G. 19
Brutus, T. 2, 3, 9
Burton, R. 52
Butcher, R. 4
Butler, J. 64
Butler, S. 6, 12n37

Cambro-British identity 51, 58n5
Cambro-Britons 7, 10; civic/political identity 49; connotations of 52; overlapping communities 54; péece of chéese 56; post-referendum polling 49; widespread cultural movement 55
Camden, W. 112
Campbell, I. 111
Carnarvon, E. 22
The case of the Commonwealth of England, stated (Nedham) 74, 91
Catholic Church 53
Catholic pope 106
Catholics Writing the Nation in Early Modern Britain and Ireland (Highley) 111
Cavanagh, E. 90
Cecil, R. 20, 21, 24, 28
Celtic Shakespeare: The Bard and the Borderers (Loughnane and Maley) 111
civic/political identity 49

civil war 21, 57
Clapham, J. 7
Coke, E. 21
Coleman, D. 63
Collignon, S. 84
comic effect 104
Commentarioli Britannicae descriptionis fragmentum (Llwyd) 50
The Compleat Angler (Walton) 112
Continuance of Albion's England (Warner) 8
Corns, T. 109
Cromwellian army 70
Cromwell's Council 85
Cromwell's military success 73
Cronica Walliae (Llwyd) 50, 56, 58n12

Daems, J. 65
Danish influence 38
Dartmoor plains 38
Dasgupta, S. 10
Defoe, D. 9, 13n64, 107
Denham, Sir John 5
discovery of England 2, 16
Drayton, M.: anti-establishment attitudes 29; *Englands Heroicall Epistles* 16–30; one-dimensional Elizabethan nostalgic 2; *Poly-Olbion* 1–5, 7, 9–11, 17, 33–47, 51, 52, 55, 87, 105; preferential royal treatment 1; topo-chronographical structure 2
Drummond, W. 2, 12n33
Dryden, J. 88
Dudley, G. 19
Dugdale, W. 4

early modern English readers 18
early modern period: Anglo-Irish interactions 111; historiography of 107; key moment of 109; nationalism theory debates 105; political aggregation of 105; post-colonial awareness 106; post-Union conceptions of 107; pre-eminent survey 110; wider historical outlook 105
Elton, O. 16
England: glory of 23; natural features of 3; poem of 1; political/regnal union 3; Princely Jewels 22; rivers of 3
Englands Heroicall Epistles (Drayton) 10, 16–30
The English-American, his travail by sea and land, or, A new survey of the West-India's (Gage) 95n42
English and Scottish policies 36
English Channel 35
English Civil War 84
English colonial rule 70
English historical materials 19
English political theory 92
English Privy Council 21, 65

English textual product 18
Essex faction 24
European communalism 108
European union 84, 92, 105
The Excellencie of a Free State (Nedham) 93

Fanon, F. 106
Farley, P. 1, 10n3
Feake, C. 74
Filmer, R. 93
"First Anniversary" 74, 75
foreign policy 22, 23, 84, 89, 93
France: battlefield in 104; catholic powers of 74; primarily political light 74
Franco-Scottish relations 98n93
free seas debates: closed seas policy 35; off-shore fishing rights 35; positions shaped national policy 35; proprietary right 37; river-sea confrontations 37; river/sea dynamics 37
The French Sea 39

Gage, T. 95n42
Gaveston, P. 20, 21
Gellner, E. 18
The Genius of the English Nation: Travel Writing and National Identity in Early Modern England (Suranyi) 112
The Ghost of Richard III (Brooke) 56
Gibson, E. 4
Gill, A. 56
Good Friday Agreement 94n17
Gower, J. 104
Graham, J. 71
Grotius, H. 36, 83
Guibbory, A. 109
Gunn, J. 85

Habington, T. 4
Hadfield, A. 6, 17, 106, 109
Hakluyt, R. 17, 56
Hardin, R. F. 19, 28
Hariot, T. 6
Harrington, J. 93
Harrison, W. 108
Hawke, M. 90
Haydn, J. 88
Heal, F. 108
Helgerson, R. 2, 3, 5, 16, 17, 45n5
Henry II 19, 27
Henry (Prince) 3, 28, 43, 87
Henry V. 104, 112
Highley, C. 111, 113n5
Hirst, D. 90
History and Antiquities of the County of Rutland (Wright) 4
History of Great Britain (Speed) 4, 53
Hole, W. 1, 9, 34

INDEX

Holland, H. 55
Holland, P. 4, 6, 12n34
Howell, J. 55, 87, 90

international coalition 42–45
intra-European activity 84
The Irish Rebellion (Temple) 67
Irish Sea 35
Italy: catholic powers of 74; Milton's treatment of 109; primarily political light 74

Johnson, R. 53
Jones, H. 67
Jones, M. 65
Jones, T. 57
Jonson, B. 2, 21, 87, 88, 96n60; *Neptune's Triumph* 87, 96n60; *Sejanus his Fall* 21

Katherine's association 20
Kerrigan, J. 71, 83, 91, 106, 107, 109, 110
Kewes, P. 107, 108
King Arthur's Table 23
Kläger, F. 18
Klein, B. 17, 45n1
Knachen, P. 83
Knox, J. 69

Lambarde, W. 112
Leicester's Commonwealth 20
Leland, J 3, 108
The Life of Henry the Fift (Shakespeare) 112
Lithgow, W. 113
Llwyd, H. 6; *Bevis of Hampton* 2; *Breviary of Britain* 3, 50, 51; *The Breviary of Britayne* 3, 12n38, 50, 51; *Commentarioli Britannicae descriptionis fragmentum* 50; *Cronica Walliae* 50, 56, 58n12
Local Negotiations of English Nationhood (Adrian) 112
local sovereign floods 43
Loughnane, R. 111; *Celtic Shakespeare: The Bard and the Borderers* 111

Mackenzie, G. 107
Maley, W. 10, 64, 106, 111, 113n5; *Celtic Shakespeare: The Bard and the Borderers* 111; *Shakespeare and Wales: From the Marches to the Assembly* 111; *This England, That Shakespeare: New Angles on Englishness and the Bard* 111
Malvezzi, V. 87
mare clausum policy 36, 37, 42, 44
Mare Clausum (Selden) 10, 83
Mare Liberum (Grotius) 36, 83
mare liberum policy 36, 37, 44
Martin Dzelzainis 85
Marvell, A. 62, 83

Marvell's republican admiration 72
mass brawl 104
McCabe, R. A. 66
McEachern, C. 17
Meadows, P. 91
Mercurius Politicus (Nedham) 64–70
Milton, J. 10, 107
Milton's ideas 109
Moryson, F. 113
Mostyn, R. 51
Murray, P. J. 10, 92

Native Tongue 25
Natural History of Staffordshire (Plot) 4
1651 Navigation Act 86
Nedham, M.: *The case of the commonwealth of England, stated* 74, 91, 98n87; *The Excellencie of a Free State* 93; *Mercurius Politicus* 64–70
Neptune's Triumph (Jonson) 87, 96n60
Norbrook, D. 21, 28, 63, 85
Nyquist, M. 109

Oceana (Harrington) 93
ocean-lapped coasts 35
off-shore fishing rights 35
old English families 67
old English Garbe 25
one-dimensional Elizabethan nostalgic 2
Ovidian feminine voice 19
The Oxford Handbook of Holinshed's Chronicles (Kewes and Archer) 107

Padwa, D. J. 90
Palmer, P. 111, 113n5
pan-Gaelic alliance 66
Parsons, R. 20
Patriarcha (Filmer) 93
Peacey, J. 84
Pict-Britans 7, 8
Plot, R. 4
Pocock, J. G. A. 17, 91, 92
Poly-Olbion (Drayton) 1–5, 7, 9–11, 17, 33–47, 51, 52, 55, 87, 105
positive English qualities 112
post-colonial awareness 106
post-war European Union 92
pre-Enlightenment era 17
Princely Jewels 22
Principal Navigations (Hakluyt) 56
pro-union positions 34
Puritan Revolution 84

Ralegh, W. 29
Raymond, J. 69, 85, 92
Red-shanks 69–71
The Rehearsal transpros'd (Marvell) 63, 75

INDEX

Renaissance Humanism and Ethnicity Before Race: The Irish and the English in the Seventeenth Century (Campbell) 111
Ricouer, P. 18
River Chore 38
River Cowen 39
River Dart: Dartmoor plains 38; dominion-based claims 45; micro-sovereignty 38; powerful role 43; Wood-nymph turns 41
River Hayle 42
River Mele 41
river-sea confrontations 37
river/sea dynamics 34
Roman rule 107
Royce, M. 84
Russell, E. 24

Salesbury, W. 51
Sandys, G. 88, 113
Saxton, C 112
Schwyzer, P. 7, 10, 17, 108, 111
Scotland: contrasting tensions 107; independence movement in 105; kingdom of 6; political/regnal union 3; pre-eminent survey 110
Scott, W. 107
sea fishing industry 36
Sejanus his Fall (Jonson) 21
Selden, J. 10, 83
The Severed Head and the Grafted Tongue: Literature, Translation and Violence in Early Modern Ireland (Palmer) 111
Severne Sea 39, 42
Shakespeare and Wales: From the Marches to the Assembly (Maley and Schwyzer) 111
Shakespeare, W. 107; *The Life of Henry the Fift* 112; *Richard II* 17
Shell, M. 86
Shore, Jane 27
Sidney, A. 17, 21, 24, 29, 51, 52, 93
Simpson, J. 74
Smith, J. 17, 56
Sobecki, S. 89
Somos, M. 90

Speed, J. 112; *History of Great Britain* 4, 53; *Theatre of the Empire of Great Britaine* 4, 112
Spenser, E. 17, 64, 65, 67, 68, 71, 72
Stanihurst, R. 108
St.Michael's Mount 39
Suranyi, A. 112, 113
Surrey-Geraldine epistles 24
The Survey and Antiquitie of the Towne of Stamforde, in the county of Lincolne (Butcher) 4
Survey of Worcestershire (Habington) 4

Temple, J. 67
Theatre of the Empire of Great Britaine (Speed) 4, 112
This England, That Shakespeare: New Angles on Englishness and the Bard (Maley and Tudeau-Clayton) 111
Thoroton, R. 4
Thoughts on the letter of Edmund Burke, esq. to the sheriffs of Bristol on the affairs of America (Bertie) 96n60
Topo-chrono-graphicall 1, 10n1
true native Muse 12, 25
Tudeau-Clayton, M. 111

unionization debates 34
Ussher, J. 76

Vanishing Primordialism 106

Walton, I. 112
Warner, W. 8
Watts, W. 90
Wentworth, P. 20
Wentworth, T. 64, 76
Wither, G. 28
Woodford, B. 83
Worden, B. 63, 73, 84, 93
Wright, G. 5
Wright, J. 4
Writing the English Republic (Norbrook) 89

Zurcher, A. 86